D0207955

*Premises and Motifs in Renaissance
Thought and Literature*

Premises and Motifs
in Renaissance
Thought and Literature

C. A. Patrides

PRINCETON UNIVERSITY PRESS
PRINCETON, NEW JERSEY

Copyright © 1982 by Princeton University Press
Published by Princeton University Press, 41 William Street,
Princeton, New Jersey
In the United Kingdom: Princeton University Press,
Guildford, Surrey

ALL RIGHTS RESERVED
Library of Congress Cataloging in Publication Data will be
found on the last printed page of this book

This book has been composed in Linotron Garamond

Clothbound editions of Princeton University Press books
are printed on acid-free paper, and binding materials are
chosen for strength and durability

Printed in the United States of America by Princeton
University Press, Princeton, New Jersey

for
Dimitri Vournas

Ἐθέλω χαλκάσπιδα Πυθιονίκαν
σὺν βαθυζώνοισιν ἀγγέλλων

Contents

Illustrations

ix

To the Reader

... there is in this Universe a Staire, or manifest Scale of creatures, rising not disorderly, or in confusion, but with a comely method and proportion.—Sir Thomas Browne

The twelve studies made available here address themselves to as many dimensions of Renaissance thought and expression in order to provide a comprehensive vision of the Renaissance at large. Variable though these studies are in their length and in their range, they converge on that pattern which, attested among others by Sir Thomas Browne in *Religio Medici* (I, 33) and by Milton in *Paradise Lost* (V, 469-90), sustains the period's tendency emotively to apprehend the created order as a hierarchical arrangement ascending "from the Mushrome to the Angels" (below, Ch. I, §3). This vertical arrangement was additionally regarded as conflated with the horizontal process along a linear path extending from the Creation to the Last Judgment. Jointly regarded, these dimensions were intended to assert—in Browne's words— "a comely method and proportion."

Such claims are writ large in the present work, especially in the course of the initial two prospects of cosmic order (Ch. I-II) and the concluding two visions of the dolorous realm (Ch. XI-XII). But the other studies uphold "proportion" no less firmly, however diverse the given premises and expansive their consequent effects. Thus the estimates of the year of creation (Ch. III) and the speculations involving numbers (Ch. IV) alike suggest efforts to impose order in particular ways; the celebration of man's upright form (Ch. V) affirms the dignity of the major link in the cosmic hierarchy; the attempt to posit Protestantism's Edenic antecedents (Ch. VI) argues yet again the predilection for "first principles"; while the remaining four studies focus on specific manifestations of order as well as disorder in the horizontal plane of history: the cessation of the oracles on the appearance of Christ (Ch. VII), the cumulative renunciations of the multitude (Ch. VIII), the providential design behind Ottoman aggression (Ch. IX), and the mystery of God's ways apropos the legendary Pope Joan (Ch. X).

Here and there, it must be acknowledged, I attend to but a minute portion of the seething cauldron that was the Renaissance; but I would all the same maintain that, not infrequently, the fervency of the whole can best be appreciated by the intensity of the part. Moreover, where my peregrinations end with a glance beyond the Renaissance, the tactic should not be regarded as strictly fortuitous. It is on the contrary designed to suggest the nature of the changes effected during the transition from a predominantly theological orientation to a largely secular one. My concern was after all to annotate certain developments in terms both of their background in our cultural heritage and of their foreground in our commonly shared literature.

All but one of these studies have been published before; but in their transit into these pages, it should be emphasized, they were far more thoroughly documented in all cases but two. In their initial state, they were indispensable in providing a background for two books I completed in 1966 and 1972 respectively;[1] but since then I also realized that they constituted an entity unto themselves, especially once I recast their arguments and revised their style. I am in consequence grateful to the editors of the following journals for their generous permission to reprint, in the revised form mentioned, the studies indicated: *Harvard Theological Review* (for Ch. XI: Copyright 1964 by the President and Fellows of Harvard College), *Huntington Library Quarterly* (Ch. III), *Isis* (Ch. IV), *Journal of the History of Ideas* (Ch. I, V, and XII), *Modern Language Review* (Ch. VII), *Shakespeare Quarterly* (Ch. VIII), *Studies in the Renaissance* (Ch. IX), *Studies in English Literature* (Ch. VI), and *Theologische Zeitschrift* (Ch. II).

At different times and in different versions, most of the ensuing studies were delivered as lectures before learned societies or at select universities. Of those occasions, one in particular deserves to be mentioned because it involved an enterprise I happen to favor (Ch. X), delivered as the Erasmus Lecture for 1981 at Victoria University in the University of Toronto. I am only too pleased to acknowledge the warm hospitality extended to me by Professor James M. Estes, Director of the Centre for Reformation and Renaissance Studies, and the patience with which numerous details were attended to by Professor Germaine Warkentin. My good friend Douglas

---

[1] *Milton and the Christian Tradition* (Oxford: The Clarendon Press, 1966; reprinted by Archon Books, Hamden, Conn., 1979) and *"The Grand Design of God": The Literary Form of the Christian View of History* (London: Routledge and Kegan Paul Ltd., and Toronto: University of Toronto Press, 1972).

Chambers provided as always the ideal context for the transformation of a formal occasion into a decidedly congenial visit.

The slow evolution of the studies that follow until they assumed their present form has involved the generous assistance I have obtained from a considerable number of individuals and institutions. Impossible as it is to name them all, I must necessarily restrict the expression of my gratitude in the first instance to Professor Philip Brockbank, Director of The Shakespeare Institute at the University of Birmingham, who encouraged my labors during the fourteen years I was fortunate to be with him at the University of York, and to Professor Roland Mushat Frye of the University of Pennsylvania, who sustained me over twenty years with his warm friendship and sage counsel. Additionally, I am grateful to Mr. C.B.L. Barr of the York Minster Library, who has given me the benefit of his vast knowledge of classical literature and scholarship, and to Professor Raymond B. Waddington of the University of Wisconsin at Madison, who has suggested several important changes in my argument and my documentation.

As most of my investigations into primary sources were undertaken at the British Library and the Bodleian Library, it gives me great pleasure gratefully to acknowledge the manifold courtesies extended to me at both. The Trustees of the British Library, it should be added, also granted me permission to reproduce the six plates appearing in this volume. I am no less obligated to still other libraries where my research encompassed secondary sources, notably the New York Public Library and the libraries of the University of California at Berkeley, the University of York, and the University of Michigan at

Ann Arbor. All three of the last named universities have in addition provided me with indispensable subsidies in the form of both travel grants and clerical assistance. When all is said, however, I am particularly grateful to the John Simon Guggenheim Memorial Foundation for the award of two fellowships, without which the present work—and much else besides—could not possibly have been realized.

It may be noted that the study of angelology (Ch. I) soon after its initial appearance in 1959 elicited a response from an entirely unexpected quarter. I am informed that it was mentioned in *Pravda* ("Truth")—or possibly in *Izvestiya* ("News")—not as the study in changing conceptions that it is but, in line with Communist premises, as a reprehensible capitalist plot to resuscitate obsolete notions. The flattering notice of my humble effort confirmed, I thought, the wise Russian saying that under the Communist dispensation *Pravda nyè Izvestiya, Izvestiya nyè Pravda.*

Ann Arbor   C.A.P.
April 1981

xv

Abbreviations

The place of publication is given only if it is other than London or New York.

ANF	*Ante-Nicene Christian Library* (Buffalo, 1884 ff.)
Augustine, *De civ. Dei*	*The City of God*, trans. John Healey (1610), revised by R.V.G. Tasker (1945)
A.V.	The King James ("Authorized") version of the Bible (1611)
BHR	*Bibliothèque d'Humanisme et Renaissance*
Browne, *BMP*	Sir Thomas Browne, *The Major Works*, ed. C. A. Patrides (Penguin Books, 1977)
BUSE	*Boston University Studies in English*
Calvin, *Inst.*	*Institutio christianae religionis* (definitive edition: 1559), trans. Henry Beveridge (Edinburgh, 1845-1846)
CH	*Church History*
CL	*Comparative Literature*
CP	*The Cambridge Platonists*, ed. C. A. Patrides (1969; repr. Cambridge, 1980)
Dante	*Inferno*, trans. J. A. Carlyle; *Purgatorio*, trans. Thomas Okey; *Paradiso*,

	trans. Philip H. Wicksteed (repr. 1941-1946), 3 vols.
Donne, *Devotions*	*Devotions upon Emergent Occasions*, ed. John Sparrow (Cambridge, 1923)
Donne, *Essays*	*Essays in Divinity*, ed. Evelyn M. Simpson (Oxford, 1952)
Donne, *Sermons*	*The Sermons of John Donne*, ed. Evelyn M. Simpson and George R. Potter (Berkeley, 1953-1962), 10 vols.
ELH	*Journal of English Literary History*
ES	*English Studies*
Herbert	*The English Poems of George Herbert*, ed. C. A. Patrides (Everyman's University Library, 1974)
HLQ	*Huntington Library Quarterly*
HTR	*Harvard Theological Review*
JHI	*Journal of the History of Ideas*
JWCI	*Journal of the Warburg and Courtauld Institutes*
LCC	*Library of Christian Classics*, ed. John Baillie *et al.* (1953 ff.)
LXX	The Septuagint: the Greek version of the Old Testament (3rd cent. B.C.?)
Milton, *MSP*	Milton, *Selected Prose*, ed. C. A. Patrides (Penguin Books, 1974)
Milton, *Works*	*The Works of John Milton*, gen. ed. Frank A. Patterson (Columbia University Press, 1931-40), 20 vols.
MLN	*Modern Language Notes*
MLR	*Modern Language Review*
MP	*Modern Philology*
N&Q	*Notes and Queries*

NPF	*Nicene and Post-Nicene Fathers* (Buffalo: 1st series, 1886 ff.; 2nd series, 1890 ff.)
PG	*Patrologia*, Series graeca, ed. J.-P. Migne (Paris, 1857 ff.)
PL	*Patrologia*, Series latina, ed. J.-P. Migne (Paris, 1844 ff.)
PMLA	*Publications of the Modern Language Association*
PQ	*Philological Quarterly*
Ralegh, *HW*	Sir Walter Ralegh, *The History of the World* (1614), ed. C. A. Patrides (1971)
RES	*Review of English Studies*
RHLR	*Revue d'histoire et de littérature religieuses*
RTP	*Revue de théologie et de philosophie*
Septuagint	(see LXX)
Shakespeare	*The Complete Works*, ed. Hardin Craig (Chicago, 1951)
SP	*Studies in Philology*
SQ	*Shakespeare Quarterly*
SR	*Studies in the Renaissance*
Thomas Aquinas	*Summa theologica*, trans. by the English Dominican Fathers (1911-1925), 22 vols.; *Summa contra gentiles*, trans. as before (1924-1929), 4 vols.
UTQ	*University of Toronto Quarterly*
Vulgate	St. Jerome's Latin version of the Bible (c. 384-404)

*Premises and Motifs in Renaissance
Thought and Literature*

✸ 1 ✸

"Quaterniond into their celestiall Princedomes":
The Orders of the Angels

. . . we know they are distinguished into Orders; the Apostle tells us so: but what, or how many their Orders are, (since S. *Gregory*, and S. *Bernard* differ from that Designe of their nine orders, which S. *Denis the Areopagite* had given before, in placing those nine . . .) we know not; But we are content to say with S. *Augustine, Esse firmissimè credo, quænam sint nescio*; that there are distinct orders of Angels, assuredly I beleeve; but what they are, I cannot tell.—John Donne

I

Pilgrims to the Parthenon at Athens still follow the Avenue of Dionysius the Areopagite leading to the Acropolis and, facing its main gate, the hill of Ares. It was on this hill that St. Paul delivered his memorable address to the Athenians, heard among others by Dionysius the Areopagite (Acts 17.34). By the time of Eusebius of Caesarea some three centuries later, the same Dionysius was thought not only to have been converted to the new faith but to have become the first bishop of Athens.[1] According to another legend, he was subsequently sent by Pope Clement I into Gaul, where he

---

[1] *Historia ecclesiastica*, III, 4; IV, 23. Eusebius is recording the statement of Bishop Dionysius of Corinth, whose works have been lost.

became the first bishop of Paris and met his martyrdom.[2] The legend, widely accepted and amply elaborated during the Middle Ages, was codified in the *Passio Sanctissimi Dionysii* written in the ninth century by Hilduin, abbot of St. Denys.[3]

St. Paul's convert in Athens was not only transmuted into the patron saint of France, however. He was also conflated with a third figure, the anonymous writer—probably a disciple of Proclus—who late in the fifth century composed the enormously influential treatises on mystical theology, the celestial hierarchy, the ecclesiastical hierarchy, and the divine names, ascribing all four to the pen of Dionysius the Areopagite.[4] The attribution

---

[2] Gregory of Tours actually mentions Dionysius as one of the seven bishops sent into Gaul (*Historia francorum*, I, 31); but, while he is referring to the original patron saint of France, later commentators interpreted his statement as a direct allusion to the Areopagite.

[3] *PL*, CVI, 14-50. The Greek biographies of Dionysius by Symeon Metaphrastes, Michael Syncellus, *et al.*, are given in *PG*, III, 577 ff. On the eventual fate of St. Paul's convert, see S. Baring-Gould, *The Lives of the Saints* (Edinburgh, 1914), XI, 190 ff.; Raymond J. Loenertz, "La légende parisienne de S. Denys l'Aréopagite: sa genèse et son premier témoin," *Analecta Bollandiana*, LXIX (1951), 217-37; and the plates reproduced in, and the commentary by, Henry Marin, *Légende de Saint Denis* (Paris, 1908).

[4] One of the best introductory accounts of the Pseudo-Dionysius is by Brooke F. Westcott, *Essays in the History of Religious Thought in the West* (1903), pp. 142-93. For summaries of his thought, see Adolph Harnack, *History of Dogma*, trans. E. B. Speirs and James Millar (1898), IV, 338n-340n; Henry O. Taylor, *The Classical Heritage of the Middle Ages*, 3rd ed. (1911), pp. 82 ff.; Otto Bardenhewer, *Geschichte der altkirchlichen Literatur* (Freiburg, 1924), IV, 282 ff.; Anders Nygren, *Agape and Eros*, trans. Philip S. Watson (1954), pp. 576 ff.; Maurice de Wulf, *History of Mediaeval Philosophy*, trans. E. C. Massinger, 3rd ed. (1954), pp. 576 ff.; Etienne Gilson, *History of Christian Philosophy in the Middle Ages* (1955), pp. 81 ff.; Jean Trouillard, "Le cosmos du Pseudo-Denys," *RTP*, V (1955), 51-57; and the articles in *Realencyklopädie für protestantische Theologie und Kirche* (Leipzig, 1898), IV, 687-96, and *The Catholic Encyclopaedia* (1909), V, 13-18. For fuller discussions consult Hugo Koch, *Pseudo-Dionysius Areopagita*

was questioned in the sixth century by Bishop Hypatius of Ephesus, in the ninth by Patriarch Photius of Constantinople, and in the twelfth by Peter Abelard; but as the first was not sufficiently authoritative, the second was less than popular in the West by reason of the schism, and the third could hardly be regarded as the anchor of orthodoxy,[5] the claims of the Pseudo-Dionysius were accepted and his four treatises eventually assumed almost canonical status among theologians in both Eastern and Western Christendom. The reverence with which St. John of Damascus approached "that most holy, and sacred, and gifted theologian, Dionysius the Areopagite,"[6] is typical of more than a millennium of orthodox thought.

The Pseudo-Dionysius as the heir of a formidable tradition in angelological thought, labored within a clearly defined circumference. His classification of the angels into nine orders arranged into three triads[7] crystallized

---

in seinem Beziehungen zum Neuplatonismus und Mysterienwesen, in *Forschungen zur christlichen Litteratur- und Dogmengeschichte*, ed. A. Ehrhard and J. P. Kirsch (Mainz, 1900), I (2-3); René Roques, *L'Univers dionysien: structure hiérarchique du monde selon le Pseudo-Denys* (Paris, 1954); Denys Routledge, *Cosmic Theology* (1964); and Stephen Gersh, *From Iamblichus to Eriugena: An Investigation of the Prehistory and Evolution of the Pseudo-Dionysian Tradition* (Leiden, 1978). Further studies are cited in the select bibliographies by Otto Bardenhewer, *Patrologie* (Freiburg, 1894), pp. 289 f., English trans. (1908), pp. 540 f.; Friedrich Ueberweg, *Grundriss der Geshichte der Philosophie* (Berlin, 1928), II, 667 f.; and E. Stéphanou, "Les derniers essais d'identification du Pseudo-Denys l'Aréopagite," *Échos d'Orient*, XXI (1932), 466-68. The Pseudo-Dionysius was even celebrated in verse: see the Latin poem by Mantuan (Baptista Spagnuoli), *Vita Dionysii Areopagita*, in *Opera* (Paris, 1513), I, 193-220.

[5] See the account and pertinent references by J. G. Sikes, *Peter Abailard* (Cambridge, 1932), pp. 18 f.

[6] *De fide orthodoxa*, II, 3; in *NPF*, IX (ii), 20. In a similar spirit, Otto of Freising later spoke of Dionysius as the "chief of theologians" (*Chronica sive de duobus civitatibus*, VIII, 30, trans. Charles C. Mierow [1928]).

[7] In Περὶ τῆς οὐρανίας ἱεραρχίας (*De cælesti hierarchia*), especially Ch. VII-IX.

speculation which ever since apostolic times tended to organize the angels into specific groups.[8] Warnings were indeed issued, often by theologians of the stature of Origen and St. Augustine, that we cannot possibly know the exact number of angelic orders.[9] But they had no effect, partly because Augustine himself readily accepted that there are "degrees" in Heaven,[10] and especially because theologians of equal authority—St. Gregory of Nyssa and St. John Chrysostom among others—anticipated Dionysius if not by providing a detailed arrangement at least by citing all his nine orders.[11] In time, once the Dionysian scheme was accepted by medieval theologians as definitive, an effort was mounted to defend his celestial hierarchy by recourse to the Scriptures. It did not prove a very arduous task since the titles of the orders

[8] On the Jewish background consult Kaufmann Kohler, "Angelology," in *The Jewish Encyclopedia*, new ed. (1925), I, especially pp. 590 ff. On developments within Christianity, see the excellent studies by Joseph Turmel in *RHLR*, III (1898), pp. 289-308, 407-34, 533-52, and IV (1899), 217-38, 289-309, 414-34, 537-62; and G. Bareille, A. Vacant *et al.*, in *Dictionnaire de théologie catholique*, I (1935), pp. 1222-71. Diverse contexts are also provided by Robert M. Grant, "Chains of Being in Early Christianity," in *Myths and Symbols*, eds. J. M. Kitagawa and C. H. Long (Chicago, 1969), pp. 279-89, and Kathi Meyer-Baer, *Music of the Spheres and the Dance of Death* (Princeton, 1970), Ch. I-II. Cf. below, note 56.

[9] Origen, *De principiis*, I, v, 1; Augustine, *Enchiridion*, LVIII.

[10] *De civ. Dei*, XXII, 30; cf. Clement of Alexandria, *Stromata*, VI, 13-14. Augustine also prepared the way for the Pseudo-Dionysius by contributing decisively to the acceptance of "three" as the most sacred of numbers: see below, pp. 75 ff. Augustinian angelology is best delineated by Emilien Lamirande, *L'Église céleste selon Saint Augustin* (Paris, 1963), Ch. IV, "L'Église angélique."

[11] Gregory, *Contra Eunomium*, I, 23, and VII, 5; John Chrysostom, *De incomprehensibili dei natura*, II and III, *passim*. The silence of these predecessors of "Dionysius" about his works, later became a strong argument against their supposed apostolic date. See below, pp. 19 (Sherman on St. Jerome) and 28 (Hakewill on Eusebius *et al.*).

are all mentioned in the Bible, two occuring in the Old Testament and the rest in the New.[12] The principal Biblical passages, together with the actual terms used in Greek and their equivalent in the Vulgate and the six principal English versions, are as follows:

Biblical source	Greek	Vulgate	English versions
Is. 6.2	σεραφὶμ (LXX)	seraphim	seraphim
Ezek. 1.5, Ps. 80.1, etc.	χερουβὶμ (LXX)	cherubim	cherubim
Col. 1.16	θρόνοι	throni	thrones[13]
Col. 1.16, Eph. 1.21	κυριότητες	dominationes	domin[at]ions[14]
Eph. 1.21	δυνάμεις	virtutes	virtues[15]
Col. 1.16, Eph. 1.21	ἐξουσίαι	potestates	powers[16]
Col. 1.16, Eph. 1.21	ἀρχαί	principatus	principalities[17]

[12] See, for example, Peter Lombard, *Sententiarum*, II, 9; Hugo of St. Victor, *Summa sententiarum*, II, 5; and Thomas Aquinas, *Summa theologica*, I, cviii, 5.

[13] "Thrones" (Wycliffe, Rheims, A.V.); but "majesties" (Tyndale, Cranmer, Geneva).

[14] "Dominions" (Cranmer, A.V.); but "dominations" (the other four versions). Tyndale, Cranmer and the Geneva Bible also translate κυριότητες (in Colossians 1.16) as "lordships."

[15] Though "virtues" is the common name for this order, only Wycliffe so translates it. Tyndale, Cranmer, the Geneva Bible, and A.V. render δυνάμεις as "mights," while the Rheims version disagrees even with the Vulgate, and reads "powers."

[16] "Powers" (all versions except the Rheims, which reads "potestates").

[17] "Principalities" (Wycliffe, Rheims, A.V.); but "rules" (Tyndale, Cranmer, Geneva).

Biblical source	*Greek*	*Vulgate*	*English versions*
Jude 9, 1 Thess. 4.15	ἀρχάγγελοι	archangeli	archangels
Romans 8.38, etc.	ἄγγελοι	angeli	angels

Twelve centuries after the Pseudo-Dionysius first proposed his scheme, Thomas Heywood apportioned each of the nine books of *The Hierarchie of the Blessed Angells* (1635) to the corresponding order of heavenly spirits. A summary account which he also provided may dull the senses by its weary poetry but conveniently reiterates the common view of the Dionysian orders:

> In three most blessed *Hierarchies* th' are guided,
> And each into three Companies diuided:
> The first is that in which the *Seraphims* bee,
> *Cherubims, Thrones*; distinct in their degree.
> The *Seraphim* doth in the word imply,
> A *Feruent Loue* and *Zeale to the Most-High*.
> And these are they, incessantly each houre
> In contemplation are of Gods great Power.
> The *Cherubim* denotes to vs the *Fulnesse*
> Of absolute *Knowledge*, free from Humane
>   dulnesse;
> Or else *Wisedomes infusion*. These desire
> Nothing, but Gods great *Goodnesse* to admire.
> The name of *Thrones*, his glorious Seat displaies;
> His *Equitie* and *Iustice* these still praise.
>   The second *Ternion*, as the Scoole relates,
> Are *Dominations, Vertues, Potestates*.
> *Dominions*, th' *Angels* Offices dispose;

The *Vertues* (in the second place) are those
That execute his high and holy Will:
The *Potestates*, they are assistant still,
The malice of the Diuell to withstand:
For God hath giuen it to their powerful hand.
  In the third order *Principates* are plac't;
Next them, *Arch-Angels*; *Angels* are the last.
The *Principates*, of Princes take the charge,
Their power on earth to curbe, or to enlarge;
And these worke Miracles. Th' *Arch-Angels* are
Embassadors, great matters to declare.
Th' *Angels* Commission hath not that extent,
They only haue vs Men in gouernment.[18]

Parallel statements in poetry abound, inclusive of Ben Jonson's celebration of

> those *Hierarchies*,
>   *Angels, Arch-angels, Principalities*,
> The *Dominations, Vertues*, and the *Powers*,
>   The *Thrones*, the *Cherube*, and *Seraphick*
>   bowers,
> That, planted round, there sing before the *Lamb*.
>   ("Elegie on my Muse," ll. 85-89)

II

The works of the Pseudo-Dionysius, available in the West by the 750's on a limited scale,[19] were first translated

---

[18] *The Hierarchie*, p. 194. See the account of this work by Percy H. Osmond, *The Mystical Poets of the English Church* (1919), pp. 56-66. K. M. Briggs in *Folklore*, LXXX (1969), pp. 89-106, is primarily interested in the work as "a rich mine of folk tradition."

[19] Between 757 and 824, they were presented as gifts on three occasions:

into Latin in the middle of the ninth century: initially but unsatisfactorily by Hilduin, and soon thereafter (*c.* 860) by John Scotus Erigena, whose version was destined to exercize a profound influence upon his contemporaries and successors.[20] As a measure of this influence we may consider the composition of an astounding number of commentaries on one or another of the works of "Dionysius," sparked by John Scotus' own lengthy exposition[21] and imitated by numerous theologians and scholars, including John Sarrazin, Hugo of St. Victor, Peter Lombard, Walter of St. Victor, Alexander of Hales, Robert Grosseteste, Vincent of Beauvais, St. Bonaventura, St. Thomas Aquinas, Dionysius the Carthusian—and especially St. Albertus Magnus, who lived up to his title of *doctor universalis* in commenting on the sum total of the Dionysian treatises.[22] But the most illustrious supporters of the Dionysian classification of the angels

by Pope Paul I to King Pippin III, by Pope Adrian I to Abbot Julrad of St. Denys, and by the Emperor Michael II the Stammerer to the Emperor Louis I the Pious (August F. Gfrörer, *Allgemeine Kirchengeschichte* [Stuttgart, 1844], III, 865).

[20] The original works of "Dionysius," with the Greek commentaries, are in *PG*, IV; John Scotus' translation is in *PL*, CXXII, 1035-70. The earlier version by Hilduin and the subsequent translations by John Sarrazin *et al.*, have been edited by Philippe Chevallier, *Dionysiaca* (Paris-Bruge, 1937-1950), 2 vols.; cf. Gabriel Théry, *Études dionysiennes* (Paris, 1932-1937), 2 vols. See also the concise account by Martin Grabman, "Ps.-Dionysius Areopagita in lateinischen Übersetzungen des Mittelalters," in *Beiträge zur Geschichte des christlicher Altertums und der byzantinischen Literatur*, ed. A. M. Koeniger (Bonn and Leipzig, 1922), pp. 180-99.

[21] *Expositiones super ierarchiam cœlestem S. Dionysii*, in *PL*, CXXII, 126-266.

[22] Albertus Magnus, *Opera omnia* (Lyons, 1651), XIII, 1-196. The Dionysian treatises were also paraphrased earlier, in the seventh century, by St. Maximus the Confessor.

were St. Thomas Aquinas and Dante, the one justifying it in his prose,[23] the other immortalizing it in his poetry.[24] St. Thomas during his appearance in Dante's *Paradiso* voices the common persuasion when he credits Dionysius with the most profound perception of "l'angelica natura e il ministero" (X, 117).

Eastern Christians, in the meantime, had accepted the Dionysian scheme just as readily; so much so, that even Byzantium's standard *Guide to Painting*, compiled by Dionysius of Fourna, expressly advised icon-makers and mosaicists to represent nine orders of angels ("according to St. Dionysius the Areopagite").[25] Yet ingenious though the Eastern Christians were in enriching the celestial hierarchy,[26] they could hardly compete with the imaginative permutations introduced by their Western counterparts. A series of correspondences upheld in the West involved, *inter alia*, the parallelism established between the nine angelic orders and the equal number of celestial

[23] *Summa theologica*, I, cviii, especially 5-6; *Summa contra gentiles*, II, 80. In line with current practice, St. Thomas regarded Dionysius as a major authority both here and in his fuller "Treatise of Angels" (*S. th.*, I, l-lxiv). For the influence of the one on the other, see J. Durantel, *Saint Thomas et le Pseudo-Denys* (Paris, 1919); cf. James Collins, *The Thomistic Philosophy of the Angels* (Washington, D.C., 1947), especially pp. 31 ff., 180 ff., 198 ff., and 294 ff.

[24] *Paradiso*, XXVIII, 98-132. The influence of Dionysius on Dante is discussed by Edmund G. Gardner, *Dante's Ten Heavens*, 2nd ed. (1900), Ch. V (ii), and *Dante and the Mystics* (1913), Ch. III.

[25] *Guide to Painting*, Part II; trans. Margaret Stokes, in Adolphe N. Didron, *Christian Iconography*, ed. E. J. Millington and M. Stokes (1886), II, 265-66. Eastern acceptance of the Dionysian scheme was determined by its endorsement by John of Damascus (as above, note 6).

[26] As in their placement of the nine orders under the aegis of the Virgin Mary—a notion eventually exported to the West (Louis Réau, *Iconographie de l'art chrétien* [Paris, 1956], I, i, 39).

11

spheres;[27] while Pico della Mirandola later reduced cabalism's malleable orders to nine in an effort to make them conform to the Dionysian scheme.[28] Where circumstances did not permit any adjustment—as in the mosaics of the octagonal cupola of the Florence Baptistery—the angelic orders were necessarily reduced[29] even as Dionysius' basic arrangement was kept firmly in view. In time, at any rate, the scheme was generously confirmed by the stipulation that the nine orders of angels correspond to an equally ninefold hierarchy among the devils.[30]

[27] I.e., the *primum mobile*, the sphere of the zodiac, Saturn, Jupiter, Mars, the sun, Venus, Mercury, and the moon. By excluding the first two, John Bishop in *The Marrow of Astrology* (1688) ended up with seven planets—and, alas, only seven orders of angels. But then the work is precisely what its author claims it is, "my unpolished Bratt."

[28] I.e., cherubim, seraphim, hasmalim, hagot, aralim, tarsisim, ophanim, thephrasim, and isim (see Frances A. Yates, *Giordano Bruno and the Hermetic Tradition* [1964], pp. 123 f.). Pico's angelology—"in accord with the teaching of Dionysius"—is set forth in his *Heptaplus*, III, 3 (*Opera* [Venice, 1557], fols. 3v ff.).

[29] I.e., to seven (from thrones down to angels), with the eighth segment of the cupola allotted to Christ in majesty who is flanked by more angels—possibly the missing cherubim and seraphim. Elsewhere, at any rate, the orders remained intact: see the miniature in the ninth-century Breviary of St. Hildegarde, reproduced by Robert Hughes, *Heaven and Hell in Western Art* (1968), p. 23.

[30] It is "a Maxime," Heywood assures us, that Satan's disciples "have amongst them Orders and Degrees" (as above, note 18: p. 411). For the similar views of Origen, Peter Lombard, Albertus Magnus, Thomas Aquinas, *et al.*, consult Arturo Graf, *The Story of the Devil*, trans. Edward N. Stone (1931), pp. 43-45; Robert H. West, *The Invisible World* (Athens, Ga., 1939), pp. 81-82, 217, 219; and Edward Langton, *Supernatural* (1934), pp. 153, 156, 158, etc. For Renaissance reports on the distribution of the devils into nine orders, see Robert Burton, *The Anatomy of Melancholy*, 6th ed. (1652), p. 44 (Part. I, Sect. 2, Memb. 1, Subs. 2); Antoine Le Grand, *An Entire Body of Philosophy*, trans. Richard Blome (1694: the Latin original was first published in 1671), I, 88-9; *et al.* The foremost Renaissance

But the Dionysian arrangement was not uniformly accepted. Two alternatives were also available; and the eventual result was, not surprisingly, galloping confusion. One alternative, introduced by St. Gregory the Great in one of his homilies and later endorsed by St. Bernard of Clairvaux,[31] had the positions of the virtues and the principalities reversed, the rest of the orders remaining intact. But the other possibility, also set forth by Gregory the Great in his *Moralia* and concurrently proposed by his contemporary Isidore of Seville,[32] was drastically different. The three schemes are as follows:

Dionysius, Thomas Aquinas *et al.*	Gregory (in *Homilia*) and Bernard	Gregory (in *Moralia*) and Isidore
seraphim	seraphim	seraphim
cherubim	cherubim	cherubim
thrones	thrones	powers
dominations	dominations	principalities
virtues	principalities	virtues
powers	powers	dominations
principalities	virtues	thrones
archangels	archangels	archangels
angels	angels	angels

exponent of this view was Heinrich Cornelius Agrippa, *Three Books of Occult Philosophy*, trans. J. F. (1651), pp. 397-99.

[31] Gregory, *XL Homiliarum in Evangelia*, III, xxxiv, 7; Bernard, *De consideratione*, V, 7.

[32] Gregory, *Moralium libri, sive expositio in librum B. Job*, XXXII, xxiii, 48; Isidore, *Etymologiarum sive originum libri XX*, VII, 5. Gregory's other formulation (see previous note) was apparently his "final and deliberate"

Least popular of these schemes was the one proposed by Gregory and Isidore; yet it managed to enlist the support of Brunetto Latini and, through him or directly from Gregory, the support of Dante in the *Convivio*— that is to say, before Dante was persuaded by Thomas Aquinas that the Dionysian arrangement should be regarded as definitive.[33] If on the other hand the Gregory-Bernard scheme enjoyed widespread approval, it may be that the crucial factor was not any conscious intention to defy the Pseudo-Dionysius so much as the likelihood of an understandable error: for the Dionysian arrangement, as already noted, becomes the Gregory-Bernard scheme through the transposition of the virtues and the principalities. Hence the frequently observed phenomenon that even self-acknowledged disciples of "Dionysius" espoused not his scheme but that of Gregory and Bernard. Among the victims of this embarrassing predicament were Bartholomeus Anglicus, the author of the thirteenth-century encyclopaedia *De proprietatibus rerum*, translated by John of Trevisa in 1398 and often published during the Renaissance;[34] Hartmann Schedel, the

version, while the one in *Moralia* was only a "rough enumeration" (F. Homes Dudden, *Gregory the Great* [1905], II, 360 ff.).

[33] Brunetto Latini, *Li Livres dou tresor*, I, xii, 5 (ed. Francis J. Carmody, *University of California Publications in Modern Philology*, XX [1948], 27); Dante, *Convivio*, II, 6. Dante's debt to Gregory the Great has been argued by Giovanni Busnelli: "L'ordine dei cori angelici nel *Convivio* e nel *Paradiso*," *Bullettino della Società Dantesca Italiana*, n.s., XVIII (1911), pp. 127-28; *Il concetto e l'ordine del "paradiso" dantesco* (Città di Castello, 1912), II, 143 ff.; and [with G. Vandelli], eds., *Il Convivio* (Florence, 1934), pp. 136n, 248-49. On Dante and Brunetto Latini consult Paget Toynbee, "Dante's Arrangement of the Celestial Hierarchies in the *Convivio*," in *Bullettino, op.cit.*, p. 205, and *Concise Dante Dictionary* (Oxford, 1914), p. 257; and Edward Moore, *Studies in Dante*, 4th series (Oxford, 1917), pp. 226-27.

[34] See, for example, *Batman vppon Bartholome, his Booke De proprietatibus*

German humanist principally responsible for the *Nuremberg Chronicle* (1493);[35] Antoine du Verdier, whose commentary on Pedro Mexía's *Silva de varia lección* (1542) later formed part of the massive work of reference compiled in England by Thomas Milles;[36] Sir John Ferne, one of the best English expositors of the Scale of Nature;[37] and the Spanish poet Hojeda, author of the epic *La Cristiada.*[38]

It is apparent, then, that the Pseudo-Dionysius was present even where he seems to have been bypassed. Of

---

rerum . . . with . . . Additions (1582), fol. 5v-10v. In other revisions of the original work the error was, of course, repeated: cf. Thomas Berthelet's version, *Bertholomevs de Proprietatibus rervm* (1535), fol. 3v-8v.

[35] *Registrum huius operis libri cronicarum* (Nuremberg, 1493), fol. 6. A later chronicler, Pieter van Opmeer, shared Schedel's fate: see his *Chronographia* (Cologne, 1625), I, 2.

[36] *Les diverses leçons d'Antoine du Verdier*, 2nd ed. (Lyons, 1580), p. 14, and Milles, *The Treasurie of Auncient and Moderne Times* (1613), p. 10—the latter being mainly a translation of Mexía's work with the commentaries on it by Francesco Sansovino, du Verdier, *et al.* Interestingly enough, a similar confusion appears to have set in concerning the colors traditionally associated with the seraphim and the cherubim: see Harry Morris, "Some Uses of Angel Iconography in English Literature," *CL*, X (1958), pp. 36-44.

[37] *The Blazon of Gentrie* (1586), p. 5.

[38] *La Cristiada* (Seville, 1611), I, 42; as noted by Sister Mary Edgar Meyer, *The Sources of Hojeda's "La Cristiada,"* in *University of Michigan Publications, Language and Literature*, XXVI (1953), pp. 94-96. The Gregory-Bernard scheme was also espoused by Robert Fludd, whose illustration—reproduced in Jocelyn Godwin's *Robert Fludd* (1979), Pl. 54 [p. 50]—provides a correspondence between the ninefold angelic world, the universal structure (the seven planets plus the *primum mobile* and the sphere of fixed stars), and the elemental world (the four elements so amended as to terminate in the requisite number nine). But Fludd was evidently tolerant enough of other variants too: see the two illustrations reproduced by S. K. Heninger, Jr., *The Cosmographical Glass: Renaissance Diagrams of the Universe* (San Marino, Calif., 1977), pp. 156-57 and 164, where Fludd appears to endorse two different schemes, neither in conformity with any of the traditional arrangements.

writers inclined to enumerate the nine angelic orders, certainly the "most part"—as William Alley correctly observed in 1571—continued strictly to follow the Dionysian scheme.[39] But as much could also be said of those who were disposed only generally to speak of "the nine Quires of Angels."[40] Such writers include a diversity of poets, noteworthy only for the monotony with which they asserted the "Nyen ordres of aungels," "the Ordrys nyne / Off haly Angelyes," "the Angellis of the Ordouris Nyne," the "nine orders . . . of Angels"—and so on.[41] Barely escaping mere repetition, Tasso alluded to three squadrons of angels, with each squadron subdivided into three unnamed orders; while Spenser twice

[39] Πτωχομουσεῖον (1571), I, 123v-124. Representative writers who listed the Dionysian orders include: Bellarmine, *De æterna felicitate sanctorvm* (Antwerp, 1616), pp. 20-24, trans. Thomas Everard, *Of the Eternall Felicity of the Saints* (St. Omer, 1638), pp. 23-27; Jodocus Clithtoveus, *Sermones* (Cologne, 1535), pp. 206 f.; Ficino (as below, note 47); Heywood (quoted above, p. 8); Matthew Kellison, *A Treatise of the Hierarchie . . . of the Chvrch* (Douai, 1629), p. 13; Le Grand (as above, note 30), I, 84-85; Guillaume de la Perrière, *Les considerations des quatre mondes* (Lyons, 1552), sig. F7v; Juan de la Pineda, *Los treynta libros de la monarchia ecclesiastica* (Barcelona, 1620), I, 4v; Robert Southwell, *A Foure-Fould Meditation of the Foure Last Things* (1606), XCV, 2; Gisbertus Voetius, *De hierarchia cœlesti*, in his *Selectae disputationes theologicae* (Utrecht, 1648), I, 882-97; and Vondel, *Lucifer*, trans. Watson Kirkconnell, *The Celestial Cycle* (Toronto, 1952), p. 369. For a fuller exposition, see John Salkeld, *A Treatise of Angels* (1613), Ch. XLVII; but his references to authorities supporting the scheme are not always reliable.

[40] Nicolas Caussin, *The Holy Court*, trans. Sir Thomas Hawkins *et al.* (1650), I, 44. See also Robert Allott's book of commonplaces, *Wits Theatre of the Little World* (1599), p. 4.

[41] *Seriatim: York Plays*, ed. L. T. Smith (1885, repr. 1963), p. 2; Andrew of Wyntoun, *The Orygynale Cronykil of Scotland*, ed. David Laing, in *The Historians of Scotland* (Edinburgh, 1872), I, 3; Sir David Lindsay, *Ane Dialog betuixt Experience and ane Courteour*, l. 6260; and Michael Drayton, *Idea*, XVIII, 5, in *Poems* (1610), p. 474.

sang of the "trinall triplicities": once near the end of the first book of *The Faerie Queene*, and again in *An Hymne of Heavenly Love* where the "angels bright" are envisaged as congregated about the throne of God:

There they in their trinall triplicities
About him wait, and on his will depend,
Either with nimble wings to cut the skies,
When he them on his messages doth send,
Or on his owne dread presence to attend,
Where they behold the glorie of his light,
And carroll hymnes of love both day and night.[42]

The pattern is far more ravelled than I have suggested, however. The galloping confusion already mentioned was a fact, the inescapable consequence of the coexistence of three different schemes. Not infrequently, therefore, to be specific about the nine orders was to court disaster, witness the experiences of four very dissimilar writers—Francesco Alunno, Andrea Vittorelli, Francisco Suárez, and Peter Hausted—each of whom transposed a different set of angelic orders in the Dionysian scheme and ended up with mutually exclusive designs.[43] Further afield were writers who like Annibale

---

[42] Tasso, *Gerusalemme Liberata*, XVIII, xcvi, 5-6; Spenser, *The Faerie Queene*, I, xii, 39, and *An Hymne of Heavenly Love*, ll. 64-70 (cf. *An Hymne of Heavenly Beautie*, ll. 85-98). F. M. Padelford is certainly mistaken in his claim that Spenser's angelology is "substantially a poetical version" of Calvin's ("Spenser and the Theology of Calvin," *MP*, XII [1914], 4).

[43] Alunno, *La fabrica del mondo* (Venice, 1581), fol. 2v; Vittorelli, *De angelorvm cvstodia* (Passau, 1605), fol. 5-6; Suárez, *Disputationes* (Venice, 1740), II, 30 ff.; and Hausted, *Ten Sermons* (1636), pp. 40-41. The first reversed the seraphim and the cherubim; the second as well as the third, the dominations and the virtues; and the fourth, the powers and the principalities.

Romei inadvertently reduced the nine orders to eight,[44] or who like Heremias Drexelius hazarded in one and the same work two schemes, the first strictly Dionysian, the second not even remotely so.[45] But the ultimate confusion appears to have been shared by three other writers— the Franciscan cabalist Jean Thenaud, the Cornish dramatist William Jordan, and the Scottish poet William Drummond of Hawthornden—whose lists of the nine orders are unique by any standards.[46]

III

It is a commonplace of scholarship that the Pseudo-Dionysius appealed greatly to the Neoplatonists of Renaissance Italy. To illustrate this appeal we need go no further than the translation of his works in 1492 by Marsilio Ficino.[47] Given in turn the well-attested intel-

[44] *Discorsi* (Ferrara, 1586), p. 6; trans. J. Kepers, *The Courtiers Academie* (1598), p. 8. William Nelson in *The Poetry of Edmund Spenser* (1963), pp. 321-22, claims that Romei—and indeed Spenser—posited the human souls as the lowermost ninth order. If so, the resultant scheme would still be the wildest on record.

[45] *Horologium auxiliaris tvtelaris angeli*, 7th ed. (Munich, 1629), pp. 22 and 37; trans. Anon., *The Angel-Gvardians Clock* (Rouen, [1621]), pp. 46 and 92.

[46] Thenaud, in the unpublished *La saincte et trescrestienne cabale*, cited by Joseph L. Blau, *The Christian Interpretation of the Cabala in the Renaissance* (1944), pp. 92-94, 130-35; Jordan, *The Creation of the World* (1611), ed. Davies Gilbert (1827), pp. 4 ff.; and Drummond, *Flowers of Sion* (Edinburgh, 1623), p. 34. The latter's scheme may be cited as an example: archangels, angels, cherubim, seraphim, thrones, principalities, dominations, powers, virtues.

[47] As we might have expected, Ficino endorsed Dionysius' nine orders without hesitation. They are listed in *De christiana religione*, XIV (*Opera* [Basle, 1576], I, 19). See also the discussion by Yates (as above, note 28), Ch. VI.

lectual relations between Ficino and John Colet in England, one is not surprised to find Colet engaged in a lengthy commentary on the Dionysian hierarchies, both celestial and ecclesiastical.[48] The surprise—and indeed astonishment—is that when Colet invited William Grocyn to speak at St. Paul's, the consequence was a series of lectures aimed at disproving the apostolic date of the Dionysian treatises.[49] In short, "Dionysius the Areopagite" was said to be a fraud.

Grocyn's pioneering labors might have passed unheeded had not two widely respected scholars also decided to express grave doubts about the authenticity of "Dionysius:" Lorenzo Valla and Erasmus.[50] It was not long before these illustrious names were invoked as a matter of course. John Sherman's discussion of the Pseudo-Dionysius in 1641 is typical: ". . . concerning the books which the Pontificians father upon his name, *De cœlesti hierarchia*, it were not very difficult to determine them not to be his. For Hierome [i.e. St. Jerome, who lived before the Dionysian treatises were penned] in his Catalogue of Ecclesiastick writers maketh no mention of them. Valla and Erasmus have proved by many arguments that they are none of his. . . ."[51] Ten years earlier

[48] The commentary was first published in 1869, ed. J. H. Lupton. See further Frederic Seebohm, *The Oxford Reformers*, 3rd ed. (1911), pp. 60-78; Ernest W. Hunt, *Dean Colet and his Theology* (1956), especially Ch. V; and Sears Jayne, *John Colet and Marsilio Ficino* (1963).

[49] Seebohm (previous note), pp. 90 f., and J.A.R. Marriott, *The Life of John Colet* (1933), pp. 103 f.

[50] The annotations on the New Testament by Valla (d. 1457) were first published by Erasmus. The editions I consulted are: Valla, *In Novum Testamentum . . . annotationes*, in his *Opera* (Basle, [1543]), p. 852, and Erasmus, *In Novum Testamentum . . . annotationes* (Basle, 1519), p. 225, where both are commenting on Acts 17.34 (as above, p. 3).

[51] *A Greek in the Temple* (Cambridge, 1641), pp. 14 f.

John Bayly had been even more contemptuous: ". . . the schoolemen, led on by *Dionisius Areopagita* who by *Valla, Erasmus*, and all the learned world, is and was long since branded for acounterfeite, haue sorted the whole heauenly society of Angells into three Hierarchies every Hierarchie conteyning three orders. . . ."[52] and so on. The two statements should not be accepted uncritically, however. Sherman's obvious prejudice against Roman Catholics ("the Pontificians"), and Bayly's sweeping celebration of "all the learned world," misrepresent the situation grossly. The "Pontificians," after all, included both Valla and Erasmus; and the "learned world," such formidable champions of the genuineness of "Dionysius" as Cardinals Baronius and Bellarmine.[53] The truth of the matter is that opinions did not divide strictly along Catholic or Protestant lines. "Dionysius" was attacked by Catholics no less than by Protestants;[54] and he was

[52] *Two Sermons* (Oxford, 1630), I, 4. The embattled Whitaker (below, note 54) also referred his opponent Campian to Valla and Erasmus.

[53] Baronius, *Annales ecclesiastici* (Cologne, 1609), II, 42 ff., and Bellarmine, *De scriptoribus ecclesiasticis Testamenti novi*, in his *Opera omnia* (Venice, 1728), VII, 27-29. Thus also the great humanist Jacques Lefèvre d'Étaples, who defended the authenticity of the Pseudo-Areopagite largely for patriotic reasons in that he provided "apostolic authority" for the Church in France. See also below, note 55.

[54] E.g., Edmundus Albertinus, *De Evcharistiæ . . . libri tres* (Deventer, 1654), pp. 260 ff.; Cardinal Cajetan, *Evangelia cvm commentariis* (Paris, 1532), fol. 283v; Martin Chemnitz (Chemnitius), *Loci theologici* (Frankfurt and Wittenberg, 1653), I, 2 f.; Jean Daillé, *The Right Vse of the Fathers*, trans. Thomas Smith (1651), p. 29; John Deacon and John Walker, *A Svmmarie Answere* (1601), p. 138; Johann Michael Dilherr, *Disputationes* (Nuremberg, 1652), II, 310 ff.; Johann Gerhard, *Patrologia*, 2nd ed. (Jena, 1668), pp. 19 ff.; Thomas James, *A Treatise of the Corruption of Scripture* (1611), p. 6; Joseph Mede, *Diatribæ* (1642), p. 172; Richard Montagu, *Immediate Addresse unto God Alone* (1624), p. 160; Joseph Justus Scaliger, *apud* John E. Sandys, *A History of Classical Scholarship* (Cambridge, 1908), II, 203; John Trapp, *A Commentary . . . upon all the Epistles* (1647), p. 658;

also defended by both in relative measure.[55] We may remind ourselves that Heywood and Spenser, who alike endorsed the Dionysian orders (above, pp. 8-9 and 17), could hardly be described as Catholics; and neither could Bacon, who had other reasons for referring in *The Advancement of Learning* to "that supposed Dionysius" (I, vi, 3).

Yet Protestants could not, and did not, fail to see that the controversy over the Pseudo-Dionysius was an ideal weapon to direct against Catholicism. True, the Catholic Church has never affirmed the number of angelic orders dogmatically;[56] and so far, at least, the controversy did not affect doctrinal issues. But as Protestants aimed at dismantling all Catholic traditions, developments centered on the Pseudo-Dionysius afforded them a perfect opportunity to ridicule yet another venerable authority of the "Pontificians." Crucial in this respect was the Protestant conviction that the Dionysian orders lack Biblical support; for even if the Bible occasionally names

Pietro Martire Vermigli, *Common Places*, trans. Anthony Marten (1574), I, 120; William Whitaker, *An Answere to the Ten Reasons of Edmund Campian*, trans. Richard Stocke (1606), p. 124; *et al.* See also below, note 72.

[55] E.g., Edmund Campian, *Rationes Decem* (published with Whitaker's *Responsio*, Antwerp, 1582), p. 116, trans. Anon., *Campian Englished. Or . . . the Ten Reasons* ([Douai?], 1632), p. 90; Richard Carpenter, *Experience, Historie, and Divinitie* (1642), II, 258-59; Martin del Rio, *Vindicæ Areopagitæ . . '. contra Iosephvm Scaligervm Ivlii F.* (Antwerp, 1607); Kellison (as below, note 39); Thomas Vaughan, *Anthroposophia theomagica* (1650), p. 5; *et al.* See also above, note 53, and below, note 69.

[56] A. Beugnet, "Angélologie dans les conciles et doctrine de l'Église sur les anges," in *Dictionnaire de théologie catholique*, I (1935), 1264-71, and Anscar Vonier, "The Angels," in *The Teaching of the Catholic Church*, ed. George D. Smith (1948), I, 266-68. Cf. above, note 8. The Eastern Orthodox Church similarly maintains that the angels are hierarchically arranged but credits no single scheme as doctrinally binding (Christos Androutsos, Δογματικὴ τῆς Ὀρθοδόξου Ἐκκλησίας [Athens, 1956], p. 126).

all nine orders, it does not endorse any coherent scheme. Luther, in consequence, did not hesitate to dismiss the Pseudo-Dionysius as "full of the silliest prattle," and his nine orders as "nothing but idle and useless human ideas."[57] Calvin was equally explicit. As he argued in his zestful attack on the "nugatory wisdom" of the Pseudo-Dionysius:

". . . if we would be duly wise, we must renounce those vain babblings of idle men, concerning the nature, ranks, and number of angels, without any authority from the Word of God. . . . None can deny that Dionysius (whoever he may have been) has many shrewd and subtle disquisitions in his Celestial Hierarchy; but on looking at them more closely, every one must see that they are merely idle talk. . . . When you read the work of Dionysius, you would think that the man had come down from heaven, and was relating not what he had learned, but what he had actually seen. Paul, however, though he was carried to the third heaven, so far from delivering anything of the kind, positively declares that it was not lawful for man to speak the secrets which he had seen."[58]

A host of Protestant theologians agreed. William Perkins, England's most widely respected Calvinist, justified the common approach with a battery of Biblical verses:

". . . that there are degrees of angels, it is most plaine. Coloss. I.16. *By him were all things created, which are in heauen, & in earth, things visible and inuisible: whether they be thrones or dominions, or principalities, or powers.* Rom. 8.38. *Neither Angels, nor principalities, nor powers, &c.* I.

---

[57] *Works*, ed. Jaroslav Pelikan (St. Louis, 1958), I, 235. See also his *Tischreden*, trans. Henry Bell in *Colloquia mensalia* (1652), p. 356.

[58] *Institutes*, I, xiv, 4. The Pauline allusion is to 2 Corinthians 12.2-4.

Thess. 4.16. *The Lord shal descend with the voice of the archangel, and with the trumpet of God.* But it is not for vs to search, who or how many be of ech order, neither ought we curiously to enquire howe they are distinguished, whether in essence, or qualities. Colos. 2.18. *Let no man at his pleasure beare rule ouer you by humblenesse of minde, and worshipping of Angels, aduancing himselfe in those thinges which he neuer saw.*"[59]

In the parallel statement of Bishop Joseph Hall:

"Heaven hath nothing in it but perfection; but even perfection it self hath degrees, as the glorified souls, so the blessed Angels have their heights of excellency and glory: He will be known for the God of Order, observeth no doubt a most exact order in his Court of heaven, nearest to the residence of his Majesty. Equality hath no place, either in earth or in hell; we have no reason to seek it in heaven. He that was rapt into the third heaven can tell us of Thrones, Dominions, Principalities, Angels and Arch-angels in that region of blessednesse. We cannot be so simple, as to think these to be but one classe of spirits; doubtlesse they are distinctions or divers orders: But what their severall ranks, offices, employments are, he were not more wise that could tell, then he is bold that dare speak: What modest indignation can forbear stamping at the presumption of those men, who . . . admitted to be the heralds, or masters of ceremonies in that higher world, have taken upon them to marshall these Angelicall spirits into their severall rooms; proportioning their stations, dignities, services, according to the model of earthly Courts; disposing them into Ternions of three generall Hierarchies."[60]

[59] *A Golden Chaine, or the Description of Theologie* (1591), sig. B5v-B6.
[60] *The Invisible World* (1659), pp. 44-46. For similar statements, see

"I know not," added Hall, "whether this soaring conceit be more seemingly pious, then really presumptuous."[61]

The impact of these massive assaults on the Dionysian scheme was decisive. Aware at last that the nine orders were "but fine cobweb-lawn, but rarefied *Metaphysical* Abstractions, and Tentered *Probabilities of Ratiocination*,"[62] an ever-increasing number of writers preferred deliberate caution to their predecessors' confidence, and studied vagueness to the erstwhile explicitness. The angels continued to be regarded as hierarchically disposed, partly because the Bible implies the existence of ranks in Heaven, and partly because the widely endorsed concept of *scala mundi* required that order and degree be maintained in every rung of the cosmic ladder "from the Mushrome to the Angels."[63] But every tendency to classify the celestial orders within any scheme whatsoever was now suppressed. The result was expertly generalized allusions to the "vnconfused orders Angellick," pointedly vague assurances that they possess "sundry names,"

Bayly (as above, note 52), I, 5 ff.; Gulielmus Bucanus, *Institvtions of the Christian Religion*, trans. Robert Hill (1606), p. 69; William Cowper, *Patmos: or a Commentary on the Revelation of Saint Iohn* (1619), pp. 181-82; Donne, *Sermons*, VIII, 105-106 [quoted in the headnote, above]; Leonardus Lessius, *Rawleigh his Ghost* [i.e., *De providentia numinis* etc.], trans. A. B. (St. Omer, 1631), pp. 210-11; William Loe, *The Mystery of Mankind* (1619), p. 129; Elnathan Parr, *The Grounds of Divinitie*, 8th ed. (1636), p. 126; John Salkeld, *A Treatise of Angels* (1613), p. 303; Andrew Willet, *Synopsis Papismi* (1594), p. 408; *et al.* For an American view see Increase Mather, *Angelographia* (Boston, 1696), pp. 15-19 (Doctr. II, Prop. II). The authority most often cited in support of this view was Augustine (as above, note 9).

[61] *Ibid.*, p. 50.

[62] The pompous phrase is Edward Sparke's, in Θυσιαστήριον, 3rd ed. (1663), p. 550.

[63] Samuel Ward, *The Life of Faith*, 3rd ed. (1622), p. 2.

and intentionally cautious claims that they are "Legion-iz'd in Rankes," else arranged "as an *Army*, one in order and degree aboue the other."[64]

Milton best illustrates the changing climate of opinion. His early reference in the *Nativity Ode* to the "ninefold harmony" of the celestial spheres (l. 131) was stilled once he became aware of the controversial issue behind his poetic flourish. Thereafter, limiting himself to the authority of the Bible, he avoided even distant echoes of the Dionysian classification of the angels, acknowledging in *The Reason of Church-Government* only that they are "distinguisht and quaterniond into their celestiall Princedomes, and Satrapies," and in *Paradise Lost* that they are generally distributed into "Thrones, Domina-tions, Princedoms, Virtues, Powers."[65] The supposition

---

[64] *Seriatim*: John Davies of Hereford, *The Holy Roode* (1609), sig. G3v; Henoch Clapham, *Ælohim-Triune* (1601), sig. C4; Davies (as before), sig. 14; and Richard Hooker, *Of the Lawes of Ecclesiastical Politie*, 4th ed. (1617), p. 10. Equally unspecific statements were ventured, for example, by Alley (as above, note 39); Jacobus Arminius, *Works*, trans. James Nichols (1825-75), II, 360; Bayly (as above, note 52), p. 5; John Boughton, *God and Man* (1623), p. 36; Heinrich Bullinger, *Fiftie . . . Sermons*, trans. H. I. (1587), p. 737; Benjamin Camfield, *A theological Discourse of Angels* (1678), pp. 43 f.; Henry Church, *Miscellanea Philo-Theologica* (1631), pp. 13 f.; Deacon and Walker (as above, note 54), p. 142; Donne, *Sermons*, VII, 129 [cf. Itrat Husain, *The Dogmatic and Mystical Theology of John Donne* (1938), p. 76]; Joseph Mede, *Diatribæ* (1642), p. 173; George Petter, *Commentary, upon . . . Mark* (1661), I, 791; Francis Quarles, *Hosanna* (1647), ed. John Horden (Liverpool, 1960), p. 8; Edmund Reeve, *The Christian Doctrine* (1631), pp. 13 f.; John Swan, *Redde debitvm* (1640), p. 17; Yates (as below, note 68); *et al.* See further the authorities cited by Heinrich Heppe, *Reformed Dogmatics*, ed. Ernst Bizer, trans. G. T. Thompson (1950), pp. 210 f., and Robert H. West, *Milton and the Angels* (Athens, Ga., 1955), pp. 13-14, 51, 135, etc.

[65] *The Reason* etc., in *Works*, III, 185; and *Paradise Lost*, V, 601 and 840. The five orders named in the latter passage are elsewhere on purpose

that the scheme of the Pseudo-Dionysius is "the basis of the whole angelical system of *Paradise Lost*"[66] requires, I should have thought, some reappraisal.

IV

In 1552 the great French apologist Pierre Viret raised a question but did not pause for an answer. "Who knoweth not," he asked, "that the book of the celestiall *Hierarchia*, is more worthy to be [of] some dreamer, then of Sainct *Denis* the Disciple of Sainct *Paul?* "[67] By 1622 John Yates felt that the time had come to be even more categorical: ". . . whereas it is supposed, that those nine orders are set downe by a disciple of S. *Paul*, it is well proued, that the alledged Dionysius is of a far newer stamp, and baser mettall."[68] In actual fact, however, proof was not forthcoming quite as readily as Yates and others would have us believe. Despite the earnest efforts of Catholic and Protestant scholars, Donald Lupton was right in declaring as late as 1640 that the works of the Pseudo-Dionysius were in the mid-seventeenth century accepted "not without some scruple or doubting, howbeit those of the best judgment give good reason why

---

reduced to four (III, 320) or, just as casually, increased to nine (V, 750-51); but in each case the basic premise of "hierarchies, of orders, and degrees" is firmly maintained as regards both the angels (V. 591) and the devils (V. 722: cf. above, note 30). See also *De doctrina christiana*, in *Works*, XV, 36 and 110, and the discussion by West (previous note), pp. 133-36.

[66] A. W. Verity, in his frequently reprinted edition of *"Paradise Lost," Books I and II* (Cambridge, 1893; 3rd. ed., 1952; repr. 1962), p. 154.

[67] *The Christian Disputations*, trans. John Brooke (1579), fol. 177v. First published in French in 1552.

[68] *A Modell of Divinitie* (1622), p. 122.

they are his."[69] Lupton's statement need not surprise; for in spite of the persuasive arguments advanced later by Nicholas le Nourry,[70] the logomachy continued and the apostolic date of the Dionysian treatises was not rejected much before the later part of the nineteenth century.[71]

It was nevertheless during the Renaissance that the movement began that led away from the long-upheld conflation of St. Paul's convert in Athens with the patron saint of France, and of both with the pseudonymous author of *De cœlesti hierarchia.* The movement, initiated by Catholics, was also extended by Catholics with the support—often the unduly enthusiastic support—of Protestants. The united crusade was in the seventeenth century undertaken by Archbishop James Ussher, by the great Protestant theologian André Rivet, and by Bishop Jacques Sirmond, S.J., among others.[72] Their arguments, and those of commentators similarly inclined, were summarized in the third edition of George Hakewill's encyclopedic, expansive, and ever-lengthening *Apologie or Declaration of the Power and Providence of God* (1635). "That this *Denise* is but a Counterfait," wrote

[69] *The Glory of their Times* (1640), p. 40. See the defenses of Dionysius' authenticity by Pierre Halloix, Martin del Rio, and Pierre Lansel, S.J., in *PG*, IV, 695 ff., 953 ff., and 981 ff., respectively; and by the writers cited earlier, in notes 53 and 55.

[70] In 1703; his arguments are reprinted in *PG*, III, 1 ff.

[71] See the numerous studies by Joseph Stiglmayr and Hugo Koch mentioned in the bibliographies by Bardenhewer, Ueberweg, and Stéphanou, above, note 4.

[72] Ussher, *Dissertatio de scriptis Dionysio Areopagitæ suppositis*, in *Works*, ed. C. R. Elrington (1847), XII, 497-520; Rivet, *Critici sacri*, I, ix-xi (Leipzig and Frankfurt, 1690), pp. 150-72; and Sirmond, *Dissertatio de duobus Dionysiis Parisiensi & Areopagita*, in *Opera varia* (Venice, 1728), IV, 241-61. See also above, notes 49-50 and 54.

27

Hakewill, "our Divines prove by sundry unanswerable arguments," namely:

"First, if these were the books of that *Denise* which was S. *Pauls* Schollar, how commeth it to passe that neither *Eusebius* in his Ecclesiasticall Historie, nor *Hierome*, nor *Gennadius* purposedly writing catalogues of all the famous writers before them; nor *Origen*, nor *Chrysostome*, nor any ancient Father (so farre as I can learne) maketh any mention of them, untill *Gregory* the great, who lived above 600 years after Christ, and speaketh very doubtfully of them too? . . . Secondly, it is well knowne that S. *Paul* was the man that converted *Denis*, and that before his coming to *Athens*, *Timothy* had bin entertained by him, & in his company had travelled over many countries, and grew so intimate and deare unto him, that he both counted and called him his Sonne;[73] which beeing so, it cannot reasonably be imagined that the true *Denise* would prove either so ungrateful, or so presumptuous as that counterfait sheweth himselfe to be. Ungrateful in that hee often speaks of one *Hierotheus*, an obscure man in comparison, as of his master: presumptuous, for that as if hee were a father to *Timothy* as well as Saint *Paul*, he calleth him his sonne, not withstanding he were farre more fit to be his Disciple. Thirdly this *Denis* citeth . . . these words out of *Ignatius*, *My love is crucified*,[74] written by him a little before his martyrdome, and yet the true *Dionysius* suffered under *Domitian*, whereas *Ignatius* both wrote his Epistle, and was martyred some good while after him under *Trajan*. . . . Lastly this *Denis* writeth that himselfe together with

[73] Acts 16.1-4; 1 Timothy 1.1-2, 8; 2 Timothy 1.1-2; etc.

[74] Ignatius of Antioch, *Epistola ad Romanos*, VII, 2: ὁ ἐμός ἔρως ἐσταύρωται; quoted by the Pseudo-Dionysius, *De divinis nominibus*, IV, 12.

Timothy and *Hierotheus*, were present at the departure and funerall of the blessed *Virgin* Mother;[75] Now story saith that shee lived 63 years, being fifteene years of age when shee bare Christ; whereunto if you add 33 years of Christs life, and fifteen more to make up her full age, it will appeare that shee dyed eight and fortie years after her sons birth, and fifteen after his ascension. But on the other side it plainely appeareth, that *Denis Areopagite* was not converted unto the Christian faith till the 18th yeare after the ascension, one and fifty years after Christs birth. Our Divines gather it thus. . . . So that it must needs bee about eighteen or at the least seventeen years after Christs ascension before S. *Denis* knew Christ. All which duly considered, it is evident that the blessed *Virgin* dyed if not three full years, yet more than two before the conversion of *Denis*; and consequently that hee could not bee one of those brethren who were present at her death and funerall. Whence also it followeth inevitably, that the Author of that booke cannot possibly bee this *Denis*."[76]

One further argument—the argument from style—had to await the linguistic tools at the disposal of later ages. But the crucial question was raised, and the implications were made clear, during the Renaissance. As Viret succinctly pointed out, ". . . the stile of those bookes, smelleth not lyke vnto that of the Apostles, nor of their time."[77]

[75] The Pseudo-Dionysius (previous note), III, 2.

[76] *An Apologie* etc., 3rd. ed. (1635), V, 222-23. Hakewill remarks that these arguments were compiled by "a learned Divine & a worthy friend," but amended "by mine observation." In the relevant section at large (pp. 208-26), the first three pages are a defense of the authenticity of Dionysius by Godfrey Goodman, and the rest Hakewill's reply.

[77] Viret (as above, note 67), fol. 126v. Thus also Whitaker (note 54).

The Dionysian arrangement of the angels was dismantled on the one hand because its author was increasingly regarded as a "counterfait," and on the other because Protestants upheld the Bible's supremacy over all the "vain babblings of idle men." In consequence, those who like Spenser celebrated the "trinall triplicities," look back upon a past that had provided a vision hallowed by time and graced by an impressive array of intellects. But those who like Milton viewed the angels as "distinguisht and quaterniond into their celestiall Princedomes," were better able to look both before and after.

✺ 2 ✺
"Ascending by degrees magnificent":
Connections Between
Heaven and Earth

. . . the ordinary way which God hath appointed to attaine felicitie, is a long and laboursome walke, a great iourney, from vertue to vertue, *from strength to strength, vntill wee appeare before GOD in Sion* [Psalm 84.7]. This was figured by the ladder which Iacob saw in a vision; extending from earth to heauen, and consisting (doubtlesse) of many steppes. Signifying, that no man can attaine that happy height, no man can approch him who standeth at the toppe, but by many degrees of vertues, whereof euery one also hath many steppes.—Sir John Hayward

I

Order in Heaven, order on earth, order even in Hell: men's minds during the Renaissance tended toward such affirmations invariably and often all too insistently. The propensity was by no means a display of excessive piety. It was on the contrary the result of a deep-seated, fully experiential awareness that chaos could come again readily enough. Disorder in sixteenth-century Europe was after all a palpable reality, its omnipresence inescapable in the political sphere as in the religious, and in the social as in the economic. It were indeed a wonder had order not become an obsession, not that it had.

The obsession was habitually articulated through the

deployment of that most characteristic of Renaissance tactics, the ahistorical and highly eclectic appeal to all "authorities" which could be invoked to sustain any given outlook. Sometimes, as we are to observe in connection with the time-honored views on man's upright stature (below, Ch. V), the authorities were coincidentally well-nigh unanimous. But where they were not—and especially where there was an evident discrepancy—the tendency was so to interpret the "evidence" that the consequence was unanimity all the same. An instructive example of how order was confirmed along these lines is provided by the juxtaposition of the account in Genesis of Jacob's dream of a ladder extending from earth to heaven (28.10-22) and the episode in *The Iliad* involving the golden chain of Zeus (VIII, 19-27).

The Homeric episode centers on the invitation by Zeus to the other gods to make a golden chain (σειρὴν χρυσείην)[1] to test his strength, only to find that he is superior to all alike. Consistently misread during the Renaissance, the episode was widely interpreted as a symbolic affirmation both of God's providential supervision of the created order and of the hierarchical structure of the universe. The single most influential interpretation in this respect had been provided long since by Macrobius:

". . . since Mind emanates from the Supreme God and Soul from Mind, and Mind, indeed, forms and suffuses all below with life, and since this is the one splen-

---

[1] "Chain," else "rope" or "cord" (cf. Georg Autenrieth, *Homeric Dictionary*, trans. Robert P. Keep [1877], p. 283). During the Renaissance, however, the word was habitually translated "catena" (Johannes Spondanus [Jean de Sponde], *Homeri quae extant omnia Ilias, Odyssea, &c.* [Basel, 1583], p. 131) or "chaine" (Chapman, *The Iliads of Homer* [1611], p. 105, and Hobbes, *Homer's Iliads* [1676], p. 108).

dor lighting up everything and visible in all, like a countenance reflected in many mirrors arranged in a row, and since all follow on in continuous succession, degenerating step by step in their downward course, the close observer will find that from the Supreme God even to the bottommost dregs of the universe there is one tie, binding at every link and never broken. This is the golden chain of Homer which, he tells us, God ordered to hang down from the sky to the earth."[2]

It was but this view that Sir Kenelm Digby among countless others resuscitated when he averred in the seventeenth century that Providence manifests itself within history as a *"Series* or chaine, . . . whose highest Linke, *Poets* say prettily, is fastned to Jupiter's chayre, and the lowest is riveted to every individuall on earth."[3] Milton in one of his prolusions maintained in a parallel utterance that "this agreement of things universal and this loving concord, which Pythagoras secretly introduced in poetic fashion by the term Harmony, Homer likewise suggested significantly and appropriately by means of that famous golden chain of Jove hanging from heaven."[4]

---

[2] *Commentary on the Dream of Scipio*, I, xiv, 15; trans. William H. Stahl (1952), p. 145. Pico della Mirandola's later deployment of the Homeric chain in his *Heptaplus* is one of the numerous instances of Macrobius' influence. See further Arthur O. Lovejoy, *The Great Chain of Being* (Cambridge, Mass., 1936); Ludwig Edelstein, "The Golden Chain of Homer," in *Studies in Intellectual History*, by G. G. Boas *et al.* (Baltimore, 1953), pp. 48-66; Pièrre Lévêque, *Aurea Catena Homeri, une étude sur l'allégorie grecque* (Paris, 1959); and, for the manifold uses of the concept in literature, the numerous references collected by "Eirionnach" in "Avrea catena Homeri," *N&Q*, 2nd series, III (1857), pp. 63-65, 81-84, 104-107, and XII (1861), 161-63, 181-83, as well as by Emil Wolff, *Die Goldene Kette: die Aurea catena Homeri in der englischen Literatur von Chaucer bis Wordsworth* (Hamburg, 1947).

[3] *Observations upon Religio Medici* (1643), pp. 10-11.

[4] "De sphærarum concentu," *Works*, XII, 151.

But it was Peter Sterry, an associate of the Cambridge Platonists, who provided the most enthusiastic exposition of the Homeric chain along the lines indicated. After citing the episode in *The Iliad*, he added: "The Throne of the most High God, is a Throne of Grace, of Love. Like the Chain doth the whole Nature of things descend from this Throne, having its top fastned to it. Whatever the weights may be of the lowermost links of this Chain, yet that Love which sits upon the Throne, with a Divine Delight, as it lets down the Chain from it self, so draws it up again by the Order of the successive Links into a Divine Ornament, an Eternal Joy and Glory to it self."[5] The evident christianization of the Homeric episode was spelled out most clearly by Bishop Robert Mossom when he wrote in 1657 that "all secondary causes are links together in one chain of Divine providence, which the *Heathens* feigned to be fastened at *Jupiters* chair, and we Christians believe to be held in Gods hand."[6]

Minor variations on the same theme abounded. Henry Reynolds, for example, maintained that the study of nature's "hidden workings" would lead one "not saucily to leap, but by the linkes of that golden chaine of *Homer*, that reaches from the foot of *Jupiters* throne to the Earthe,

[5] *A Discourse of the Freedom of the Will* (1675), sigs. C4v-d1; the passage is more readily available in *Peter Sterry*, ed. V. de S. Pinto (Cambridge, 1934), p. 140. See also Burton, *The Anatomy of Melancholy*, 6th ed. (1652), p. 416 [Part. 3, Sect. 1, Memb. 1, Subs, 2], and several "popular" summaries of the same notion, as by Lewis Thomas, *Demegoriai* (1600), sig. K2v: "[God's] holy love is like a golden chaine, that by an inseparable vnion linketh together God and vs."

[6] *The Preachers Tripartite* (1657), II, 67. But the episode could also be invoked to serve the opposite purpose, as in Thomas Cheaste, *The Christian Path-Way* (1613), p. 21: "The world, is as the devils golden chaine, to hinder men from following of Christ."

more knowingly and consequently more humbly [to] climbe vp to [God]."[7] But the same commonplace could be made to serve a very different purpose, as in Sir Richard Barckley's exposition of the adverse effects of the Fall:

". . . where all the meane causes of things euen from the vppermost heauen, vnto the lowest part of the earth, depended each vpon other in such an exact order & vniformity to the production of things in their most perfection and beautie, so as it might be likened to that *Aurea Cathena* as *Homer* calleth it, by the grieuous displeasure, which God conceiued against man, he withdrew the vertue which at the first he had giuen to things in these lower parts, and nowe through his curse the face of the earth and all this elementarie world, doth so much degenerate from his former estate, that it resembleth a chaine rent in peeces, whose links are many lost and broken, and the rest so slightly fastened as they will hardly hangtogether."[8]

Poets argued more "prettily" still, witness Ben Jonson, who in *The Forrest* described love as "a golden chaine let downe from heauen, / Whose linkes are bright, and even," and in *Hymenaei* arranged the dancers with linked

---

[7] *Mythomystes* (1632), in *Critical Essays of the Seventeenth Century*, ed. J. E. Spingarn (Oxford, 1908), I, 174.

[8] *A Discourse of the Felicitie of Man* (1598), pp. 5-6. Still other interpretations are collected in a learned note by John Ogilby—the same "Ogilby the great" so massively satirized in *The Dunciad*, I, 141. See his translation of *Homer his Iliads* (1660), p. 177, which draws on the standard summaries of interpretations as provided by Archbishop Eustathius of Thessalonica (d. *c.* 1194) in Κέρας ᾿Αμαλθείας, ἤ ᾿Ωκεανὸς τῶν ᾿Εξηγήσεων ᾿Ομηρικῶν (Basel, 1558), p. 187, and by Spondanus (as above, note 1). See also the extensive commentary in an unexpected study: Geoffroy Troy, *L'art & science de la vraye proportion des lettres antiques*, 2nd ed. (Paris, 1549), fols. 52v-56.

hands "in manner of a chaine" to the accompaniment of a spoken commentary:

> Svch was the *Golden Chaine* let downe from
> *Heauen*;
> And not those linkes more euen,
>
> Than these: so sweetly temper'd, so combin'd
> By VNION, and refin'd. . . .[9]

Herbert and Milton were at once more traditional and more individualistic. Herbert's adaptation occurs in the concluding lines of "The Pearl," where a survey of the labyrinths of learning, honor, and pleasure, terminate with an acknowledgment before God:

> But thy silk twist let down from heav'n to me,
> Did both conduct and teach me, how by it
> To climb to thee.[10]

---

[9] *The Forrest*: XI, "Epode," 11. 47-48, and *Hymenaei*, 11. 320-23. Jonson pointedly affixed a learned note to the latter, citing both Homer and Macrobius ("to whose interpretation, I am specially affected in my Allusion"): see *Ben Jonson*, ed. C. H. Herford, Percy and Evelyn Simpson (Oxford, 1941), VII, 221. D. J. Gordon remarks on the sacrosanctity of this concept in *"Hymenaei*: Ben Jonson's Masque of Union," *JWCI*, VIII (1945), p. 119.

[10] Herbert's allusion was in turn adapted by Vaughan, who has God inform man, "My love-twist held thee up, my unseen link" ("Retirement" [I], 1. 22). Cf. Traherne, "Fullnesse." Spenser's earlier reference in the *Hymne in Honour of Love* to the "adamantine chains" linking the diverse aspects of the created order (1. 89) is rightly said by James Hutton not to form part of the tradition emanating from the Homeric chain; see his essay in *The Classical Tradition*, ed. Luitpold Wallach (Ithaca, N.Y., 1966), especially pp. 576-77.

Milton's adaptation is equally characteristic of his particular mode of thought and articulation. It occurs in *Paradise Lost* at the crucial moment when Satan emerges from Hell and Chaos to behold the newly created earth linked to the domain of God with a golden chain (II, 1005, 1051-2). Clearly symbolic both of the order pervading the universe and of the connection between Heaven and earth, the golden chain is later transfigured into a ladder. Satan is by now en route to Eden; and he suddenly beholds

> Ascending by degrees magnificent
> Up to the wall of heaven a Structure high,
> At top whereof, but farr more rich appeerd
> The work as of a Kingly Palace Gate
> With Frontispiece of Diamond and Gold
> Imbellisht; thick with sparkling orient Gemmes
> The Portal shon, inimitable on Earth
> By Model, or by shading Pencil drawn.
> The Stairs were such as whereon *Jacob* saw
> Angels ascending and descending, bands
> Of Guardians bright, when he from *Esau* fled
> To *Padan-Aram* in the field of *Luz*,
> Dreaming by night under the opn Skie,
> And waking cri'd, This is the Gate of Heav'n.
>
> (III, 502-15)

The concurrent deployment of the golden chain and Jacob's ladder had by Milton's time become all too common. The polymath Andrew Willet, for example, enumerated several interpretations of Jacob's ladder but concluded that: ". . . the proper and literal [*sic*] meaning of the ladder is, to set forth Gods prouidence, both in generall, wherby he gouerneth all things in heauen and in earth, Psal. 113.6. The degrees of the ladder are the diuers meanes, which God vseth: the Angels ascending and descending, are the ministring spirits, which God sendeth forth for the execution of his will: euen the heathen Poet *Homer*, by the like similitude of a golden chaine, which Iupiter sent downe from heauen to earth, describeth the diuine prouidence."[11]

It is not an accident that the transfiguration in *Paradise Lost* of the golden chain into Jacob's ladder is followed by their modulation into two other ladders, first the Scale of Nature (V, 469 ff.) and then the Scale of Love (VIII, 589 ff.). They are, of course, equally providential.

II

Jacob's ladder was inherited by the Renaissance fraught with a diversity of suggestive interpretations. It may well be that, as a scholar has assured us, the ladder as a ladder is "a timeworn symbol for sexual congress."[12] But the overwhelming evidence appears to indicate that the ladder in general, and Jacob's ladder in particular, were most frequently used to reinforce metaphysical claims and spiritual principles. The foremost interpretation, in-

---

[11] *Hexapla in Genesin* (Cambridge, 1605), p. 300. Don C. Allen in "Two Notes on *Paradise Lost*," *MLN*, LXVIII (1953), pp. 360-61, avers that Milton regarded the chain and the ladder as one—a possibility that occurs only in Jean Bodin's *Heptaplomeres*. But this is justly denied by Harry F. Robbins, "Milton's Golden Scale," *MLN*, LXIX (1954), p. 76, in that the two figures are different aspects of one idea.

[12] Helen F. Dunbar, *Symbolism in Medieval Thought* (New Haven, 1922), p. 392n.

deed, involved a typologically oriented identification of Jacob's ladder with Christ.

That Jacob has been habitually regarded as a type of Christ is a commonplace of theology;[13] nor is it surprising to assert as much for Jacob's ladder in view of the express words of Jesus that "hereafter ye shall see heaven open, and the angels of God ascending and descending upon the Son of man" (John 1.51). Such an authoritative statement could not but condition the responses of any number of scholars and preachers: in England, "silver-tongued" Henry Smith, Gervase Babington, Henry Ainsworth, Richard Sibbes, James Ussher, John Lightfoot and Benjamin Whichcote among many others;[14] and on the Continent, respected authorities like Johann Mi-

[13] For references, see the general index to *PL*, CCXXI, 984. The *loci classici* are Augustine's *De civ. Dei*, XVI, 37-38, and *In Joannis Evangelium tractatus VII*, 23. See also below, note 21.

[14] Smith, *Iacobs Ladder* (1595), sigs. B2v-B3; Babington, as below, note 18; Willet, *Thesaurus Ecclesiae* (Cambridge, 1604), p. 94, and *Hexapla* (as above, note 11), pp. 301, 304; Ainsworth, *Annotations upon . . . Genesis* ([Amsterdam], 1616), sig. XIv; Sibbes, as below, note 17; Ussher, *Immanuel* (1638), p. 53; Lightfoot, *The Harmony, Chronicle and Order of the Old Testament* (1647), p. 30; and Whichcote, *Several Discourses* (1703), III, 81. Thus also: William Hunnis, *A Hyve Fvll of Hunnye* (1578), fol. 67v; Eusebius Pagitt, *The Historie of the Bible* (1613), p. 27; Sebastian Benefield, *Eight Sermons Pvblikely Preached in the Vniversity of Oxford* (Oxford, 1614), p. 50; Walter Sweeper, *Israels Redemption by Christ* (1622), p. 11; Griffith Williams, *Seven Govlden Candlestickes* (1624), p. 258; Richard Senhouse, *Fovre Sermons* (1627), p. 3; Alexander Ross, *Three Decads of Divine Meditations* ([1630]), p. 8; Alexander Grosse, *Swet and Soule-Perswading Indvcements* (1632), p. 14; Meric Casaubon *et al.*, *Annotations vpon . . . the Old and New Testament* (1645), sig. g4; John Trapp, *A Clavis to the Bible* (1650), p. 226; George Hughes, *An Analytical Exposition of . . . Genesis* (1672), pp. 354-55; Thomas Vaughan, quoted by R. A. Durr, *On the Mystical Poetry of Henry Vaughan* (Cambridge, Mass., 1962), p. 161; and the authorities quoted and cited by George W. Whiting, *Milton and this Pendant World* (Austin, 1958), pp. 71 ff.

chael Dilherr and Giovanni Diodati, whose works were alike translated into English—and, far more important than all, Luther and Calvin.[15] Sometimes an exposition tended to take flight into excessively spiritual realms, as was the case with Jakob Boehme's mystical speculations.[16] But the common preference was for statements which, as in the Geneva Bible's gloss on the Genesis account, annotated Jacob's ladder as a "notable representation" of Christ in tradition-bound ways. One such statement was provided by the widely respected Puritan divine Richard Sibbes ("Heaven was in him," said Izaac Walton, "before he was in heaven"):

"Iacob's Ladder, it reached from Earth to Heaven; and that pointed to Christ himselfe, who is *Emanuel*, God and man, who brought God and man together: He was a Mediator betweene both, and a friend to both: He was that *Ladder*, that touched Heaven and Earth, and joyned both together. Now it is said, the *Angels* ascended and descended upon that *Ladder*: so the *Angels* descending upon us, is, because they ascend and descend upon *Iacobs Ladder* first; that is, upon Christ."[17]

Gervase Babington—Bishop in succession of Llandaff, Exeter and Worcester—had earlier attempted to explain

---

[15] Dilherr, *Contemplations*, trans. William Style (1640), pp. 46-50; Diodati, *Pious and Learned Annotations upon the Bible*, trans. Anon., 3rd ed. (1651), sig. E4; Luther, *Vber das Erst Buch Moses* (Wittenberg, 1527), fol. 249v; Calvin, *A Commentarie . . . upon the first Booke of Moses called Genesis*, trans. Thomas Tymme (1578), p. 596. The latter is quoted at length by Whiting (previous note), p. 72.

[16] *Mysterium Magnum. Or an Exposition of . . . Genesis*, trans. John Elliston and John Sparrow (1654), Ch. LVI, "Of Jacobs Ladder."

[17] *Light from Heaven* (1638), I, 100-101. For parallel statements by Sibbes, see also his *Yea and Amen* (1638), p. 29; *The Christians Portion* (1638), pp. 7, 116; and particularly *The Fovntaine Opened* (1638), I, 100.

the "mystery" more precisely, with particular reference to Christ's dual nature: "The ladder is Christ. The foot of it in earth noteth his humanitie, man of the substance of his mother borne in the world. The top reaching vp to heaven, noteth his diuinitie, *God of the substance of the Father begotten before all worlds, perfit God, and perfit man*, by which vnion of natures, he hath ioyned earth and heauen together, that is, God and man."[18] There were moreover convenient tabular expositions like the comprehensive one attempted by William Gould:

Iacobs Ladder, Gen. 28. [10-22]

1. *Iacobs* Ladder, which hee saw in a Vision, stood vpon the earth, but the top reached to Heauen: and so it ioyned as it were heauen and earth together, *Gen.* 28.12.

So Christ, albeit he was humbled in shape of sinfull flesh, touching the earth as it were, yet he was the most High God, reaching so to heauen, and reconciling, as the two natures in himselfe by personall Vnion: so God and vs together by his death and mediation, Ro. 5.10.

2. The Angels went vp and downe by it.

So by Christ Iesus they are become ministring spirits, comming and returning for the good and protection of the godly, Heb. 1.[14.] *as also by him our prayers ascend, and Gods blessings descend.*

3. No ascending vp to heauen, but by the Ladder.

So no attaining to that inheritance, but by Iesus Christ alone, Ioh. 10.7.

[18] *Certaine . . . Notes vpon . . . Genesis* (1592), fol. 114.

4. *Iacob* in his Pilgrimage saw the Ladder onely in a Vision.

So wee see Christ heere in our pilgrimage but in a glasse, as it were, darkely and in part, 1. Cor. 13.[12.]

5. The Lord stood aboue it, and made his promise of *Canaan* to *Iacob, verse* 13.

So in Christ, and through him, are the Lords promises of heauen, made and ratified to vs, Ioh. 2.1.

6. In the place which was the House of God, and gate of Heauen, was the Ladder seene, *verse* 19.

So in Christs Church (which is the foresaid truely) through Faith can wee onely get a spirituall sight of Christ.

7. At the foote of this Ladder, *Iacob* did repose and sleepe.

Shadowing the rest and peace of conscience, which the godly haue vnder the shadow of Christs intercession.

The Disparitie.

It was a Ladder wheron to climbe, but not giuing strength to that effect: but Christ Iesus, that blessed Ladder, is both. That Ladder at *Iacobs* awaking vanished, and begate feare by the vision thereof: but Christ Iesus, at our awaking in the Resurrection, shall more cleerely appeare, whose sight by faith heere expels feare, and begets confident joy, and whose cleere sight then shall beget farre greater.[19]

Other similarly extensive annotations were not wanting. Far more eloquent, however, were briefer utterances like Traherne's in *Centuries of Meditations*: "The Cross of Christ is the Jacobs ladder by which we Ascend into the Highest Heavens" (I, 60).

Yet the view of Jacob's ladder as a type of Christ,

---

[19] *Moses Vnailed: or those Figures which served vnto the patterne and shaddow of heauenly things, pointing out the Messiah CHRIST IESVS* (1620), pp. 33-35. As Gould's title suggests, the work is encyclopedically typological. So is an earlier companion volume, *The Harmony of all the Prophets*, (1619).

though by far the most widespread interpretation during the Renaissance, was by no means the only one available. Several alternative theories were also entertained, each duly fortified with numerous precedents. According to St. Gregory the Great, for example, the ladder is a symbol both of man's contemplation of God and of man's compassion toward man;[20] according to St. John Chrysostom, it signifies "the gradual ascent by means of virtue, by which it is possible for us to ascend from earth to heaven, not using material steps, but improvement and correction of manners;"[21] while St. Augustine, as we are reminded by a Renaissance commentator, "by God standing vpon the ladder vnderstadeth Christ hanging vpon the crosse: by the angels ascending, the preachers handling mysticall doctrines, by the angels descending preachers applying themselues to morall doctrine."[22] In time, too, Jacob's vision also became an exemplum freely used, its "lesson"—so far as St. Jerome was concerned—that "the sinner must not despair of salvation nor the righteous man rest secure in his virtue."[23]

These diverse interpretations were only the beginning, however. During the Middle Ages, certainly, Jacob's ladder became the mainstay of still other theories inclusive of the ladder of merit and the analogical ladders of speculation and of mysticism, which jointly attest to the powerful impact of two hierarchically minded writers in particular, the Pseudo-Dionysius and St. John

---

[20] *Liber regulae pastoralis*, II, 5; in *PL*, LXXVII, 33. For a variation of this idea, see St. Thomas Aquinas, *Summa theol.*, II (II), 181, 4.

[21] *In Joannem Homilia LXXXIII*, 5; in *NPF*, 1st series (1890), XIV, 312.

[22] Andrew Willet, *Hexapla in Genesin* (Cambridge, 1605), p. 300. Augustine's original statement is in his *Enarrationes in Psalmos*, CXIX, 2; in *Opera omnia* (Paris, 1836), IV, 1948.

[23] *Epistola* CXXIII, 15; in *NPF*, 2nd series (1893), VI, 236.

surnamed Climacus.[24] The celebrated vision of Jacob's ladder in the *Paradiso* (XXI-XXII) would seem to appeal largely if not exclusively to the ladder of contemplation, it is true. Actually, however, it encompasses suggestively all the other ladders erected during the Middle Ages. "It is," we have been authoritatively informed, "the archetype of all the hierarchies, philosophical, theological, and social, which medieval thinkers used to organize and interpret experience.[25]

In the emergent universe of the Reformers the promiscuity of the Middle Ages was curtailed dramatically. Weary as Luther was of the viability of the overlabored symbolism of the ladder, he tolerated but its usefulness in suggesting the descent of God's love through Christ.[26] However, as Protestantism gradually evolved a scholasticism of its own, opinions began to proliferate yet again. Partial as Protestants were to the early Fathers, they revived the interpretations of Jacob's ladder by St. Augustine as representative of preaching[27] and by St. John Chrysostom as an invitation to ascend to God through virtue.[28] But St. Gregory's view of the ladder as symbolic of man's contemplation of God was also en-

[24] See the comprehensive study by Anders Nygren, *Agape and Eros*, trans. Philip S. Watson (1932-1939), pp. 295-99 and 403-19. On the pseudo-Dionysius see also above, Ch. I; and on John Climacus: below, note 43.

[25] Joseph A. Mazzeo, *Structure and Thought in the "Paradiso"* (Ithaca, N.Y., 1958), pp. 162-63. On the Dantesque ladder in relation to Milton, see C. Schaar, " 'Each Stair Mysteriously Was Meant,' " *ES*, LVIII (1977), pp. 408-10.

[26] Nygren (as above, note 24), pp. 489-91.

[27] See Clifford Davidson, "Style and the Heavenly Ladder," *Gordon Review*, XI (1968), pp. 159-67.

[28] Thus, for example, Sir John Hayward in *Davids Teares* (1623), p. 297. His statement is quoted in the headnote, above.

dorsed—and endorsed all the more enthusiastically by the *literati* of the Renaissance when it was noted that Pico della Mirandola's oration on the dignity of man had also invoked Jacob's experience in order to commend the contemplation of the divine by means of the natural:

 "Sleeping in the lower world but keeping watch in the upper, the wisest of the fathers [i.e., Jacob] will advise us. But he will advise us through a figure (in this way everything was wont to come to those men) that there is a ladder extending from the lowest earth to the highest heaven, divided in a series of many steps, with the Lord seated at the top, and angels in contemplation ascending and descending over them alternately by turns."[29]

Refinements abounded. Some writers, we are informed, "by this ladder insinuate a Christian profession, in which are diuers degrees and vertues," and while "by angels ascending, such are vnderstood, as are giuen to contemplation: by the angels descending, such as follow an actiue and practicall life."[30] Several other writers espoused the essentially Lutheran interpretation of the ladder as a symbolic affirmation of the love of God that extends—"like to Iacobs ladder"—from heaven to earth, while still others viewed it as a figurative declaration of the "course and order of mans Saluation," else a representation of the way prayers "maintaine our traffique with

---

[29] Trans. Elizabeth L. Forbes, in *The Renaissance Philosophy of Man*, ed. Ernst Cassirer *et al.* (Chicago, 1948), p. 229. For an illustration of the ladder of perfection reaching to God, see Joscelyn Godwin, *Robert Fludd* (1979), Pl. 86 (p. 71).

[30] *Apud* Willet (as above, note 22).

Heauen."[31] Two more suppositions may also be recorded: on the one hand the identification of the ladder
with "the genealogie of Christ," and on the other its use
as a warning lest we rest in "the naturall cause" at the
expense of "the supreme and supernaturall"—for Jacob,
it was claimed, "when he saw the Angels ascending and
descending, enquired who stood at the top of the ladder."[32]

Much more responsible—and certainly far more broadly
disseminated—was the association of Jacob's ladder with
the elaborate "world picture" current during the Renaissance, according to which the universe is an imposing
system of interdependent levels of existence arranged hierarchically "from the Mushrome to the Angels."[33] The
same association, as we have seen, obtained in connection with the Homeric chain; and it generated in both
cases any number of formulations similar to those by the
Cambridge Platonists, who asserted with Benjamin
Whichcote "the Scale of the Creatures," with Henry More
the arrangement of all beings in "distinct degree," and
with Ralph Cudworth "a *Scale* or *Ladder of Perfection* in
Nature, one above the other, as of *Living* and *Animate
Things*, above *Senseless* and *Inanimate*; of *Rational* things
above *Sensitive*."[34] But it was Peter Sterry who once again

[31] *Seriatim*: Lewis Thomas, *Demegoriai* (1600), sig. K2v; Anthony Maxey,
The Sermon preached . . . at White-Hall (1605), sig. E2; and Henry King,
Two Sermons Preached at White-Hall (1627), II, 31. The last-named inter-
pretation was also favored by Paul Wentworth, *The Miscellanie . . . of
Orizons* (1615), pp. 62-63, and Henry Valentine, *Noahs Doue* (1627), p.
35.

[32] *Apud* Willet (as above, Note 22), and John Trapp, *Gods Love-Tokens*
(1637), p. 10; respectively.

[33] See above, Ch. I, §3.

[34] *CP*, p. 35.

penned one of the most eloquent expositions of this *scala mundi* in terms of Jacob's ladder:

"Being it self, in its universal Nature, from its purest heighth, by beautiful, harmonious, just degrees and steps, *descendeth* into every Being, even to the lowest shades. All ranks and degrees of Being, so become like the mystical steps in that scale of Divine Harmony and Proportions, Jacobs Ladder. Every form of Being to the lowest step, seen and understood according to its order and proportions in its descent upon this *Ladder*, seemeth as an *Angel*, or as a *Troop* of Angels in one, full of all Angelick Musick and Beauty."[35]

Parallel affirmations by others repeatedly aver that "the creatures be vnyted so to gethers that eche one hangeth on other, & al of god, in such wise that they make a ladder."[36] Not all statements, of course, allude expressly to Jacob's ladder; but even where they do not, the vaguest of references to the cosmic scheme as "the Ladder and scale of creatures"—to quote Sir Thomas Browne[37]—sufficed to put one in mind of the episode recounted in

[35] *A Discourse* (as above, note 5), p. 30; more readily available in Pinto's edition, p. 152. See also Sterry's *The Appearance of God to Man in the Gospel* (1710), also in Pinto, p. 176. Consult further Donne, *LXXX Sermons* (1640), pp. 376-77; F. M. van Helmont, *Paradoxal Discourses* (1685), p. 17; and the lengthy passage from John Weemes (1610) quoted by Sister Mary Irma Corcoran, *Milton's Paradise with reference to the Hexameral Background* (Washington, D.C., 1945), p. 42. For still other symbolic extensions of the Scale, see Karl Josef Höltgen, "Arbor Scala und Fons vitae," in *Emblem und Emblematikrezeption*, ed. S. Penkert (Darmstadt, 1978), pp. 72-109.

[36] Bernardino Ochino, *Certayne Sermons*, trans. Richard Argentine (1550?), sig. A8v.

[37] *Religio Medici*, I, 30; in Browne, *BMP*, pp. 97-98. For a similarly generalized reference, cf. John Smith the Cambridge Platonist on "those golden links that unite as it were the World to God" (*Select Discourses* [1660], facsimile edition with an introduction by C. A. Patrides [Delmar, N.Y., 1979], p. 431).

Genesis. Jacob's ladder, like the Homeric chain, had clearly become one of the period's most widely credited commonplaces.

Not all of the interpretations proposed were accepted during the Renaissance, however. The line was drawn, firmly, so as to exclude the more extreme view of Hebrew "doctors" and Catholic theologians. One Jewish interpretation was fathered upon Maimonides: "The things made known to a prophet by prophetical vision, were made knowen unto him by way of parable; and immediately, the interpretation of the parable, was written in his hart, and he knew what it was. As the Ladder which Jakob our father saw, and the Angels ascending and descending on it. And that was a parable of the (fowr) monarchies."[38] "All this," Bishop Simon Patrick noted drily, "is the pure invention of idle Men, who dream upon the Holy Scriptures."[39] Even more "idle," however, were the Roman Catholics, predictably the object of unrestrained Protestant vituperation. Thus John Stoughton, enumerating their numerous "strange devices," was particularly abusive concerning their claim that "there are two Ladders up to Heaven: a red Ladder by *Christs blood*, and a white Ladder by *Maries beautie*, which is farre the easier: me thinks these men mistake *Iacobs* Ladder, but yet something like it was, for they

[38] *Apud* Ainsworth (as above, note 14). Maimonides had confined himself but to a report that Jacob's ladder is said to have had four steps and four angels (*The Guide of the Perplexed*, X). The source of the tradition quoted is, in fact, the *Mishne Torah*, I,vii, 3 (ed. Elias Soloweyczik [1863], p. 47); cf. Louis Ginzberg, *The Legends of the Jews*, trans. Henrietta Szold (Philadelphia, 1909-38), I, 350-51. Philo's elaborate interpretation of Jacob's dream—discussed by Erwin R. Goodenough, *By Light, Light* (New Haven, 1935), pp. 168 ff.—was greeted during the Renaissance with stony silence.

[39] *A Commentary upon . . . Genesis* (1695), p. 411.

are in a dreame, as *Iacob* was."[40] The rest of the passage
is unprintable.

III

We must of course demand whether the variegated attitudes sketched here could have influenced the period's
major talents at all. In brief, one's response must be
negative—but only so far as the more extreme surmises
are concerned. Otherwise Jacob's ladder, like the Homeric chain, was so adapted as to stiffen the sinews of
dispositions whether in poetry or prose. Deprived of the
symbolic language provided by the one concept as by
the other, the articulation of the Ladder of Nature as of
the Chain of Being would have been seriously compro-
mised; and denuded of the figurative range of reference
afforded by both, the allusiveness of each would have
been radically abridged. As it is, Vaughan could detail
the universal hierarchy ("all / Strive upward still") in
order forcefully to oppose man who sleeps on earth to
Jacob who dreamt of Heaven:

> All have their *keys*, and set ascents: but man
> Though he knows these, and hath more of his own,
> Sleeps at the ladder's foot . . .
> ("The Tempest," ll. 37-39)

As it is, too, Milton could concatenate the Homeric chain
and Jacob's ladder in order not only to affirm both the
reality of universal gradation and the link between God
and man, as before stated, but to urge in particular the

---

[40] *XI. Choice Sermons* (1640), II, 105. For a parallel statement, see
Theophilus Wodenote, *Eremicus Theologus* (1654), p. 7.

presence of Christ throughout the course of history. To be aware of the persistent typological identification of Jacob's ladder with Christ—and, more generally, that "the proper and literall meaning of the ladder is, to set forth Gods prouidence"—is to appreciate the massive irony which in *Paradise Lost* is directed against Satan at the very moment of his greatest expectations. Prevenient Grace may not prevent. But it does anticipate.

By way of an epilogue we might glance at the visual interpretations of the two concepts explicated here. The Homeric chain has surprisingly elicited no response from artists; so far as I know, indeed, there are but two engravings of it in the form of a Chain of Being, neither a noteworthy example of the visual imagination.[41] Far more impressively, however, Jacob's dream has been delineated visually on several memorable occasions, sometimes in Western Europe—e.g., the painting in the Vatican attributed to Giovaŋ Francesco Penni (d. 1528) and the serenely evocative one in the Prado by Ribera (d. 1652)[42]—but most often in Byzantium, whose artists, as the direct heirs of the Pseudo-Dionysius and, in turn, John Climacus, were vastly influenced by the for-

[41] The first—brought to my attention by Professor D.D.C. Chambers of the Univesity of Toronto—is a literalistic interpretation of the Chain in Didacus Valades' *Rhetorica christiana* (Perugia, 1579); it is reproduced in my essay "Hierarchy and Order," in *Dictionary of the History of Ideas*, ed. Philip P. Wiener (1973), II, 436. The second is a more attractive but less detailed exposition in Kircher's *Mundus subterraneus* (Amsterdam, 1678); it is reproduced in Joscelyn Godwin, *Athanasius Kircher* (1979), Pl. 79 (p. 86).

[42] The former is reproduced in Arnold Hauser, *Mannerism*, trans. Eric Mosbacher (1965), Vol. II, Pl. 6; the latter, in Elizabeth du Gué Trapier, *Ribera* (1952), Fig. 113.

mer's visions of cosmic hierarchy and the latter's treatise *The Heavenly Ladder* with its numerous visual interpretations in illuminated manuscripts as well as in countless frescoes and mosaics.[43] The interpretation most relevant to our purposes, however, is Blake's *Jacob's Ladder* (c. 1800).[44] A radiant watercolor, it is suggestive of infinite spiritual dignity as graceful angelic figures are seen ascending and descending the ladder against a luminously blue, starlit background. The single most estimable commentary on its subject, its imaginative range is matched not by any other visual interpretation as by an oratorio, Schoenberg's *Jacob's Ladder*, where prayer informs its resounding dimensions in order to suggest—as it did so often in the preceding centuries—"the upward movement between earth and heaven."[45]

[43] Of the numerous frescoes, a particularly energetic one in the monastery of St. Dionysius in Mount Athos shows the saints ascending the ladder supported by angels, while the damned fall precipitously toward hell. On the versions in illuminated manuscripts, consult John Rupert Martin, *The Illustration of the "Heavenly Ladder" of John Climacus* (Princeton, 1954).

[44] Reproduced in color in Kathleen Raine, *William Blake* (1970), Pl. 93. Blake also made use of the "golden chain," but with understandable ambiguity; see Désirée Hirst, *Hidden Riches: Traditional Symbolism from the Renaissance to Blake* (1964), p. 55.

[45] Berthold Viertel, "Schoenberg's *Die Jakobsleiter*," in *Schoenberg*, ed. Merle Armitage (1937), pp. 165-81.

❦ 3 ❧

"The exact compute of time":
Estimates of
the Year of Creation

Concerning the World and its temporall circumscriptions, who ever shall strictly examine both extreams, will easily perceive there is not only obscurity in its end but its beginning; that as its period is inscrutable, so is its nativity indeterminable: That as it is presumption to enquire after the one, so is there no rest or satisfactory decision in the other.—Sir Thomas Browne

I

The Bible's absolute authority during the Renaissance was an open invitation totally to rely on its impossible chronology. True, responsible thinkers like Sir Thomas Browne declined the invitation promptly. But a massive majority accepted it, fully in agreement with Hugh Broughton who in 1594 declared: "He that wyll deny the course of tyme to be in Scripture cleerely observed, even unto the fulness, the yeere of salvation, wherein our Lord dyed, may as wel deny the Sunne to have brightness."[1] Broughton's choice of image is not accidental. Time and again the clarity of the Bible was compared to the sun's impact upon our sublunary darkness.

[1] *A Seder Olam, that is: Order of the Worlde* (1594), p. 1.

Alas, Biblical chronology, far from being illuminated, fell into greater obscurity whenever anyone tried to bring order into it. The degree of frustration suffered is measurable in the ever-increasing number of Biblical chronologists, each with something different to contribute to the subject. William Nisbet in 1650 was compelled to acknowledge: "There is great disagreement among Chronologues, in counting of the years from the Creation of the World to the death of our Saviour."[2] The statement's tact was not likely to appeal to Sir Thomas Browne, who drily remarked that the efforts of chronologists "have left the history of times far more perplexed then Chronology hath reduced."[3] Equally perplexed, and desperate to account for the discrepancies, Edward Leigh in 1663 propounded the ultimate theory: ". . . some say the holy Ghost did obscure some things in Chronology to sharpen mens wits."[4]

The difficulties of the chronologists are understandable. Should their choice of text in determining the year of creation be the Hebrew Bible or the Septuagint? The spokesmen for Judaism had long since fixed the year of creation at 3760 B.C.E. ("Before the Common Era"), a

[2] *A Golden Chaine of Time* (Edinburgh, 1650), p. 1. Summaries of the chronologists' endeavors are available in Michael Beuther, *Ephemeris historia* (Paris, 1551); Jacques Cappel, *Historia sacra et exotica ab Adamo* (Sedan, 1613); Gilbert Génébrard, *Chronographia*, with its continuation by Arnauld de Pontac (Leyden, 1609); Georg Horn, *Arca Noæ* (Leyden and Rotterdam, 1666); *et al.* Cf. John Gregory, *Gregorii posthuma* (1649), Tract VI, "De Æris & Epochis." The problems involved, and Ralegh's efforts to solve them, are discussed by Ernest A. Strathmann, "Ralegh on the Problems of Chronology," *HLQ*, XI (1947-1948), pp. 129-48, and *Sir Walter Ralegh* (1951), pp. 197 ff.

[3] *Pseudodoxia Epidemica*, 2nd ed. (1650), p. 125 [Bk. VI, Ch. I].

[4] *Fœlix consortium* (1663), p. 34.

date still used as the basis of the Jewish calendar. But the Septuagint chose to differ from the Hebrew Bible by nearly two thousand years because of variants introduced principally in the Hexateuch, the unit comprising the five books of the Torah (Genesis to Deuteronomy) together with the Book of Joshua. From the early Greek Fathers through the Byzantines, accordingly, the Eastern Orthodox Church resorted to a variety of estimates which generally predicated that the world was created in 5500 B.C. or shortly thereafter.[5] The Septuagint during the Renaissance had a number of champions, notably Achilles Gasser, Jerónimo de Chaves, Francesco Sansovino, Christoph Lauret, Isaac Voss, and Giovanni Battista Riccioli.[6] But the majority of chronologists preferred to limit the age of the world in accordance with the Hebrew Bible. Yet even they were rarely in agreement.

Gilbert Génébrard did not exaggerate when he observed that "touching the number of the yeares of the world, a man shall finde as many opinions as writers."[7] The following estimates proposed by well over a hundred Renaissance chronologists[8] bear him good witness:

[5] The Graeco-Hebrew differences are summarized in tabular form by Christoph Lauret, *La Doctrine des temps* (Paris, 1598), fol. 72. The various Greek proposals deriving from the Septuagint are also enumerated by Browne (as above, note 3), p. 123.

[6] Gasser, *Historiarum et cronicorum mundi epitome* (Antwerp, 1533); Chaves, *Chronographia* (Seville, 1561); Sansovino, *Cronologia del mondo* (Venice, 1580); Lauret (as above, note 5); Voss, *Chronologia sacra*, in *De Septuaginta interpretibus* etc. (The Hague, 1661); and Riccioli, *Chronologiæ reformatæ tomi tres* (Bologna, 1669). The comparative veracity of the Septuagint is now vindicated: see Adam Rutherford, *Treatise on Bible Chronology* (Stanmore, Middx., 1958).

[7] Quoted by Matthew Brookes, *The . . . History of Mans Redemption* (1657), p. 6.

[8] Documented for the greatest part in the study cited below, note 20.

Date of creation	*Advocates*
3928 B.C.	Matthieu Beroalde, Henoch Clapham, Thomas Hayne, John Lightfoot, David Pareus, Anthony Rudd
3934 B.C.	Thomas Allen
3935 B.C.	Andrew Willet
3939 B.C.	John More
3946 B.C.	G. J. Voss
3947 B.C.	Johann Heinrich Alsted, Johann Ludwig Gottfried, Henry Isaacson, Johann Micraelius, Joseph Scaliger, Christiaan Schotanus
3948 B.C.	Albert Otto Horn, Robert Pont, William Slatyer, Griffith Williams
3949 B.C.	John Gregory
3950 B.C.	Ubbe Emmen, Seth Kallwitz (Calvisius), Theobald Meuschius, Henri de Samrez (Samerius), Friedrich Spanheim, Girolamo Vecchietti
3951 B.C.	Cornelis van den Steen (à Lapide)
3954 B.C.	Alonso Maldonado
3955 B.C.	Valerius Rud (Anshelm), Heinrich Wolff
3959 B.C.	Stephen Bateman
3960 B.C.	Hugh Broughton, Giovanni Doglioni, Philipp van Lansbergen, Giovanni Lucido, William Nisbet, Matthias Prideaux, Giuseppe Rosaccio
3962 B.C.	Michael Beuther, David Chytraeus, Thomas Cooper, Paul Krauss (Crusius), Manuel de Faria y Sousa, Johann Thomas Freig, Thomas Lanquet, Christian Masseeuw, Clemens Schubert, István Székely

3963 B.C.	Johann Carion, Johann Funck, Richard Grafton, Jacobus Kimedoncius, Anthony Munday
3964 B.C.	Abraham Fleming
3966 B.C.	Gerhard Kremer (Mercator), Pieter van Opmeer, John Taylor the Water Poet
3967 B.C.	Girolamo Bardi, William Perkins
3968 B.C.	Heinrich Bünting
3969 B.C.	Francisco Vicente de Tornamira
3970 B.C.	Abraham Bucholzer, Johann Clüver, Matthaeus Dresser, Hendrik Guthberleth, Meredith Hanmer, Leonhard Krentzheim, Heinrich Pantaleon, Elias Reusner, David Tost (Origanus)
3974 B.C.	Heinrich Bullinger
3979 B.C.	Theodor Buchmann (Bibliander)
3980 B.C.	Lambert Daneau
3983 B.C.	Charles de Bouelles, Denis Pétau (Petavius)
3984 B.C.	Robert Bellarmine, Walter Lynne
3992 B.C.	Kepler
3996 B.C.	F. M. van Helmont
4000 B.C.	Jacques Cappel, Agostino Ferentilli, Christoph Helwig (Helvicus), Luther, Francisco Suárez, Orazio Torsellino
4002 B.C.	Jens Bircherod, James Gordon
4004 B.C.	Georg Horn, William Howell, Antoine Le Grand, James Ussher
4005 B.C.	John Swan
4020 B.C.	Thomas Pie
4022 B.C.	Patrick Anderson, Benito Pereyra (Pererius)
4032 B.C.	Sir Walter Ralegh
4040 B.C.	Wilhelm Lange
4051 B.C.	Henri de Sponde (Spondanus), Agostino Tornielli

4052 B.C.	Gabriel Bucelin, Jean de Bussières, Jacques Salian
4053 B.C.	Claude Clément
4054 B.C.	Philippe Briet, Philippe Labbé
4089 B.C.	Giuseppe Biancani, Gilbert Génébrard, Arnauld de Pontac
4103 B.C.	Brian Walton

In England, the date of creation proposed by Archbishop James Ussher—4004 B.C.—was destined to be the one most widely accepted. The respect that Ussher commanded among scholars of every religious denomination ensured this. The praise of the noted Hebraist, John Lightfoot, was typical; Ussher, said Lightfoot, is "the magazine of all manner of Literature and knowledge."[9] By 1660 William Winstanley was able to report that Ussher ("learned to a miracle") had left in his *Annales* "a Work acknowledged by the learnedst men of this Age for the admirable Method and Worth of it, not to have hitherto been parallel'd by any preceding Writers."[10] William Howell, in full agreement, a year later adopted Ussher's date as the basis for the chronology of his massive world history, observing firmly that it is a date "we most approve."[11] Ussher's chronology was decisively established with its incorporation into the margins of the Bible edited by Bishop William Lloyd in

[9] From the Epistle Dedicatory to *The Harmony, Chronicle, and Order of the New Testament*; in *Works* (1684). The reference is to Ussher's celebrated volumes, *Annales Veteris Testamenti, a prima mundi origine dedvcti* (1650), and *Annalium pars posterior* (1654); both translated as *The Annals of the Old and New Testament* (1658). Ussher's reputation may be gathered from the four studies of his various activities in *Hermathena*, LXXXVIII (1956), pp. 3-80.

[10] *England's Worthies* (1660), pp. 469, 476-77.

[11] *An Institution of General History* (1661), p. 767.

1701. For nearly two centuries thereafter it remained uncontested. Then it simply died.[12]

Renaissance chronological reckonings are among the most characteristic products of the period. For thoroughness, they are well-nigh astonishing; and in terms of quantity, extraordinary. Girolamo Vecchietti's *Tabulae maiores*[13] well illustrates such features. It comprises an exhaustive series of tables listing in sequence not simply the years but the sum total of all the *days* from the creation of the first Adam to the nativity of the second (total: 1,442,801); yet it continues, still day by day, to *anno mundi* 6000. But Vecchietti was no exception. Numerous other writers, even if much less ambitious, were similarly preoccupied with specific days. At what precise date had the world begun? For Lightfoot there were but two alternatives: "That the world was made at *Æquinox*, all grant, but differ at which, whether about the eleventh of *March*, or twelfth of *September*."[14] Lightfoot himself paused, reflected, and finally decided that God began to create on September 12, 3928 B.C. But, being a man of precision, he went even further: Adam, he affirmed, was created on September 18th "about the third hour of the day, or nine of the clock in the morning." Another Englishman disagreed on both counts: in the opinion of John Swan,[15] the world was created during the last week of April, so that the first day of creation was April 23, 4005 B.C. Continental writers were just as divided. If a consensus of opinion could be taken (which

---

[12] On the rise and fall of Biblical chronology, see Francis C. Haber, *The Age of the World: Moses to Darwin* (Baltimore, 1959).

[13] In *De anno primitivo ab exordio mundi* (Augsburg, 1621).

[14] *Works* (1684), II, 1322. The next quotation is from I, 692.

[15] In *Calamus mensurans* (1635), I, 35-36.

it cannot), it might show that Adam was created on March 25th. It was a date fraught with typological implications; for, as calendars like Pantaleon's *Diarium historicum* remind us at a glance, we should celebrate on one and the same day both Adam's creation and the Annunciation.[16]

II

The marked refusal of Renaissance chronologists to date the year of creation more than a century either side of 4000 B.C. was not an accident. It was a necessity. Had they accepted the Septuagint's chronology, they would have been driven to the conclusion that by the time of the Renaissance the world was over 7,000 years old. But this was a manifest impossibility since it was widely expected that the world would end on or before its 6,000th year. As Hugh Latimer categorically pointed out, the world "was ordained to endure (as all learned men affirme and proove it with Scripture) six thousand yeares." The same chronological span, Donne also maintained, is "vulgarly esteemed to be the age and terme of this world."[17]

---

[16] I consulted the Basle edition of the *Diarium* (1572?), p. 91. In England, so far as I know, the creation of Adam on March 25th was not greeted with wild enthusiasm. Leonard Wright reported the notion with the observation that he found it in "an old booke, of what credite I knowe not" (*A Display of Dutie* [1589], p. 39).

[17] Latimer, *Fruitfull Sermons* (1635), fol. 141v; Donne, *Sermons*, II, 352. For typical statements to the same effect, see the extended discussions by Sheltoo à Geveren, "That the world shall not endure above six thousand yeares," in *Of the Ende of The World*, trans. Thomas Rogers (1577), fols. 5v ff., and Richard Baxter, *The Reasons of the Christian Religion* (1667), pp. 582 ff.

The calculation was based on two traditions which respectively divided temporal history into Three Eras and Six Ages. The earliest formulation of the Three Eras was ascribed by the Talmud to the Tanna debe Eliyahu ("the school of Elijah").[18] According to a typical Renaissance version, "The world shall last sixe thousand yeeres; two thousand thereof there shall be a vacuitie or emptinesse; two thousand the Law shall continue; and the dayes of the Messiah shall make out two thousand more; of which if any be lacking, by reason of our many and grievous sinnes they shall be lacking."[19]

The early Christians, persuaded that the end of the world was imminent, paid little attention to this "prophecy." Modified in time, however, it gained ground steadily. St. Augustine—much in character—readily accepted the notion of the Three Eras yet preferred to be silent concerning the precise duration of history. Concurrently, still another concept began to emerge, the division of world history into Six Ages (Adam to Noah, thence to Abraham, to David, to the Babylonian captivity, to the birth of Jesus, and to the Last Judgment). Once endorsed by Augustine, Isidore of Seville, and Bede,[20] it became securely entrenched. Sometime, some-

[18] *Sanhedrin*, 97a-b; in *The Babylonian Talmud*, ed. I. Epstein (1935), Sanh. II.

[19] Daniel Featley, *Clavis mystica* (1636), p. 83. The earliest reference in England to the "prophecy" of Elijah was in an anonymous work, *The Complaynt of Scotlande* (1549); but thereafter it was disseminated widely, more often than not in connection with the period's rampant apocalyptic expectations. See Katharine R. Firth, *The Apocalyptic Tradition in Reformation Britain 1530-1645* (Oxford, 1979), p. 113 and *passim*, as well as Richard Bauckman, ed., *Tudor Apocalypse* (1978), pp. 282-83 etc.

[20] Augustine: *De civitate Dei*, XII, 30; *De genesi contra manichaeos*, I, 23; and *De catechizandis rudibus*, XII; Isidore: *Etymologiae*, V, 39; and Bede: *De temporibus*. See further my study *"The Grand Design of God": The Literary Form of the Christian View of History* (1972), *passim*.

how, this idea converged with the psalmist's assertion that a thousand years in the sight of God are but as yesterday (Psalm 90.4), later held to be confirmed by the Petrine statement that "one day is with the Lord as a thousand years, and a thousand years as one day" (2 Peter 3.8). In the light of this "equation," the Six Ages were said to be analogous to the six days of creation. The "excellent mystery" of this analogy positively transfixed the orthodox thinkers of the Renaissance. To quote a commonplace elaboration: "As in the worlds sixth day God did make man: so in the worlds sixth age hee did redeeme man. In the worlds sixth day the first *Adam* was made, in whom wee are deformed: and in the worlds sixth age was the second *Adam* made, in whom wee are reformed."[21] But this was not all. Since a day "equals" a millennium, the Six Ages or "Days," collectively at least, must comprise six thousand years. For Renaissance expositors ever in search of further correspondences, this was an open invitation to associate the Six Ages with the Three Eras of "the school of Elijah": both add up to six thousand years. It must be confessed nevertheless that the prophecy of the Three Eras is often encountered by itself, both in England and on the Continent.[22] So is the legend of the Six Ages, which Pedro Mexía confidently described as upheld "by $\tilde{y}$ moste parte of approued Authours."[23] But on the whole the two concepts were conflated, witness Luther's *Supputatio annorum mundi* (1541),

[21] William Jones, *The Mysterie of Christs Nativitie* (1614), sig. Blv.

[22] Among the authorities citing the "prophecy" were Pico, Melanchthon, Osiander, Matthaeus Dresser, Georg Horn, Pietro Martire Vermigli, Simon Goulart, *et al.*

[23] *Silva de varia lection* (Valladolid, 1551), Part I, Ch. XXVI; trans. Thomas Fortescue in *The Foreste* (1571), sig. F3v. Cf. Griffith Williams, *Seven Goulden Candlestickes* (1624), p. 403, and *The Best Religion* (1636), p. 853.

where the verso of the title page displays prominently the following solitary entry:

ELIA Propheta.
Sex milibus annorum stabit Mundus.
Duobus milibus inane.
Duobus milibus Lex.
Duobus milibus Messiah.
Isti sunt Sex dies hebdomadae coram Deo
Septimus dies Sabbatum æternum est.
Psalm. 90. Et 2. Pet. 2 [*sic*]
Mille anni sicut dies unus.

But the Renaissance is a period of transition and we should therefore not conclude this excursion into one of its byways without reporting exceptions to traditional views. More often than not, such exceptions were phrased hesitantly. Most writers preferred the cautious words of Daniel Featley that the tradition of "the house of Elias" is not "of infallible certaintie."[24] But a handful were more outspoken. One was the widely respected Anglican apologist John Dove;[25] another was Sir Thomas Browne, who not only included "the prophecy of Elias the Rabbin" among the vulgar errors of his age, but was also of the opinion that while it is possible to "sit down with the common and usuall account" of chronology, it should be understood that "we cannot satisfie our selves in the exact compute of time."[26] John Lightfoot, though unwilling to accept the latter attitude, nevertheless agreed that the "prophecy" must be dismissed as unreliable. According to his militant statement, heavy with shrewd

---

[24] *Clavis mystica* (1636), p. 84.
[25] *A Sermon preached at Pauls Crosse* (1594), sigs. A8 ff.
[26] In the work cited earlier (note 3), p. 127.

sarcasm, "Every one knows the old conceit of the worlds lasting six thousand years, because it was made in six days: and of Elias Prophesie among the Jews, of the worlds ending, at the end of six thousand: which Prophesie of his is flat against the words of Christ:[27] Many believe these opinions, yet few prepare for the end which they think is so near. . . ."[28]

But an even more sweeping attack had already been delivered by Gabriel Harvey's younger brother John, in *A Discoursive Probleme Concerning Prophesies* (1588). Manifestly bent on stemming the tide of the ever-increasing apocalyptic prophecies current during the Renaissance in England, John Harvey proclaimed the concept of the Three Eras to be a "conjectural fansie," the legend of the Six Ages simply "fantasticall," and all chronological computations "ambiguous, uncertaine, fallible, erronious, deceitfull."[29] It was for a young man aged only twenty-five a giant step to have taken, anticipatory of developments normally associated with the ensuing century and beyond.

[27] I.e., his express admonition that the precise day of the Last Judgment is known only to the Father (Mark 13.32).

[28] *Works* (1684), I, 1021. Blake in *The Marriage of Heaven and Hell* adapted the same "old conceit" to his own purposes: "The ancient tradition that the world will be consumed by fire at the end of six thousand years is true, as I have heard from Hell."

[29] *A Discoursive Probleme* (1588), pp. 16, 34. The work may have been written at the request of the government, perhaps of Queen Elizabeth herself, who strongly disapproved of "prophecies" anticipatory of catastrophes (Garrett Mattingly, *The Defeat of the Spanish Armada* [Penguin ed., 1962], pp. 202-203).

❦ 4 ❧
"Those mysterious things they observe in numbers":
Approaches to Numerology

[ἡ μαθηματικὴ] τήν τε τῶν λόγων εὐταξίαν
ἀναφαίνουσα, καθ'ἥν δεδημιούργηται τὸ πᾶν,
καὶ ἀναλογίαν τὴν πάντα τὰ ἐν τῷ κόσμῳ συν-
δήσασαν, ὥς που φησὶν ὁ Τίμαιος.—Proclus

I

The narrator in Swift's *A Tale of a Tub* (1704) advances
from one questionable preocupation to another. Among
them is an obsession with numerology—"in imitation,"
we are told, ". . . of that prudent method observed by
many other philosophers and great clerks, whose chief
art in division has been to grow fond of some proper
mystical number, which their imaginations have rendered sacred, to a degree, that they force common reason
to find room for it, in every part of nature; reducing,
including, and adjusting every genus and species within
that compass, by coupling some against their wills, and
banishing others at any rate."[1] His own tendency, we
are informed, is to favor "the profound number THREE."
But a threatened "panegyrical essay" on that number

[1] *A Tale of a Tub*, Everyman ed. (1909, repr. 1964), p. 44.

remained only a threat, in part at least because by the Renaissance the subject had been exhausted altogether. Yet the numerological obsession of Swift's narrator is by no means the last on record. It encompasses in our own time the labors of several scholars who appear intent on establishing numerology as a preeminent structural principle in a variety of literary works, some of them relevant, most of them only coincidentally so.[2] A fair example of the strategies involved concerns the claim that the division of Milton's *De doctrina christiana* into two rather than three parts is "tantamount to a rejection of that Trinity which the book itself rejects in no uncertain terms."[3] The claim should have been equally relevant to every other theological treatise, and to works of literature like Sir Thomas Browne's *Religio Medici*, that happen to be similarly divided; but in the event this is

---

[2] In chronological sequence, the relevant studies are: A. Kent Hieatt, *Short Time's Endless Monument: The Symbolism of Numbers in Edmund Spenser's "Epithalamion"* (1960); Maren-Sofie Røstvig, "The Hidden Sense: Milton and the Neoplatonic Method of Numerical Composition," in *The Hidden Sense and Other Essays* (Oslo, 1963), Part I; Alastair Fowler, *Spenser and the Numbers of Time* (1964); Røstvig, "Milton and the Science of Numbers," in *English Studies Today*, 4th series, ed. Ilva Cellini and Giorgio Melchiori (Rome, 1966), pp. 267-88; Gunnar Qvarnström, *The Enchanted Palace: Some Structural Aspects of "Paradise Lost"* (Stockholm, 1967); Fowler, *Triumphal Forms: Structural Patterns in Elizabethan Poetry* (Cambridge, 1970); and the even more wide-ranging collection of essays *Silent Poetry: Essays in Numerological Analysis*, ed. Fowler (1970). There are several extensions of these theses, their argument based on coincidental patterns which can be easily disproved by emphasizing such poems, and such aspects of poems, that do *not* conform to the carefully selected "evidence." A representative study whose argument can be thus easily undermined is Sibyl L. Severance, "Numerological Structures in *The Temple*," in *"Too Rich to Clothe the Sunne": Essays on George Herbert*, eds. Claude J. Summers and Ted-Larry Pebworth (Pittsburgh, 1980), pp. 229-49.

[3] Røstvig, *The Hidden Sense* (as in previous note), p. 39.

not so at all. By the same token, generalized numerological patterns—whether in connection with three as diversely predicated by Dante in the *Commedia* and Herbert in "Trinitie Sunday," or with five as variously upheld by Spenser in Book V of *The Faerie Queene* and Chapman in the Fifth Sestiad of *Hero and Leander*—could be transmuted into primary structural components only if we are prepared adventurously to assert that every line in, say, *Paradise Lost* is fraught with arithmomantic import. In short, the espousal of numerology during the Renaissance, widespread though it was as a way of sustaining belief in cosmic order or of reinforcing a variety of parallel themes, need not argue its actual application to the very structure of works of literature in any substantive way. Even where particular numbers were invoked—such, for example, as the two numbers to be considered here—care must be taken not to mistake the conscious deployment of numbers within an analogical framework as a principle at once all-embracing and literally applicable to every given literary structure. Numerology was operative during the Renaissance primarily as a sustained *thematic* concern often—perhaps, indeed, all too often—attesting to "form," but not habitually and incontestably as an axiom relevant to structure *qua* structure. To credit otherwise could result—and, in one case, did result—in the ironic "discovery" that the work of a numerologically minded scholar happened itself to contain positive evidence of strictly unintended "hidden senses"![4]

[4] William Nelson, reviewing Fowler's *Spenser and the Numbers of Time* (as above, note 2), in *Renaissance News*, XVIII (1965), pp. 52-57. See also Douglas Bush, "Calculus Racked Him," in his *Engaged and Disengaged* (Cambridge, Mass., 1966), pp. 58-66. On numbers used to reinforce the

Numerology as a thematic concern is certainly well-nigh omnipresent in the literature of the Renaissance, its "evidence" extending from the firm declaration of St. Augustine ("numbers and combinations of numbers are used in the sacred writings to convey instruction under a figurative guise, and ignorance of numbers often shuts out the reader from this instruction") to the countless efforts mounted thereafter to comprehend, explicate, and apply the mysteries variously penetrated.[5] Yet it is imperative to accept that such efforts were not an isolated activity: they formed part of a cumulative endeavor to reinforce the order believed to pervade the universe at large. As we have had occasion to observe earlier (Chs. I and II), order was proclaimed to be the foremost characteristic not only of the celestial and the sublunar realms but, it was often averred, of Hell too. The widespread belief was fortified in a variety of ways, principal among them the fabrication of a multitude of correspondences connecting the diverse levels of being into a unified whole. Fundamentally an analogical mode of thought, the elab-

---

structure of the universe and, by way of analogy only, the structure of literary works too, consult S. K. Heninger's balanced discussion in *Touches of Sweet Harmony: Pythagorean Cosmology and Renaissance Poetics* (San Marino, Calif., 1974).

[5] Augustine, *De doctrina christiana*, II, xvi, 25; trans. J. F. Shaw, in *Works*, ed. Marcus Dods (Edinburgh, 1877), IX, 53. The most comprehensive study of the period leading to the Renaissance is by Vincent F. Hopper, *Medieval Number Symbolism: Its Sources, Meaning, and Influence on Thought and Expression* (1938). But see also F. Flanders Dunbar, *Symbolism in Medieval Thought* (New Haven, 1929), Ch. I, and Christopher Butler, *Number Symbolism* (1970). On the sixteenth century, consult Lynn Thorndike, *A History of Magic and Experimental Science* (1941), VI, Ch. XLIV. Russell Fraser's premise ("Number is the annulling of decay") is an eloquent testimony of tradition-bound modes of thought (*The Language of Adam* [1977], p. 168); but its further extensions may not be hazarded without due caution.

orate correspondences devolved into analogies between the divine, the human and the political planes.[6] The correspondence between the celestial plane and the macrocosm, for example, was habitually centered on analogies posited between the Godhead and the sun. As John Dove typically maintained in 1605, ". . . in the Sunne which shineth in the firmament, there are the bodie of the Sunne, the brightnes which proceedeth from the body, and the heate which procedeth from them both. So in the Trinitie, there is the Father from whome all thinges are, the Sonne which is the brightnes of his Fathers glorie, and the ingrauen forme of his person, and the holy Ghost, which is the heate and loue of them both."[7] As the sun corresponds in one direction to the Godhead, so it does in another to the heart of man. In the words of Du Bartas,

> Je veux tout sur-le-champ trompeter qu'en la sorte
> Qu'au milieu de son corps le Microcosme porte
> Le cœur, source de vie, et qui de toutes parts
> Fournit le corps d'esprits par symmetrie espars,
> Que de mesme, o soleil, chevelu d'or, tu marches
> Au milieu des six feux six plus basses arches
> Qui voutent l'univers, à fin d'esgalement,
> Riche, leur departir clarté, force, ornement.[8]

[6] In accordance with the tabulations of E.M.W. Tillyard, *The Elizabethan World Picture* (1943), Ch. VI-VII.

[7] *A Confutation of Atheisme* (1605), p. 37. For a version of the same idea in verse, see Thomas Heywood, *The Hierarchie of the Blessed Angells* (1635), p. 279.

[8] *La Creation du monde*, 1ère semaine, 4me jour, pp. 531-38. More detailed elaborations of the macrocosm-microcosm analogy include: Henry Cuffe, *The Differences of the Ages of Mans Life* (1607), pp. 1 ff.; Sir Walter Ralegh, *The History of the World* (1914), p. 30; Thomas Adams, *Mysticall Bedlam* (1615), p. 9; Samuel Purchas, *Purchas his Pilgrim* (1619), pp. 30-

Equally, however, the sun corresponds within the body politic to the king, witness in particular the frequency with which the analogy was deployed by Shakespeare.[9] Most interestingly representing the habitual conflation of the various levels of being is the analogy between the body politic, the microcosm of man, and the greater world, unexpectedly set forth by William Harvey. In his dedication of *De motu cordis* to Charles I in 1628, the eminent anatomist began with the statement that "Cor animalium, fundamentum est vitæ, princept omnium, Microcosmi Sol, à quo omnis vegetatio dependet, vigor omnis & robur emanat. Rex pariter regnorum suorum fundamentum, & Microcosmi sui Sol, Reipublicæ Cor est, à quo omnis emanat potestas, omnis gratia provenit."[10] But such was the number of correspondences possible, and such the regularity with which they were expounded, that the habit could prove tiresome. Du Bartas was at least honest enough to confess, after using an inordinate number of analogies, that the enterprise was rather "teadious; how ever sweet we sing."[11]

As with the correspondences, so with the numerological patterns: the intention in each case was to

31; Helkiah Crooke, *Mikrokosmographia*, 2nd ed. (1631), pp. 4-8; Person (as below, note 29), I, 27; Comenius (note 34), pp. 226-27; etc.

[9] *Richard II*, III, iii, 62-67; *1 Henry IV*, I, ii, 221-27; *2 Henry IV*, II, iii, 18-21; etc. The analogy's frequency is discussed by Caroline Spurgeon, *Shakespeare's Imagery* (Cambridge, 1935), pp. 235-38.

[10] *Exercitatio anatomica de motu cordis et sanguinis in animalibvs* (Frankfurt, 1628). For the most detailed exposition of the correspondence between the microcosm and the body politic, see Edward Forset, *A Comparative Discourse of the Bodies Natural and Politique* (1606), partially reprinted in *The Frame of Order*, ed. James Winny (1957), pp. 89-103.

[11] *Op.cit.* (above, note 8), lère semaine, 7me jour, 712; trans. Joshua Sylvester. The original French states that repetition "Enuie l'auditer, pour bien qu'il soit chante."

strengthen the concept of cosmic order by a multiple association of all parts of the universe to one another. With the "new philosophy" calling all in doubt, analogical thinking became all the more important. However vain an endeavor it proved to be, it was undertaken at the time with all gravity and earnestness.

II

The preoccupation with numbers arose from two independent sources, the astrological lore of ancient Babylonia and the Pythagoreanism of ancient Greece. The two currents of thought merged as they made their entry into Christianity, and though number symbolism appealed particularly to the Gnostics, it was frequently invoked by the Fathers—notably Irenaeus, Tertullian, Lactantius, and Ambrose—and given "the final stamp of approval" by St. Augustine.[12] Inherited and greatly elaborated by the Middle Ages, the concern with numbers was in turn transmitted to the Renaissance, which provided not only surveys such as Heinrich Cornelius Agrippa's *De occulta philosophia* (1531, translated into English in 1651) but textbooks such as Pietro Bongo's highly regarded *De numerorum mysteria* (1591) and, in England, William Ingpen's *The Secrets of Numbers* (1624).[13]

But it should not be assumed that obsession with numbers distinguished only the theologians and the *literati* of the Renaissance. On the contrary, scientists of

[12] Hopper (as above, note 5), p. 78.

[13] The relevant portions of Agrippa's *Three Books of Occult Philosophy*, trans. J. F. (1651), are pp. 167-238 [Bk. II, Ch. 1-21]. The full title of Ingpen's effort is *The Secret of Numbers; According to Theologicall, Arithmeticall, Geometricall and Harmonicall Computation* (1624).

the first order often turned to numerology; nor is it a long way from this to the revived Pythagoreanism of the fifteenth and sixteenth centuries over which Copernicus, Galileo, and Kepler were eventually to reign supreme.[14] The structure of the universe revealed by these astronomers was founded squarely on mathematics, then coming to the forefront of attention throughout the universities and academies of Europe. Standing in the line of descent that includes Pythagoras and Plato and Proclus ("[mathematics] discloses the order of those relations by which the universe is fabricated, and that proportion which binds, as Timaeus says, whatever the world contains"),[15] Galileo proclaimed: "Philosophy is written in that vast book which stands forever open before our eyes, I mean the universe; but it cannot be read until we have learnt the language and become familiar with the characters in which it is written. It is written in mathematical language, and the letters are triangles, circles and other geometrical figures, without which means it is humanly impossible to comprehend a single word."[16]

[14] On Pythagoreanism, see the summaries by William P. Wightman, *The Growth of Scientific Ideas* (New Haven, 1953), Ch. III, and particularly George Sarton, *A History of Science* (Cambridge, Mass., 1952), Ch. VIII; yet one of the best accounts I know is still the comprehensive survey by E. Zeller, *A History of Greek Philosophy*, trans. F. Alleyne (1881), I, 368-480. Its revival during the Renaissance and its influence on the astronomers mentioned are discussed by Edwin A. Burtt, *The Metaphysical Foundations of Modern Physical Science*, 2nd ed. (1932), pp. 40-60, and Abraham Wolf, *A History of Science, Technology and Philosophy in the 16th and 17th Centuries*, 2nd ed. (1952), Ch. II and VI, *passim*.

[15] Proclus, *In primum Euclidis elementorum librum commentarii*, ed. G. Friedlein (Leipzig, 1873), p. 22; trans. Thomas Taylor, *The Philosophical and Mathematical Commentaries of Proclus* (1788), I, 63-64. The original Greek is quoted in the headnote, above.

[16] *Il Saggiatore*, Q. 6; trans. A. C. Crombie, *Augustine to Galileo* (1957), p. 295.

In England, John Dee, in his famous address "To the Vnfained Lovers of Truthe" prefixed to Sir Henry Billingsley's translation of Euclid's *Elements* (1570), not only stressed the importance of "arithmetike" but maintained that the universe consists of "numbryng." In a fusion of the popular conception of the scale of nature with aspects of Pythagoreanism and Neoplatonism, Dee affirmed that we may best comprehend the cosmic scale by considering the behavior of "number" under the guidance of God: ". . . by degrees, by litle and litle, [it will be seen to be] stretchyng forth, and applying some likenes of it, as first, to thinges Spirituall: and then, bryngyng it lower, to thynges sensibly perceived . . . : then to the least thynges that may be seen, numerable: And at length, (most grossely,) to a multitude of any corporall thynges seen, or felt."[17]

On the Continent, the scientist who best exemplified this mystico-mathematical conception of the universe was Kepler. Though unquestionably an exact mathematician and an empirical astronomer, Kepler never abandoned astrology and frequently devoted his energies to numerical curiosities that were for him—as they were to be for Newton—much more important than we are wont to credit. In an effort to demonstrate the "harmonical proportions" of the mathematical universe, he claimed, first in his *Mysterium cosmographicum* (1596) and again in *Harmonices mundi* (1619), that "the number of the planets or circular routes around the sun was taken by the very wise Founder from the five regular solids"; in other words,

[17] *The Elements of Geometrie of the most Auncient Philosopher Euclide* (1570), sig. *i verso. For a discussion of the views of Dee and other English mathematicians, see Paul H. Kocher, *Science and Religion in Elizabethan England* (San Marino, Calif., 1953), pp. 150 ff.

each of the five regular polyhedra may in turn be placed within each of the spheres containing the orbits of the six planets—manifest evidence, Kepler asserted, that God is "Geometriæ fons ipsissimus, et, vt Plato scripsit, 'æternam exercans Geometriam' " ("the very source of geometry and, as Plato wrote, 'practices eternal geometry' ").[18] It was in *Harmonices mundi*, too, that Kepler, while formulating his third great law of planetary motion, celebrated also the "music of the spheres" which directly associates him with the Pythagoreans, who "supposed," as Aristotle reported, "the elements of numbers to be the elements of all things, and the whole heaven to be a musical scale and a number."[19]

The structure of the universe so eloquently divulged by Kepler would have been accepted readily by the guardians of orthodoxy during the Renaissance were it not that he and the other expositors of the new cosmology denied the validity of the Ptolemaic system, adhering either to the heliocentric theory of Copernicus or to the modified geocentric theory of Tycho Brahe. In consequence, the exponents of orthodox thought, while in agreement with the "new philosophers" so far as the "harmonical proportions" of the universe were concerned, on the whole renounced the assailants of the time-honored cosmology of Ptolemy and endeavored to fortify the traditional conception partly through the series of

[18] In *Gesammelte Werke*, ed. Max Caspar (Munich, 1940), VI, 298 and 299; trans. C. G. Wallis, *The Harmonies of the World*, in *Great Books of the Western World*, ed. R. M. Hutchins (Chicago, 1952), XVI, 1016 and 1017. For a discussion of Kepler's treatise, see Francis Warrain, *Essai sur l'Harmonices Mundi* (Paris, 1942). Kepler's concurrent respect for experimental science and for astrology is clearly evident throughout his correspondence: see Carola Baumgart, *Johannes Kepler: Life and Letters* (1952).

[19] *Metaphysica*, 985b; trans. W. D. Ross.

correspondences we have noted and partly through the equally vital series of analogies involved with numbers. Persuaded that "there is no knowledge, either rationall, morall, physicall, or metaphysicall, which hath not some cognation or participation with numbers,"[20] they sought—and of course found—much evidence to support their predetermined thesis. The ages of man, for example, were variously claimed to be three, four, six, or seven.[21] Where they were said to be three, reference was promptly made to the Trinity and other triads; where four, a comparison was made to the four seasons, the four complexions, or the four elements; where six, the six ages of the world were normally invoked; and where seven, it was generally agreed that the seven planets were involved. The ultimate number—"the perfect number in the universe," Robert Grosseteste had long since called it—was widely affirmed to be ten. As Henry More explained, "The number of ten among the ancients called παντέλεια, is an emblem of perfection: for it comprehends all numbers, sith we are fain to come back again to one, two, &c. when we are past it."[22]

When all is said, however, the numbers that received the greatest stress were three and seven. Both have been regarded ever since Eratosthenes as "prime numbers,"

---

[20] Ingpen (as above, note 13), p. 1.

[21] The differences of opinion are summarily treated by Sir Godfrey Fenton, *Golden Epistles* (1575), fols. 148v-157v.

[22] Grosseteste, *De luce*, trans. Clare C. Riedl (Milwaukee, 1942), p. 17; More, *Philosophical Poems* (Cambridge, 1647), p. 360. Ingpen's treatise (above, note 13) devotes each of its ten chapters to the numbers one through ten. One other highly favored number should also be mentioned: "four," which was particularly relevant to Pythagorean conceptions of the universe (see S. K. Heninger, as above, note 4).

irresolvable into smaller factors and therefore of particular significance to numerologists.

III

"*Tria sunt omnia*, is as old as father Time," declared Francis Meres in 1598.[23] Within Christianity, commitment to the Trinity dictated an extreme partiality to the number three and whatever triads could be discerned—or, as often as not, imagined to exist—in the created order. The path that Christians were to traverse was carved principally by St. Augustine, who sought to establish any number of *vestigia trinitatis* at every level of the universal structure.[24] By the Middle Ages three had become "easily the favorite number,"[25] while for Dante it was no less than his "key number."[26] A host of writers during the Renaissance similarly regarded three as "an incompounded number, a holy number, a number of perfection, a most powerful number," or even—so it was proclaimed with rising enthusiasm and declining sense—as "the fountain and well-spring of all things produc-

---

[23] *Palladis Tamia* (1598), "The Epistle Dedicatorie." On triadic thought in diverse cultures, see Philip Wheelwright, *The Burning Fountain: A Study in the Language of Symbolism* (Bloomington, Ind., 1954), pp. 130 ff. ["The Primal Triad"].

[24] *De civ. Dei*, XI, 24-26. Consult especially Rudolf Allers, "The Notions of Triad and of Mediation in the Thought of St. Augustine," *New Scholasticism*, XXXI (1957), 499-525. Cf. Thomas Aquinas, *Summa theologica*, I, xlv, 7.

[25] Hopper (as above, note 5), p. 128.

[26] Howard Candler, "On the Symbolic Use of Number in the *Divina Commedia* and elsewhere," *Transactions of the Royal Society of Literature*, XXX (1910), 3. While the *Commedia* is fully committed to three, *La vita nuova* (XXIX-XXX) favors especially nine ("un miracolo, la cui radice è solamente la mirabile Trinitade").

tive, the beginning of all procession, the continuance of all immutable substance."[27] A very popular analogy centered on three involved the Trinity in relation to the Augustinian concept of the threefold distinction of the soul into *intelligentia, voluntas,* and *memoria.* As Thomas Milles rendered this view:

". . . the Soule . . . is said to bee the *Image of God,* like as in a Trinity. For albeit, that (by Nature) she can bee but one, yet it is most certaine, that she hath in her selfe three seuerall Dignities, to wit, *Vnderstanding, Will,* and *Memory.* And looke how the Sonne is begotten of the Father, and the Holy-Ghost proceedeth both of the one and the other: In like manner, is the *Will* engendred of the *Vnderstanding,* and *Memory* hath her procreation from them both. And euen as the three persons of the Trinitie are but one God; so the three powers of the Soule, are but one only Soule."[28]

But one should glance farther afield in order to appreciate the lengths to which many writers were prepared to go. Thus David Person, who believed that "three

---

[27] Agrippa, p. 179, and Ingpen, p. 20 (both as above, note 13).

[28] *The Treasurie of Auncient and Moderne Times* (1613), p. 18; translated from *Les diverses leçons d'Antoine Du Verdier,* 2nd ed. (Lyon, 1580), p. 27, in turn an adaptation from Pedro Mexía's *Silva de varia lección* (Seville, 1542). For other parallel statements, see Henry Ainsworth, *The Orthodox Foundation of Religion* (1641), p. 22; Edward Benlowes, *Theophila,* VIII, 42-43; John Donne, *Six Sermons upon Severall Occasions* (Cambridge, 1634), I, 28-31; Dove (as above, note 7), p. 37; Joseph Fletcher, *The Historie of . . . Man* (1629), pp. 8-9; William Loe, *The Mysterie of Mankind* (1619), p. 47; Purchas (as above, note 8), pp. 120-21; John Swan, *Speculum mundi* (Cambridge, 1635), p. 500; Andrew Willet, *Hexapla in Genesin* (Cambridge, 1605), p. 15; John Woolton, *A Newe Anatomie of Whole Man* (1576), fol. 11; *et al.* The ultimate source of this idea is Augustine, *De Trinitate,* XIV, 8.

of all numbers should be held in greatest veneration," drew his examples from a multitude of fields: from the queen of the sciences, the three theological virtues; from politics, the three kinds of government, monarchy, aristocracy, and democracy; from biology, the three kinds of living things, men, animals, and plants; from mythology, the three destinies, the three sirens, the three sons of Saturn, the three daughters of Acheron, the three names of Diana, and so forth.[29] It was not difficult for the analogies to be multiplied to absurdity, especially when the number three was used as a springboard for moral discourses. One of the numerous instances offered by Person will suffice: "Three things [are] incident to man: To fall to sinne, which is humane; to rise out of it againe, which is Angelicall; and to lye in sinne, which is Diabolicall."[30] But Person's moralized triplicities were not unique. At least two other books had already been compiled—Simson Robson's *The Choise of Change* (1585) and Charles Gibson's *The Remedie of Reason* (1589)—with a similarly exclusive purpose in mind.

Person's enthusiasm for the number three was tolerant enough to accommodate an equal enthusiasm for the number seven, which "by many learned men hath beene held the most mysticall, and by some entitled the most sacred of Numbers."[31] Seven was indeed often hailed as "singular," "absolute," "a number universall and accom-

---

[29] *Varieties* (1635), V, 2-9. For other exhaustive examples, see Thomas Tymme, *A Dialogue Philosophicall* (1612), pp. 26 ff. [Part I, Ch. IV-VI]. Cf. John Lightfoot, *Erubhin* (1629), pp. 151 ff.

[30] *Ibid.*, V, 5. The formula "There are three things" reigns supreme in most numerical apophthegms (E. R. Curtius, *European Literature and the Latin Middle Ages*, trans. William R. Trask [1953], pp. 510 ff.).

[31] *Ibid.*, V, 10 ff.

plished," "the most excellent of all others."[32] In the very first book of the Bible, after all, it is said that God rested on the seventh day; and in the very last, the Book of Revelation, it is even more evident that seven is so omnipresent that commentators were in effect obliged to regard it as "the nombre of fulnes," "perfection," "an universall number, by whose revolution, all tymes are framed, al ages beinge in like manner wheerled upon this Pole."[33] No wonder that the great Comenius should have expressed his enthusiasm over the sacred number: ". . . now what mean the seven planets in heaven? what mean the seven continents on earth? the seven kinds of meteors, seven kinds of metalls, seven kinds of stones, &c? the seven combinations of tangible qualities? the seven differences of taste? the seven vitall members in man? the seven tones in musick? and other things which we meet with throughout all nature? yea, and in the Scripture the number of seven is every where very much celebrated, and sacred: For what do the seven dayes of the week point at? what are the seven weeks betwixt the

---

[32] *Seriatim*: Walter Charleton, *The Harmony of Natural and Positive Divine Laws* (1682), pp. 161 ff.; Pierre de la Primaudaye, *The French Academie*, trans. T. B. (1586), p. 563; Fenton (as above, note 21), fol. 149; and Ingpen (note 13), p. 47.

[33] *Seriatim*: Heinrich Bullinger, *A Hundred Sermons vpō the Apocalips*, trans. John Daws (1561), p. 165; Giovanni Diodati, *Pious and Learned Annotations upon the Holy Bible*, 3rd ed. (1651), sig. Xxxl; and Thomas Brightman, *A Revelation of the Reuelation* (Amsterdam, 1615), p. 6. The number seven figures prominently elsewhere in the Bible too, most strikingly in Joshua 6.2-20. For still other references, consult Eduard König in the *Dictionary of the Bible*, ed. James Hastings (Edinburgh, 1900), III, 562-63. The enthusiasm for this number extends thereafter from its celebration in Macrobius' *Commentary on the Dream of Scipio*, I, vi (trans. William H. Stahl [1952], pp. 99 ff.) to treatises variously devoted to *The Seauen Champions of Christendome* (by Richard Johnson, in 1616) or *The Seuen Deadly Sinnes of London* (by Thomas Dekker, in 1606).

Passeover and Pentecost? what the seventh year of rest? what the seven times seventh of *Jubilee*? what do all these portend I say, but that it is, the expresse Image of that *God, whose seven eyes passe through the whole earth?* (Zach. 4. 10.) *and whose seven spirits are before his Throne?* (Apoc. I. 4.)"[34]

John Donne, one of the foremost numerologists of his age, likewise believed that "seven is infinite."[35] On one occasion he also dwelt at length on the "remarkable" things limited to the number seventy, itself miraculously compounded of "the two greatest Numbers (for *Ten* cannot be exceeded, but that to express any further Number you must take a part of it again; and *Seven* is ever used to express infinite)."[36] Not surprisingly, therefore, God asked Moses for seventy elders; Adonibezek died after slaying seventy kings; the life of man is normally confined to seventy years; and the disciples of the Apostles numbered seventy. By the same token, both the Babylonian and the Avignon captivities lasted seventy years each, while the seventy-two translators of the Old Testament into Greek significantly called their version the Septuagint.[37]

[34] *Naturall Philosophie reformed by Divine Light*, trans. Anon. (1651), pp. 241-42.

[35] *Devotions upon Emergent Occasions*, ed. John Sparrow (Cambridge, 1923), p. 22.

[36] *Essays in Divinity*, ed. E. M. Simpson (Oxford, 1952), pp. 59-61. A notable predecessor was St. Cyril of Alexandria, who likewise favored the numbers seven and ten as well as their multiples; see the passages from his work collected by Alexander Kerrigan, *St. Cyril of Alexandria, Interpreter of the Old Testament* (Rome, 1952), pp. 383 ff.

[37] Actually the papal court was at Avignon only sixty-eight years (1309-1377). On the Babylonian captivity see Jeremiah 25.11, Daniel 9.2, and Zechariah 7.5. The other Biblical references are Numbers 11.36, Judges 1.7, Psalm 90.10, and Luke 10.1.

The "remarkable" events enumerated by Donne tended to pale, however, before the dire threat that the multiplication of seven by ten posed for the life of man. What this alarming prospect entailed was made quite clear by the historian Camden, whose account of the reign of Elizabeth I ends with the ominous remark that the Queen died "in her Climactericall yeare, to wit, the seventyeth yeare of her age."[38] In point of fact, however, Camden had forced the issue ever so slightly, in that only every seventh and ninth year—and of course their multiples—were generally regarded as "cretick" (critical), while one's sixty-third year (7×9) was held to be "most dangerous."[39] According to the fuller exposition by John Chamber: ". . . vpon the numbers of 7 and 9 some haue grounded their clymactericall years, that euery seuenth yeare & euery 9. yeare should be climacterical, and 63, which is made of both those numbers, that is of 7 multiplyed into 9, is counted and called *Clymactericus magnus*, the great clymactericke. These yeares they count to bring great alteration to the life of man, dying in these years, but especially, when they are 63 yeares olde."[40] Chamber himself considered such an outlook to be "follie"; and, skeptic that he was, added that "if any die, not only in that year but any thing neare it, as in the 62, or 64 yeares of his life, they will fetch him into the

---

[38] *Annals*, trans. R. Norton, 3rd ed. (1635), p. 584. For a lengthy discussion of this aspect of the Queen's death, see the appendix to the 1604 edition of Thomas Wright's *The Passions of the Minde*.

[39] Antonio de Guevara, *Familiar Epistles*, trans. Edward Hellows (1574), pp. 259 ff. Thus also Person (as above, note 29), V, 17, and Levinus Lemnius, "Of the *Climacterick* or graduall year," in *The Secret Miracles of Nature*, trans. Anon. (1658), pp. 142 ff. [Bk. II, Ch. XXXII].

[40] *A Treatise of Judicial Astrologie* (1601), p. 106.

63 yeare, and say that his age was mistaken."[41] As the narrator in *A Tale of a Tub* was to say, partisans of one number or another "force common reason to find room for it, in every part of nature."

Yet whether or not one regards the speculations on the climacteric year as "follie" and shares the sweeping condemnation by John Selden of all "those mysterious things they observe in Numbers,"[42] many individuals during the Renaissance discerned in numerology the means further to strengthen the structure of the universe and none was prepared readily to retreat before the assaults of the emancipated wits. Perhaps the best weapon to have directed against them was the sort of devastating irony deployed by Sir Thomas Browne. Decidedly enthusiastic in *Religio Medici* (1643) over "the mysticall way of *Pythagoras*, and the secret Magicke of numbers,"[43] Browne displayed next, in *The Garden of Cyrus* (1658), an apparently total commitment to the number five as manifest especially in the omnipresent pattern of the quincunx. But the pattern was in fact annihilated through a maximum of hyperbole and an optimum of eccentricity; and so, overtaking every numerologist am-

---

[41] *Ibid.* But see the passionate reaffirmation of the climacteric year by Sir Christopher Heydon, *A Defense of Judiciall Astrologie* (Cambridge, 1603), pp. 409-12. Chamber and Heydon were the protagonists in one of the period's numerous logomachies over astrology; they were later joined by George Carleton (*Astrologomania: The Madnesse of Astrologers*, 1624). Another series of exchanges involved Nathanael Homes (*Dæmonologie and Theologie*, 1650) and William Ramsey (*Lux Veritatis. Or, Christian Judicial Astrology Vindicated*, 1651), with a survey of the battlefield by William Rowland (*Judiciall Astrologie, Judicially Condemned*, 1652). See the studies by Don C. Allen, *The Star-Crossed Renaissance* (Durham, N.C., 1941), Ch. III, and Kocher (as above, note 17), Ch. X.

[42] *Table-Talk*, 2nd ed. (1696), pp. 109-10.

[43] Browne, *BMP*, p. 73.

bling along, Browne disproved both his case and theirs. Yet he did not forsake order. He affirmed it all the more passionately, not indeed in terms of any particular number, but in terms of the more comprehensive sense whereby it can be said that "All things began in order, so shall they end, and so shall they begin in again; according to the ordainer of order and mystical Mathematicks of the City of Heaven."[44]

[44] *Ibid.*, p. 387.

❧ 5 ❧
"With his face towards Heaven":
The Upright Form of Man

> Wee attribute but one priviledge and advantage to Mans
> body, above other moving creatures, that he is not as others,
> grovelling, but of an erect, of an upright form, naturally
> built, and disposed to the contemplation of *Heaven.* Indeed
> it is a thankfull forme, and recompences that *soule,* which
> gives it, with carrying that soule so many foot higher,
> towards *heaven.*—John Donne

I

The nature of God's image in man has exercized many
minds in Christendom. The crucial dimension was best
affirmed by St. Augustine when he wrote, "It is in the
soul of man, that is, in his rational or intellectual soul,
that we must find that image of the Creator which is
immortally implanted in its immortality."[1] Traditionally, however, there has also been an inclination to aver
that man's resemblance to God is in some way reflected
in the human frame as well. Even Calvin was of the
opinion that "though the primary seat of the divine image was in the mind and the heart, or in the soul and
its powers, there was no part even of the body in which
some rays of glory did not shine."[2]

[1] *De Trinitate,* XIV, 4; *apud* Reinhold Niebuhr, *The Nature and Destiny
of Man* (1941), I, 165.

[2] *Institutes,* I, xv, 3. The statement has numerous counterparts in Eastern
Christian thought, for example the parallel affirmation by St. Gregory Pa-

Man's upright form is foremost among the physical characteristics claimed as aspects of *imago Dei*. It suggests, wrote a popular author in 1652, man's distinction from animals no less than his natural heavenward propensity; for "whereas God hath made all other creatures to goe with their faces groveling towards the earth, he hath made man to go upright, and with his face towards Heaven."[3] More expansively stated, the idea is encountered in the collection of commonplaces gathered by Thomas Milles (1613 ff.):

"Man . . . was Created, to the end that he might acknowledge his God, and in knowing him, to honour him; and in honouring him, to loue him; and louing, to serue and obey him: and all this to no other end, but that finally he might attaine to that end, for which he was created: to wit, the fruition of his God and Maker. For this cause, he made him with an erected and vpright Body; not so much for his dissimilitude frō the brutish Beasts, who are crooked, bended and looking downe vpon the Earth: as to mount vp his vnderstanding, and eleuate his eyes vnto the Heauens, his originall, to contemplate there Diuine occasions and permanent, leauing the Terrestriall as vaine."[4]

Milton was sufficiently attracted by the idea to men-

lamas: see Vladimir Lossky, *The Mystical Theology of the Eastern Church* (1957), p. 116.

[3] Richard Gove, *The Saints Hony-comb* (1652), p. 42.

[4] *The Treasurie of Auncient and Moderne Times* (1613-9), I, 18-19. Milles is here drawing on Pedro Mexía's formulation in *Silua de varia lection* (Valladolid, 1551), I, 19 f., which was also available in the translations into French by Claude Gruget, *Les diverses leçons* (Lyon, 1592), pp. 68 f., and into English by Thomas Fortescue, *The Foreste* (1571), fols. 15v ff. Milles's words were lifted almost *verbatim* by Thomas Heywood in *The Hierarchie of the Blessed Angells* (1635), p. 375: see my note in *PQ*, XXXIX (1960), 118-22.

tion it twice in *Paradise Lost*. On the first view of Adam
and Eve in the Garden, it is carefully noted that in contrast to the animal creation beneath them, they are "of
farr nobler shape erect and tall, / Godlike erect" (IV,
288-89). A much fuller account is given in Raphael's
statement that God had resolved to create man as

> a Creature who not prone
> And brute as other Creatures, but endu'd
> With Sanctitie of Reason, might erect
> His Stature, and upright with Front serene
> Govern the rest, self-knowing.
>
> (VII, 506-10)

II

Few commonplaces of thought have been so enthusiastically supported by authorities of the first magnitude and,
in close pursuit, by a legion of lesser talents. It is an
idea which, traceable to Plato, was clearly articulated by
Aristotle and Cicero, and more fully expressed by Ovid:

> where all other beasts
>   behold the ground with grovelling eie,
> [God] gave to Man
>   a stately looke replete with majestie:
> And willde him to behold
>   the Heaven wyth countnance cast on hie,
> To marke and understand
>   what things were in the starrie skie.[5]

[5] Ovid, *Metamorphoses*, I, 84-86, according to the free version by Arthur
Golding (1567). The other authorities are: Plato, *Cratylus*, 399c (cf. *Timaeus*, 90a); Aristotle, *De partibus animalium*, 686a; and Cicero, *De natura
deorum*, II, 56. Milton's use of the idea has been traced to Ovid by Davis
P. Harding, *Milton and the Renaissance Ovid* (Urbana, Ill., 1946), pp. 77-
78; but it is clearly impossible to isolate a single influence when Milton
must have known any number of other formulations.

In the Christian era the idea was accepted by Justin Martyr and even more readily by Lactantius, identified by Augustine as an aspect of the image of God in man, upheld by Basil the Great, Gregory of Nyssa, Ambrose, and Peter Lombard, maintained by Boethius, and adopted among the Reformers by Calvin.[6] Its Renaissance adherents include among English poets not only Milton but Chapman, Benlowes, and Wither; among Continental poets, Tasso, Alonso de Acevedo, Du Bartas, Vondel, and Hugo Grotius; among English divines, William Perkins, Thomas Adams, Joseph Hall, Donne, Henry King, and Richard Baxter; and among Continental theologians and philosophers, Luis de la Puente, Peter Martyr, Levinus Lemnius, Philippe de Mornay, Andreas Gerardus Hyperius, Annibale Romei, Pierre Charron—and inevitably a host of minor writers as well.[7] Evidence

---

[6] *Seriatim*: Justin, *Apologia*, I, 50; Lactantius, *Divinae institutiones*, II, i, 15-18; Augustine, *De genesi contra Manichaeos*, I, xvii, 28; Basil, *Homilia IX in Hexaemeron*, II; Gregory, *De hominis opificio*, VIII; Ambrose, *Hexaemeron*, IV, ix, 55-58; Peter Lombard, *Sententiarum*, II, xvi, 5; Boethius, *De consolatione philosophiae*, V, 5; and Calvin, *Institutes*, I, xv, 3. For other references consult Mary Irma Corcoran, *Milton's Paradise with reference to the Hexameral Background* (Washington, D.C., 1945), p. 47n.

[7] The writers just cited, merged in an alphabetical roll-call with others, are: Alonso de Acevedo, *Creación del mundo* (1615), in *Bibliotheca de autores españoles* (Madrid, 1854), II, 280; Thomas Adams, *Heaven and Earth Reconcil'd* (1613), sig. E3v; Andreini, *apud* Corcoran (previous note); Baxter, *The Saints Everlasting Rest*, 2nd rev. ed. (1651), IV, 56; Benlowes, *Theophila* (1652), II, 20; Immanuel Bourne, *The True Way* (1622), p. 44; Nicholas Byfield, *The Rule of Faith* (1626), p. 196; Richard Carpenter, *Experience* etc. (1642), I, 67; Vicenzo Cartari, *The Fountaine of Ancient Fiction*, trans. Richard Lynche (1599), sigs. B1 f.; Jacob Cats, *Grondt-Houwelijck*, cited by Geoffrey Bullough in *Essays in English Literature*, eds. Millar MacLure and F. W. Watt (Toronto, 1964), p. 108; Chapman, *Hymnus in noctem*, ll. 124-26; Charron, *Of Wisdome*, trans. Samson Lennard (1640), pp. 9f.; Francis Cheynell, *The Man of Honour* (1645), p. 26; William Chub, *The True Trauaile* (1585), sig. B5v; Donne, *Devotions*, p. 10 [quoted in the head-

to confirm the widespread belief was provided not only
by the apparent differences between man and the animal
kingdom beneath him, but by the claim of etymologists
that ἄνθρωπος (man) derives from ἄνω (upward) and
θρῴσκω (leap).

note, above], as well as *Essays*, p. 30, and *Sermons*, III, 105, and VIII,
243; Du Bartas, *apud* George C. Taylor, *Milton's Use of Du Bartas* (Cambridge, Mass., 1934), p. 99; John Edwards, *A Demonstration of the Existence
and Providence of God* (1696), II, 3; Simon Goulart, *A Learned Summary upon
. . . Bartas*, trans. Thomas Lodge (1621), I, 268; Robert Greene, *Planetomachia* (1585), sig. A1; Grotius, in *The Celestial Cycle*, ed. Watson Kirkconnell (Toronto, 1952), pp. 134 f.; Peter Heylyn, Μικρόκοσμος, 7th ed.
(Oxford, 1636), p. 9; Hyperius, *The Course of Christianitie*, trans. John
Ludham (1579), pp. 3 f.; Henry King, *Two Sermons preached at White-Hall*
(1627), II, 11 f., and *An Exposition vpon the Lords Prayer* (1634), p. 165;
Edward Leigh, *A Systeme or Body of Divinity* (1654), pp. 290 f.; Lemnius,
The Secret Miracles of Nature, trans. Anon. (1658), p. 6; William Lilly, *The
Worlds Catastrophe* (1647), p. 4; Martyr (Pietro Martire Vermigli), *Common
Places*, trans. Anthony Marten (1574), I, 121; Henry Montagu, *Manchester
al mondo*, 7th impr. (1658), p. 98; Philippe de Mornay, *The Truenesse of
Christian Religion*, trans. Sir Philip Sidney and Arthur Golding (1617), p.
209; Pierre du Moulin, *The Love of God*, 5th ed. (1628), p. 11; Thomas
Nabbes, *Microcosmos* (1637), sig. C2; John Paget, *Meditations of Death* (Dort,
1639), pp. 120 f.; Perkins, *Works* (Cambridge, 1605), p. 170; Puente,
Meditations, trans. John Heigham (St. Omer, 1619), II, 756; Samson Price,
The Two Twins (1624), p. 33; Annibale Romei and Louis Le Roy, *apud*
Theodore Spencer, *Shakespeare and the Nature of Man*, 2nd ed. (1951), pp.
4-5; Alexander Ross, *Questions and Answers upon Genesis* (1620), p. 38; Francis Sabie, *Adams Complaint* (1596), sig. B1v; Michael Scott, *The Philosophers
Banquet*, 2nd ed. (1614), p. 12; Archibald Simson, *Heptameron* (St. Andrews, 1621), p. 29; Peter Sterry, *The Teachings of Christ in the Soule* (1648),
p. 24; John Swan, *Speculum mundi* (Cambridge, 1635), p. 428; Tasso, *apud*
Maury Thibaut de Maisieres, *Les Poèmes inspirés du début de la Genèse a
l'époque de la Renaissance* (Louvain, 1931), pp. 54 f.; Thomas Traherne,
Meditations on the Six Days of Creation (1717), p. 78; Robert Turner, in the
preface to his translation of Paracelsus' *Archidoxes magicae* (*Of the Supreme
Mysteries of Nature* [1656]); William Vaughan, *The Golden-Grove* (1600),
sig. D1; Vondel, *apud* George Edmundson, *Milton and Vondel* (1885), pp.
46-48; Michael Wigmore, *The Good-Adventure* (1620), p. 17; Andrew Willet, *Hexapla in Genesin* (Cambridge, 1605), p. 31; Griffith Williams, *The

Moralists expatiated on man's upright form frequently, and sometimes to advantage. Giambattista Gelli in *La Circe* (1549) annexed the time-honored idea to the belief in man's dual nature, and warned:

". . . yf [man] wyll gyue hym selfe holely vnto the belly holdynge hys countenaunce, and face continually fyxed on the earth, he shal become as one that perceueth nothynge, and like to the plantes: and yf he shall drowne himselfe to much in the sensytiue pleasure, he shall become like to the brute beastes: but yf he lyftynge hys face towardes heauen, playing the philosopher, shal consider the beautye of the heauens, and the marueyllous order of nature, he shal chaunge himselfe from an erthly beast, vnto an heuenly creature."[8]

But if man upright could be usefully moralized, so could man turned upside down to resemble an inverted tree. The aim in both cases was the same, in that man as *arbor inversa* is also upwardly disposed: ". . . he has his roots, or his hair, in the air, while other trees have their hairs, or their roots, in the earth."[9] The unlikely comparison was destined to appeal most to a mind like Marvell's, who used it in *Upon Appleton House* to confirm aims at once playfully articulated and seriously intended (l. 568).

Best Religion (1636), p. 518; George Wither, *Emblemes* (1634), I, xliii, 11-13; John Yates, *A Modell of Divinitie* (1622), p. 153; *et al.* See also the references cited by Charles Trinkaus, *In Our Image and Likeness* (1970), 2 vols., *passim*.

[8] *Circes*, trans. Henry Iden (1557), sig. S8v.

[9] From *The Hermetic Museum* (1677), quoted by A. B. Chambers who also unravels the diverse strains of the tradition in " 'I was but an inverted Tree': Notes toward the History of an Idea," *SR*, VIII (1961), pp. 291-99. The idea harks back to Plutarch's view of man "inverted to point to heaven" (*De exilio*, V [600F]).

Man "with his face toward Heaven" was not unanimously accepted as a valid concept, however. Two writers out of a handful who decided to oppose the intimidating number of authorities just cited are of interest to the student of the history of thought chiefly because of their profession. Both were doctors, and both must have been cognizant of Galen's sardonic claim that a skyward carriage is characteristic not of man but of a certain fish![10] Walter Charleton, physician to Charles I, denied that man has any reason "to boast a singularity" in his upright form since the penguin, the mantis, and other animals are similarly structured. As much had already been argued by another physician, Sir Thomas Browne, who ironically proposed that the antithesis between upward-looking man and downward-tending animals "may admit of question," and that "the end of this erection [which is] to look up toward heaven" is "not so readily to be admitted."[11] Before long Browne was vociferously challenged.[12] But authority had been questioned yet again, and the door to the new age was inched open further still.

[10] "Called *uranoscopos* ['beholder of the skies'], from the eye which it has in its head," reported Pliny (XXXII, xxiv, 69). Man, on the contrary, cannot look at the skies unless he actually leans back! (Galen, *De usu partium corporis humani*, Book III, Ch. III, ed. N. R. Calabrio [Paris, 1528], p. 69; for the original Greek see Περὶ χρείας μορίων, ed. G. Helmreich [Leipzig, 1907], I, 133).

[11] Charleton, *The Darknes of Atheism* (1652), pp. 86-87; Browne, *Pseudodoxia Epidemica* (1st ed., 1646), IV, 1, in *BMP*, pp. 224-25. While anticipating Charleton, Browne was himself anticipated by Henry More the Cambridge Platonist, who had earlier rejected the "conceit" of man's upright form since "Baboons, and Apes, as well as th' *Anthropi* / Do go upright" (*Psychozoia* [1642], II, 47; in *Philosophical Poems*, ed. Geoffrey Bullough [Manchester, 1931], p. 48).

[12] By Alexander Ross, in *Arcana microcosmi* (1652), pp. 154 f.

❦ 6 ❧

"The first promise made to man":
The Edenic Origins
of Protestantism

Before the *Law*, I pray, what was the Religion of *Adam*?
Moses touches it in a word, *The seed of the woman shall
breake the head of the Serpent*: see the first prophecie concerning
Christ, and that by God himselfe: he that *promised* him,
prophecyed of him: for *Christ* was that *Seede*.—John Stoughton

I

The sentence that God passes on Satan in *Paradise Lost*
is framed within the "mysterious terms" of Genesis 3.15:

Between Thee and the Woman I will put
Enmitie, and between thine and her Seed;
Her Seed shall bruise thy head, thou bruise his
    heel.

(X, 179-81)

To prevent any misunderstanding, Milton himself explains that the prophecy was verified

When *Jesus* son of *Mary* second *Eve*,
Saw Satan fall like Lightning down from Heav'n
Prince of the Aire; then rising from his Grave
Spoild Principalities and Powers, triumphd
In op'n shew, and with ascension bright

90

Captivity led captive through the Aire,
The Realme it self of Satan long usurpt,
Whom he shall tread at last under out feet.

(X, 182-90)

Milton throughout Books XI and XII made generous use
of the "mysterious terms" in the expectation of an appropriate response from his readers. That such a response
is not presently forthcoming may be attributed to a variety of reasons, not least to the tendency of modern
theologians to deny the validity of Genesis 3.15 as the
first "good news" in the process of fulfilment leading
from the first Adam to the second. At present, it has
been said, "we are not justified in going to the full length
of this interpretation"; it has been questioned indeed
"whether, even in the broad sense, this is a Messianic
text at all."[1] Given Milton's contrary view, however, it
may be that an investigation of the views of Renaissance
theologians will shed some light on the "mysterious terms"
beyond his own attempt at explication.

Only in a few other instances is Milton so strongly
supported by tradition generally, and by Protestant
apologists particularly, as he is in his identification of
the "seed" with the Christ Jesus. "Das ist das erste Eu-
angelion," declared Luther of the passage in Genesis,
"vnd verheyssung von Christo geschehen auff erden."[2] A

---

[1] Herbert E. Ryle, *The Book of Genesis* (Cambridge, 1921), p. 54, and
J. E. McFadyen in *The Abingdon Bible Commentary* (Nashville, 1922), p.
177; respectively. Thus also August Dillmann, *Genesis*, trans. W. B. Ste-
venson (Edinburgh, 1897), I, 161; W. H. Bennett, *Genesis* (Edinburgh,
1904), pp. 109-10; and John Skinner, *Commentary on Genesis* (1910), p.
81. S. R. Driver is somewhat more "traditional" in *The Book of Genesis*,
2nd ed. (1904), pp. 48, 57.

[2] *Vber das Erst Buch Mose* (Wittenberg, 1527), fol. 6v. Thus also in his
Special and Chosen Sermons, trans. William Gace (1578), pp. 37, 299.

host of commentators assented readily, most of them stressing the remarkable swiftness with which God displayed his mercy ("scarce was there Sinne, ere Christ was promised to Come")[3] and nearly all hailing the prophecy as the "grand Charter of our Salvation," "the first promise of mans redemption."[4]

[3] John Gaule, *Practiqve Theories . . . Upon Christs Prediction* (1629), p. 7.

[4] John Trapp, *A Clavis to the Bible* (1650), p. 39, and Thomas Jackson, *Nazareth and Bethlehem* (Oxford, 1617), p. 14; respectively. For other equations of the "seed" with Christ, see Henry Ainsworth, *Annotations upon . . . Genesis* ([Amsterdam], 1616), sig. D1: Thomas Aylesbury, *The Passion Sermon at Pavls-Crosse* (1626), p. 6; Gervase Babington, *Certaine . . . Notes vpon euerie Chapter of Genesis* (1592), fols. 19v-20; Thomas Becon, *The Actes of Christe* (1577), sig. D1; Immanuel Bourne, *The Rainebow* (1617), p. 10; Matthew Brookes (as below, note 13), pp. 2 ff.; Meric Casaubon *et al., Annotations vpon . . . the Old and the New Testament* (1645), sig. 62; Henoch Clapham, *A Brief of the Bible* ([Edinburgh,] 1596), p. 22; Richard Clerke, *Sermons* (1637), pp. 281 ff.; Thomas Cooper, *A Briefe Exposition of . . . the Olde Testament* (1573), fol. 99r; Ezekiel Culverwell (as below, note 23), p. 164; Giovanni Diodati, *Annotations vpon the Holy Bible*, 3rd ed. (1651), sig. D2; Donne, *Sermons*, I, 301, II, 256 and 332, III, 268 and 365, IV, 231-32 and 355, V, 102, VI, 195 and 272, VIII, 360, IX, 143, X, 48, 165, 185, 219, 244, etc.; Nicholas Gibbens (as below, note 8), p. 145; Thomas Goodwin, *Christ Set Forth* (1642), p. 17; John Gordon, Ἑνωτικόν (1604), p. 18; Simon Goulart, *A Learned Summary upon the famous Poeme of . . . Bartas*, trans. Thomas Lodge (1621), II, 66; Thomas Heywood, *The Hierarchie of the Blessed Angells* (1635), p. 343; William Hunnis, *A Hyve Fvll of Hunnye* (1578), fol. 4v; Thomas Jackson, *Nazareth and Bethlehem* (Oxford, 1617), p. 59; Jacobus Kimedoncius, *Of the Redemption of Mankind*, trans. Hugh Ince (1598), p. 100; Arthur Lake, *Sermons* (1629), II, 3; Thomas Lanquet, *An Epitome of Chronicles* (1559), fol. 6v; William Lesk, *A Sermon Preached . . . by the Cape of Good Hope* (1617), p. 3; John Lewis, *Ignis Coelestis* (1617), p. 3; John Lightfoot, *Ervbhin* (1629), pp. 163 ff., and *The Harmony, Chronicle and Order of the Old Testament* (1647), p. 4; Benjamin Needler, *Expository Notes* (1655), pp. 94 ff.; Eusebius Pagitt, *The Historie of the Bible* (1613), p. 5; Simon Patrick, *A Commentary upon . . . Genesis* (1695), pp. 72 ff.; Alexander Ross, *An Exposition of . . . Genesis* (1626), p. 67; Francis Sabie, *Adams Complaint* (1596), sig. D1; Edwin Sandys, *Sermons* (1585), p. 330; John Stoughton, *Choice Sermons* (1640), II, 45 [quoted in

Nearly all, but not all; for there were also those who preferred to interpret the "first gospel" in a radically different fashion. The most important theologian to diverge from the common view was Calvin. Fully aware that his interpretation would be unexpected, he began on a defensive note:

". . . concerning the sense, I doe not agree with others. For they take without controuersie the seede for Christ: as if it were saide, that One should arise out of the womans seede, which shoulde wounde the serpentes head. I would gladly approue their sentence with my opinion, were it not that I see that the word (Seede) is too violently wrested of them. For who will graunt, that a Nowne collectiue is vnderstoode of one man onely? Also, as the perpetuitie of the enmitie is noted: so by the continuall order and successe of ages, victorie is promised to mans seede and posteritie. Therfore I do generally interprete (Seede) of posterities. But seeing experience teacheth, that it cannot be, by any meanes, that all the sonnes of Adam shoulde be victors or conquerers of the diuell, we muste needes come vnto one heade, that we may finde to whome the victorie perteineth. So Paule leadeth us from the seede of Abraham vnto Christ. . . . Wherefore the sense shall be in my iudgement, that mankinde, which Sathan went about to oppresse, shall at the last haue the victorie and preeminence. In the meane time

---

the headnote, above]; Alice Sutcliffe, *Meditations of Mans Mortalitie* (1634), p. 150; Lewis Thomas, *Demegoriai* (1600), sig. K8v; William Whately, *Prototypes* (1640), I, 7; Benjamin Whichcote, *Select Sermons* (1698), pp. 331-32; John White, *A Commentary upon . . . Genesis* (1656), III, 169-200; Hieronymus Zanchius, *Confession of the Christian Religion*, trans. Anon. (Cambridge, 1599), p. 44; *et al.* The emergence of this tradition from a group of related ideas—Moslem, Hebrew, and early Christian—is surveyed by John M. Steadman (as below, note 17).

. . . all the faithful haue power giuen vnto them to treade down Sathan vnder their feete, and to subdue him, and that so the blessing shall belong to the whole Church."[5]

There were a number of other views which, though not nearly so drastic as Calvin's, may be mentioned in order to appreciate the lengths to which commentators were wont to go. For a convenient list we turn to Andrew Willet, whose prolixity might have given us cause to complain were it not that his output is often "the plaine-mans path-way to Heaven:"

"Where the Lord saith, *I will put enmitie betweene thy seede and her seede.* 1. This first is truly vnderstood of Christ. . . . 2. We may also vnderstand by the seede of the woman, all the elect, and by the seede of the serpent, all the wicked, who are the sonnes of the deuill, as Christ to the vnbeleeuing Iewes, *ye are of your father the deuill*, Ioh. 8.44. betweene whome, the elect and the wicked, there shall be perpetuall enmitie. . . . 3. Part of this sentence is literally true in the serpent: for . . . betweene man and those venemous creatures, there is a natural hatred, that one cannot endure the sight and presence of the other. 4. Some doe maruell, why the serpent is not made mute and dumbe, seeing Sathan abused his tongue and mouth to tempt the woman: the Hebrewes thinke that the punishment is included, in that dust is appointed to be his meate: for such, whose mouthes are filled with earth, cannot speake. And to this day we see that the punishment remaineth vpon the ser-

[5] *A Commentarie of John Caluine, vpon the First Booke of Moses called Genesis*, trans. Thomas Tymme (1578), pp. 108-109. Some other Protestant theologians, notably Pareus and Rivet, endeavored to follow Calvin, but their efforts were at best half-hearted. See Arnold Williams, *The Common Expositor* (Chapel Hill, 1948), p. 129.

pent, who maketh no perfect sound, as other cattell doe, but hisseth onely. 5. Sathan was accursed before God, nor any hope of recouerie remained, but now the sentence is declared to be irrepairable. . . . 6. Some by the heele, vnderstand . . . the inferiour part of the soule: some the humanitie of Christ, which Sathan pinched at when Christ was put to death: but thereby Christ gaue him a deadly blow vpon the head. But generally it signifieth, the weaker parts of Christs bodie, which is the Church: that Sathan shall be nibling and biting at the heele, as a serpent doth, when he is ouerwhelmed and turned vpon his backe: that is, he shall touch the members of Christ, and trie them with many temptations, but he shall not be able to hurt them."[6]

One particular interpretation, however, all Protestants rejected categorically: the assignment of the role of redemption prophesied in the "first gospel" to the Virgin Mary. The obvious culprits and their sinister methods are named for us by Nicholas Gibbens. Referring to the pronoun in the phrase "it shall bruise," he maintained that ". . . it may onlie be translated, as some doe, *it*; that is, that same seed; but much better, *he*: namelie, that one person; as manie other, & euen *Hierom* himselfe, and the Septuagint translation, and our English[7] hath it. But some of the Fathers, misguided by the translations of *Aquila*, of *Symmachus*, and *Theodotion*, which chieflie in their time were in vse, doe read it, *she shall*

---

[6] *Hexapla in Genesin* (Cambridge, 1605), p. 51.

[7] I.e., The Geneva Bible (1560), which is the only version to use "he." Wycliffe and the Douai Old Testament read "she"; the Bishops' Bible and the King James Version, "it." In three cases, the pronoun was cleverly bypassed: Tyndale and Rogers alike read "that seed shall tread," while Coverdale reads "the same [seed] shall tread."

breake: so also doth the Iewish Targhum which those translatours followed, as Iewish heretikes: yet none of these expound it of any other woman than of *Heua*, sauing that in a mysticall sense they take it for the affections of the minde. But the church of Rome will needes read it, *she shall breake*, & vnderstand it of the virgin *Marie*, giuing vnto her the glorie of breaking the Serpents head."[8] For Gibbens as for Protestants generally, this was a clear instance of extreme "follie." Worse still, he complained, Catholics persist in their folly: "they do not onlie not acknowledge this for an errour and reforme it, but they allow it, confirme it, bind men vnto it."[9]

II

The terms characteristic of most Protestant attacks on the Catholic Church were not commonly deployed by Milton; but he did share the violent opposition of all Protestants to the occasional Catholic claim that "the obedience of *Mary* was the cause of salvation to her selfe, and all mankind."[10] His interpretation of the "first gospel," as we noted at the outset, took the form of an

---

[8] *Questions and Dispvtations concerning the Holy Scripture* (1601), p. 146. For Donne's similar view, see *Sermons*, I, 100, and VI, 313.

[9] *Ibid.*, p. 149. For a typical Catholic statement of the sort that irritated Protestants, cf. John Falconer's view that the Virgin is "that woman which was ordayned to crush the Serpents head long before, and vtterly to vanquish him" (*The Mirrour of Created Perfection* [St. Omer, 1632], p. 107). Since Falconer's time, however, the Catholic Church has elected to "reforme" this view: consult *A Catholic Commentary on Holy Scripture*, trans. Bernard Orchard *et al.* (1951), Sect. 144a-c, 145d-e.

[10] *Of Prelaticall Episcopacy*, in *Works*, III, 94. On Milton's Mariological views, see especially Mary Christopher Pecheux, "The Concept of the Second Eve in *Paradise Lost*," *PMLA*, LXXV (1960), 359-66.

explicit equation of the "seed" with Christ. Thereafter in the poem, the prophecy is recollected at a crucial moment in the relations between Adam and Eve. Long after it was pronounced by God, Adam attempts to console his repentant wife with these words:

> let us seek
> Som safer resolution, which methinks
> I have in view, calling to minde with heed
> Part of our Sentence, that thy Seed shall bruise
> The Serpents head.
>
> (X, 1028-32)

For the time being, however, the terms are still "mysterious" to both. But not for long. The archangel Michael was already receiving his charge from God to

> reveale
> To Adam what shall come in future dayes,
> As I shall thee enlight'n, intermix
> My Cov'nant in the Womans seed renewd;
> So send them forth, though sorrowing, yet in
> peace.
>
> (XI, 113-17)

In line with the divine behest, Michael—"milde," "benigne," "gentle"—unfolds the future before an expectant Adam. But the crucial word is not mentioned until the appearance in the vision of Abraham, at which point Michael states that "in his Seed / All Nations shall be blest" (XII, 125-26). Shortly after that, the word is repeated—with a significant addition:

> all Nations of the Earth
> Shall in his Seed be blessed; by that Seed

Is meant thy great Deliverer, who shall bruise
The Serpents head; whereof to thee anon
Plainlier shall be reveald.

(XII, 147-51)

Michael's failure to be precise is calculated: being the
excellent storyteller that he is, he increases suspense by
withholding the information Adam is seeking until the
appropriate moment. So the gradual revelation of the
identity of the "seed" continues. Typology is invoked
next so that Adam can be informed

> by types
> And shadowes, of that destind Seed to bruise
> The Serpent, by what meanes he shall achieve
> Mankinds deliverance.

(XII, 232-35)

At the mention of David, Michael pauses to look both
before and after:

> of the Royal Stock
> Of *David* (so I name this King) shall rise
> A Son, the Womans Seed to thee foretold.
> Foretold to *Abraham*, as in whom shall trust
> All Nations, and to Kings foretold, of Kings
> The last, for of his Reign shall be no end.

(XII, 325-30)

Then, at last, the Nativity:

> His place of birth a solemn Angel tells
> To simple Shepherds, keeping watch by night;
> They gladly thither haste, and by a Quire
> Of squadrond Angels hear his Carol sung.
> A Virgin is his Mother, but his Sire

98

The Power of the most High; he shall ascend
The Throne hereditarie, and bound his Reign
With Earths wide bounds, his glory with the
    Heav'ns.

(XII, 364-71)

As Michael falls silent, Adam, with "joy / Surcharg'd,"
exclaims:

O Prophet of glad tidings, finisher
Of utmost hope! now clear I understand
What oft my steddiest thoughts have searcht in
    vain,
Why our great expectation should be calld
The seed of Woman . . .

(XII, 375-79)

But he has not, in fact, "understood" as yet. Patiently,
therefore, Michael explains what is meant by the stroke
that is to "bruise the Victors heel." This leads to an
account of the redemption, to Adam's acknowledgment
of that wondrous mystery, and to Michael's final statement explicitly linking his narrative with the "mysterious terms" of the "first gospel:"

The Womans Seed, obscurely then foretold,
Now amplier known thy Savior and thy Lord.

(XII, 543-44)

In the moving confession of faith that follows, Adam
acknowledges the "seed" to be his "Redeemer ever blest"
(XII, 573). He has finally "understood." He has become, in fact, a Christian.

John Durie, in a sermon preached in 1645, averred
that God "told *Adam* in plain tearms from the begin-

99

ning, the end of the whole work of our salvation, which is, that *the seed of the woman should tread down the head of the Serpent.*"[11] Such a statement does not merely recognize the "first gospel" as a typological proclamation of the Christ to come; it asserts, too, Adam's awareness of the *precise* meaning of that gospel. Catholics did not, and indeed could not, venture such a claim; as Cristóbal de Fonseca cautiously observed, Adam knew "by revelation" certain aspects of the ministry of Christ, "but he knew not the *Media*, or means that led thereunto."[12] On the contrary, Protestants countered, Adam was fully cognizant of the "meanes"—and, what is more significant, he was saved.

The Protestant inference was grounded upon the doctrine of justification by faith only. Hence the statement of Matthew Brookes in 1627, that when Adam "apprehended by faith" the meaning of the first gospel, "he was then built vpon the Rocke . . . the *Redeemer.*"[13] Hence, also, this decisively Protestant interpretation by the celebrated Biblical scholar John Lightfoot:

"Christ is promised before the man and the woman are censured. . . . *Adam* apprehendeth and layeth hold upon the promise by Faith, and in evidence of this his faith he calleth his wives name *Eve* or *Life*, because shee was to be the mother of Christ according to the flesh, by whom life should come; and of all beleevers that by faith should live in him, for an outward signe and seale of this his Faith,[14] and for a further and more lively

---

[11] *Israels Call to March out of Babylon* (1646), p. 4.

[12] *Devovt Contemplations*, trans. James Mabbe (1629), p. 608.

[13] *The House of God* (1627), p. 25.

[14] The phrase "an outward signe and seal" is intentionally borrowed from the Protestant definition of the Sacrament—as by Calvin, *Inst.*, IV, xiv, 1, and the Westminster Confession of Faith, XXVII, 1. Thus also Milton in *De doctrina christiana* (*Works*, XVI, 165).

expression of the same; God teacheth him the rite of sacrifice, to lay Christ dying before his eyes in a visible figure: And with the skins of the sacrificed beasts God teacheth him and his wife to cloath their bodies. And thus the first thing that dyeth in the world is Christ in a figure."[15]

But if Adam was able to live in Christ "by faith," could this be true also of the other patriarchs—and, indeed, of humanity at large to the advent of the Savior? Brookes, cited earlier, may be quoted again. As he affirmed in a later work, the divine promise of the "seed" was "the *Originall promise*, the *Covenant of Grace*, the sum and substance of the *Gospel*: which promise all the righteous faithfull, from *Adam* to *Abraham* (though they knew no more of *Christ*) did believe, that they might be saved."[16] More than a century earlier, John Bale had ventured the same sweeping—and characteristically Protestant—generalization. According to the concluding verses of his singularly dreadful work, *A Tragedye or enterlude manyfestyng the chefe promises of God vnto man* (1547?),

In the womans sede, was Adam first iustyfyed,
So was faythfull Noah, so was iust Abraham.
The faythe in that sede, in Moses fourth
    multyplyed,
Lyke wyse in Dauid, and Esaye, that after cam.
And in Johan Baptyst, whych shewed the very
    lam.

The English writers I have invoked were by no means "original" in their emphases. Behind them stood the

---

[15] *A Few, and New Observations, vpon the Booke of Genesis* (1642), pp. 5-6. The episode recounted by Lightfoot occurs also in *Paradise Lost*, X, 211-19.

[16] *The Sacred and Most Mysterious History of Mans Redemption* (1657), p. 6.

Continental Reformers, notably Heinrich Bullinger, whose full exposition of 1537 was translated by Miles Coverdale in 1541.[17] But here is the equally adequate summary statement of Bullinger's master Philip Melanchthon, in an English translation published in 1548 as *The Iustification of Man by Faith Only*:

"God gaue [to Adam] a comfortable voyce promysynge deliuerance from sinne and death, and the restoring agayne of mankynde, sayenge that the sede of a woman shulde breake the head of the Serpent. The whiche voyce spoken and declared by God: streyght way the son of God mouynge and styrrynge the hert of Adam: dyd poure into hym a newe lyfe and lyghte. At that tyme the sonne of God was constituted and ordeyned to be a keper, a gouernour, and sauyour of the churche. . . . Thus dyd Adam take and vnderstand the promyse. So did al the fathers after him beleue, that for thys sede sake which was promised, they shuld obteyn remission of theyr sinnes with deliuerance from sinne and deathe. By thys faythe they were made iuste."[18]

---

[17] The editions I consulted are: *Der alt gloub. Das der Christen gloub von anfang der wält gewärt habe* (Zurich, 1539); trans. Coverdale, *The Olde fayth* etc. (1547). Bullinger's treatise is most ably discussed by John E. Parish, "Pre-Miltonic Representations of Adam as a Christian," *The Rice Institute Pamphlet*, XL (1953), No. 3, pp. 1-24. Equally fundamental is the study by John M. Steadman, "Adam and the Prophesied Redeemer," *SP*, LVI (1959), pp. 214-25. This survey of earlier parallels culminates in Reuchlin's *De arte cabalistica* (1517); *Paradise Lost*, it is shown, shares "several significant features" with Reuchlin's exposition despite occasional divergences on "important points."

[18] *The Iustification* etc., trans. Nicholas Lesse (1548), fols. 24v, 25-25v. See further the 1521 version of Melanchthon's *Loci communes*, trans. Charles L. Hill (Boston, 1944), pp. 144 ff., 165, 189 ff., and 224, as well as Luther's parallel comments in *De captivitate babylonica* (*Reformation Writings*, trans. B. L. Woolf [1953], I, 235).

It is in terms of such "iuste" individuals that the vision of the future unfolds in *Paradise Lost*,[19] culminating in the incarnation of the Son of God, whom Adam accepts as his redeemer "by faith only."

For Protestants, in short, Adam's recognition of the Savior made him not merely a Christian but, more precisely, the first Protestant. But even as the theory witnessed to the Protestant doctrine of justification by faith only, it assisted Protestants to combat the charge of a number of "braynles and madde fellowes"[20]—obviously the Catholics—that Protestantism was a "new" religion. Profoundly disconcerted by the charge, Protestants rallied their forces to still the opposition's "outcries and clamours that our Religion was not heard of before *Luthers* time."[21] The result was a veritable flood of polemical literature, its nature indicated by the titles of such works as Richard Bernard's *Looke beyond Luther: or an Answere to the Question, so often and so insvltingly proposed by our Aduersaries, asking vs; Where this our Religion was before Luthers time?* (1623) and Henry Rogers' *The Protestant Church existent, and their Faith professed in all Ages, and by whom: with a Catalogue of Councels in all Ages, who professed the same* (1638)—a catalogue extended, I might

---

[19] In Book XI, notably Abel (436 ff.), Enoch (665 ff., 700 ff.), Noah (719 ff.); and in Book XII, Abraham (113 ff.), Isaac (153 ff.), Moses (169 ff.), Joshua (310 ff.), and David (321 ff.).

[20] The phrase is from Rhegius' treatise (below, note 22).

[21] Robert Abbot, *The Old Waye* (1610), p. 17. Among the "braynless" Catholic attacks: John Colleton, *The Theatre of Catholique and Protestant Religion* ([St. Omer,] 1620), Bk. I, Ch. I; Paulus Veridicus (pseud.), *A Brief Confvtation of Certaine Absurd Doctrines*, 2nd ed. (Antwerp, 1639), pp. 51 ff.; and particularly Richard Smith's brilliant *De auctore et essentia protestanticae ecclesiae et religionis libri duo* (Paris, 1619), trans. W. Bas., *Of the Author and Substance of the Protestant Church and Religion* ([St. Omer,] 1621).

add, so as to include not only the Latin fathers and the entire range of medieval theologians but all Eastern Orthodox Christians as well.[22] It was this frantic search for "origins" that drove Protestants as far back as the Garden of Eden, to locate there the first man whose justification "by faith only" established him as the ultimate Protestant. The efforts to confirm this persuasion are best—and in any case summarily—reflected in the revised title of Bullinger's treatise, in the version by Coverdale, that appeared in 1624: *Looke from Adam, and behold the Protestants Faith and Religion, evidently proved ovt of the holy Scriptures against all Atheists, Papists, loose Libertines, and Carnall Gospellers: and that the Faith which they professe, hath continued from the beginning of the world.*

The "mysterious terms" attending the sentence passed on Satan in Genesis 3.15 as in *Paradise Lost* constituted "the first promise made to man, and the foundation of all others."[23] But they constituted, it appears, much else besides.

[22] For still other Protestant *apologiae*, see Thomas Bedford, *Luther's Predecessours* (1624); Simon Birckbeck, *The Protestant Evidence* (1634); Edward Bowen, *An Account of the Church Catholick* (1653), *passim*; Donne, *Sermons*, VIII, 67; Joseph Hall, *The Olde Religion* (1628); Thomas Jackson, *A Treatise of the Holy Catholike Faith* (1627), Ch. XVI; Andrew Logie, *Cv{m} Bono Deo* (Aberdeen, 1634); Wolfgang Musculus, *Common Places of Christian Religion*, trans. John Man (1563), fols. 349 ff.; Jean Paul Perrin, *Lvthers Fore-Rvnners*, trans. Samson Lennard (1624) from *Histoire de Vaudois* (Geneva, 1619); Urbanus Rhegius, *A Cōparison betweene the Olde Learnynge & the Newe*, trans. William Turner (1537); Thomas Taylor, *Christs Victorie over the Dragon* (1633), pp. 303 ff.; and George Webbe, *Catalogus Protestantivm* (1624).

[23] Ezekiel Culverwell, *A Treatise of Faith*, 8th ed. (1648), p. 163.

❧ 7 ❧

"That great and indisputable miracle":

The Cessation of the Oracles

ex quo mortalem praestrinxit Spiritus alvum,
Spiritus ille Deus, Deus et se corpore matris
induit atque hominem de virginitate creavit,
Delphica damnatis tacuerunt sortibus antra,
non tripodas cortina regit, non spumat anhelus
fata Sibyllinis fanaticus edita libris.—Prudentius

I

The legend of the cessation of the pagan oracles appears in Milton's poetry twice. The version in *Paradise Regained* is voiced by Jesus, who tells Satan:

No more shalt thou by oracling abuse
The Gentiles; henceforth Oracles are ceast,
And thou no more with Pomp and Sacrifice
Shalt be enquir'd at *Delphos* or elsewhere,
At least in vain, for they shall find thee mute.
God hath now sent his living Oracle
Into the World, to teach his final will,
And sends his Spirit of Truth henceforth to dwell
In pious Hearts, an inward Oracle
To all truth requisite for men to know.

(I, 455-64)

A fuller version was set forth earlier, in the ode *On the Morning of Christ's Nativity*, which majestically enumerates the oracles in retreat before the emerging Christ:

> The Oracles are dumm,
> No voice or hideous humm
>   Runs through the arched roof in words
>   deceiving.
> *Apollo* from his shrine
> Can no more divine,
>   With hollow shreik the steep of *Delphos*
>   leaving.
> No nightly trance, or breathed spell,
> Inspire's the pale-ey'd Priest from the prophetic
>   cell.[1]

As six more stanzas are devoted to this theme, Milton's treatment is easily the most sustained exposition of the legend in English poetry. Its finest counterpart in English prose is the equally sweeping roll-call of the fallen angels by Sir Walter Ralegh:

"The houses and sumptuous buildings erected to *Baal*, can no where bee found upon the earth; nor any monument of that glorious Temple consecrated to *Diana*. There are none now in *Phœnicia*, that lament the death of *Adonis*; nor any in *Lybia, Creta, Thessalia*, or elsewhere, that can aske counsaile or helpe from *Iupiter*. The great God *Pan*

---

[1] *Nativity Ode*, ll. 173-80. Appropriately enough this stanza (XIX) is quoted by H. W. Parke and D.E.W. Wormell in their standard work, *The Delphic Oracle* (Oxford, 1956), I, 289. There is an indispensable commentary on the poem by Albert S. Cook, "Notes on Milton's *Ode on the Morning of Christ's Nativity*," *Transactions of the Connecticut Academy of Arts and Sciences*, XV (1909), especially pp. 335-38, 349-50. See also Helga Spevack-Husmann, *The Mighty Pan: Miltons mythologische Vergleiche* (Münster, 1963), pp. 88 ff.

hath broken his Pipes, *Apolloes* Priests are become speechlesse. . . ."²

Few readers of Spenser need be reminded of the comment by his annotator "E.K."—quoted by nearly every editor of Milton—that upon the Incarnation "all oracles surceased, and enchaunted spirits, that were wont to delude people, thenceforth held theyr peace."³ The frequent invocations of E.K. are always well advised, if only because he points to the ultimate source of the legend in the seventeenth chapter of Plutarch's *De defectu oraculorum* (Περὶ τῶν ἐκλελοιπότων χρηστηρίων). Plutarch's treatise was readily available during the Renaissance in the original Greek and in the 1566 Latin version by Adrien Turnèbe,⁴ as well as in the famous English translation by Philemon Holland.⁵ Its most pertinent passage, however, was all too often extracted in several other works. Here, for example, is the version in Thomas Milles' encyclopedic compilation *The Treasurie of Auncient and Moderne Times* (1613). "I remember," observes Plutarch,

". . . that I haue heard (concerning the Dæmons death) of Æmilianus the Orator, an humble, wise, and worthy man, and well knowne to some of you; that his Father comming (on a time) by Sea towardes Italy, pass-

² Ralegh, *HW*, p. 152 (I, vi, 8).
³ Commentary on *The Shepheardes Calender: May*, 1. 54; in Spenser's *Minor Poems*, Variorum ed. (Baltimore, 1943), I, 55-56.
⁴ The editions I consulted are: Πλουτάρχου Χαιρωνέως τὰ σωζόμενα συγγράμματα. *Plutarchi Chaeronensis quæ extant opera* (Geneva, 1572), especially I, 206-207, and *Plvtarchi Chaeronei de oracvlorvm defectv liber, ab Adriano Turnebo latinitate donatus, & annotationibus quibusdam illustratus*, 1st ed. (Paris, 1556), especially fols. 14v-15; respectively.
⁵ *Of the Oracles that have ceased to give Answere*, being part of *The Philosophie, commonlie called, The Morals* (1603), especially pp. 1331-32.

ing and coasting (in the night time) an inhabited Island, named [Paxi],[6] at what time, all the men in the Shippe were in silence and repose: they heard a great & feareful voyce, which came out of the Island, and the voyce called [Thamus][6] (for so was the Pilot of the Ship named, who was a natiue of Ægipt.) And albeit that this voyce was heard once or twice by [Thamus], and others: yet had they not so much hardinesse, or to returne any answere, vntill the third time. And then hee said: Who is there? Who is it that calleth mee? What wouldst thou with me? then the voice spake much louder then before, and said vnto him. [Thamus], my desire is, that when thou shalt passe by the Gulfe, called [Palodes]:[6] that there thou remember to cry aloud, and giue it to vnderstand; that the great God Pan is dead. This being thvs vnderstood, all in the Shippe were in great feare and terrour, and aduised the Patrone of the Shippe, to make no account thereof, neyther to speak one word, or make any stay at the Gulfe: but if the time prooued fauourable; to passe on further, and entend the finishing of the voyage. But beeing come to ioyne with the place, whereof the voyce had spoken and made designement: the Shippe stayed, the Sea was becalmed, and no winde stirred, so that (indeede) they could sayle no further. By meanes whereof, they all resolued, that [Thamus] should deliuer his message. And that he might the better performe it,

[6] Milles, following Mexia and Gruget (below, note 11), writes "Paraxis," but I have substituted the more accurate "Paxi" (the common classical name of the Ionian isles). Moreover, I have changed "Ataman" to "Thamus" (thus Lavater, more or less in agreement with Plutarch and Eusebius), and "Laguna" to "Palodes" (thus Plutarch, Eusebius, Lavater *et al.*). The precise location of "Palodes" is still unknown; in 1603 Philemon Holland evaded the issue by remarking that "Some take it to be a place of manie shelves and shallowes."

he went vp vpon the poupe of the Shippe, and there hee cryed out so loud as possible he could, saying: I giue ye to know, that the Great God Pan is dead. But so soone as he had vttered these wordes, they heard so many voyces crying and complaining, that all the Sea resounded their dreadfull Echoes, and this wofull lamenting continued a long while, to the no little amazement of all them in the Shippe. But finding the wind immediatly prosperous, they sayled on-ward, and arriuing afterward at Rome; there they declared the whole aduenture. Which comming to the eare of the Emperour Tyberius, he would needes be further informed thereof, and found it to bee most true."[7]

[7] *The Treasurie* etc. (1613), I, 641-42. Milles's version was made from Gruget's translation of Mexía (below, note 11). On Pan's birth, activities, and death—with references to the primary sources—see Robert Graves, *The Greek Myths* (1955), Ch. XXVI, and the concise account by H. J. Rose, *A Handbook of Greek Mythology*, 6th ed. (1958), pp. 167 ff. For broader studies, consult A. Bouché-Leclercq, *Histoire de la divination dans l'antiquité* (Paris, 1880, repr. 1963), II, 383-89; Walter Immerwahr, *Die Kulten und Mythen Arkadiens* (Leipzig, 1891), I, 192-206; and Lewis R. Farnell, *The Cults of the Greek States* (Oxford, 1909), V, 431-34, 464-68. The standard Renaissance account is by Natalis Comes, *Mythologiæ* (Frankfurt, 1584), pp. 451-63 (Book V, Ch. VI). On the iconography of Pan, there was always Vicenzo Cartari's compendium, *Le imagini degli dei antichi* (Venice, 1556), trans. Richard Lynche, *The Fovntaine of Ancient Fiction* (1599), sigs. 13 et seq. Bacon's summary observations on Pan are in *De sapientia veterum* (1609; trans. Sir Arthur Gorges, *The Wisdome of the Ancients* [1619], Ch. VI, and commented upon by Charles W. Lemmi, *The Classic Deities in Bacon* [Baltimore, 1933], pp. 61-74). For the diverse uses of Plutarch's story over the ages, see G. A. Gerhard, "Der Tod des grossen Pan," *Sitzungsberichte der Heidelberger Akademie der Wissenschaften: Philosophisch-historische Klasse*, VI (1915), No. 5; and for modern interpretations of Pan's death: Salomon Reinach, "La mort du grand Pan," *Bulletin de correspondance hellénique*, XXXI (1907), 5-19; Hermann Haakh, "Der grosse Pan ist tot," *Das Altertum*, IV (1958), 105-10; and Sir James Frazer, *The Golden Bough: The Dying God*, 3rd ed. (1935), pp. 6 ff.

Besides this version by Milles there were a number of similarly full accounts,[8] together with a host of notices to the effect that "under the raigne of *Tiberius*"—to quote William Perkins' statement—"the great god *Pan* (as they say) then dyed."[9] But of all the available accounts, three were particularly decisive in the dissemination of Plutarch's story. One was its quotation in full by Eusebius, in *Praeparatio evangelica*;[10] another, Pedro Mexía's equally full relation in his popular collection *Silva de varia lección* (1543);[11] and the third, Ludwig Lavater's account in his widely read treatise *De spectris, lemuribus et magnis atque insolitis fragoribus* (1570).[12] There is no adequate

---

[8] In addition to that by E. K. (as above, note 3), see: Baronius, *Annales ecclesiastici* (Mainz, 1601), I, 237-38; Richard Bovet, *Pandæmonium* (1684), ed. Montague Summers (Aldington, Kent, 1951), p. 41; Francesco Giorgio, *De harmonia mundi* (Paris, 1545), fols. 99v ff.; Henry Howard, Earl of Northampton, *A Defensative against the Poyson of supposed Phophecies*, 2nd ed. (1620), fols. 49v-50 (1st ed. in 1583); Paulus Marsus, *P. Ovidii Nasonis Fastorvm libri diligenti emendatione* (Venice, 1520), fols. 23v-24 (frequently published both before and after 1520); C. Stephanus, *apud* D. T. Starnes and E. W. Talbert, *Classical Myth and Legend in Renaissance Dictionaries* (Chapel Hill, N.C., 1955), p. 307; Rabelais (as below, note 15); Noël Taillepied, *Psichologie ou Traité de l'apparition des esprits* (1588), trans. Montague Summers, *A Treatise of Ghosts* (1933), pp. 103-104; Antonius van Dale, *De oraculis ethnicorum* (Amsterdam, 1683), pp. 26-27; Peter Hausted, *Ten Sermons* (1636), pp. 14-15; *et al.*

[9] *The Whole Treatise of the Cases of Conscience* (1636), p. 129.

[10] Εὐσεβίου τοῦ Παμφίλου Προπαρασκευὴ εὐαγγελικὴ. *Evsebii Pamphili Præparatio evangelica* (Paris, 1628), I, 206-207 (Book V, Ch. XVII). The pertinent passage is more readily available in *PG*, XXI, 353-56.

[11] *Silua de varia lection* (Valladolid, 1551), I, 86-86v. Besides a host of editions of this work in Spanish, there were versions of it in French, Italian, German and English. The French translation by Claude Gruget was crucial (*Les diverses leçons* [Lyons, 1592], pp. 292-93; first published in 1552), for it yielded two versions in English: Thomas Fortescue's *The Foreste* (1571), fols. 93-94, and Milles's *Treasurie* (quoted above, pp. 107-109).

[12] I consulted the Geneva edition (1575), pp. 114-17. The work was translated into French, Dutch, German, and English. The English version was by Robert Harrison: *Of ghostes and spirites walking by night, and sundry*

reason for doubting that Spenser and Milton derived their knowledge of the story directly from Plutarch. But both poets must have been also familiar with the story's reiteration—and certainly its interpretation—especially by Lavater.[13]

II

Ever since the early Christian apologists endeavored to prove that their faith was not a novel religion but the culmination of God's gradual revelation to mankind, the temptation to enlist Plutarch's story to the services of Christianity has been irresistible. We may suppose it inevitable that some significance would be attached to an incident reputed to have occurred during the reign of Tiberius (A.D. 14-37), moreover involving a "great god" whose death had occasioned such wondrous lamentation. E.K., as we know, was categorical enough. Pan, he wrote, is "Christ, the very God of all shepheards, which called himselfe the greate and good shepherd. The name is most rightly (me thinkes) applyed to him, for Pan signifieth all or omnipotent, which is onely the Lord Iesus."[14] Rabelais had already agreed:

"For my part, I understand it [i.e. the death of Pan]

forewarnynges (1572), pp. 94-95, ed. J. Dover Wilson and Mary Yardley (Oxford, 1929). Lavater's account is quoted in the original Latin by Charles G. Osgood, *The Classical Mythology of Milton's English Poems* (1900), p. xlvii.

[13] Milton had certainly consulted Lavater's Biblical commentaries: see A. I. Carlisle, "Milton and Ludwig Lavater," *RES*, n.s., V (1954), 249-55.

[14] As above, note 3. It should be noted that E. K.'s reference to Pan as "god" is an interpolation: Plutarch and Eusebius alike speak solely of the "great" Pan (ὁ μέγας Πάν). But the interpolation had already appeared in Rabelais, Lavater *et al.*, and was to survive well beyond the Renaissance. See the study by Screech (next note).

of that Great Saviour of the Faithful, who was shamefully put to Death at Jerusalem. . . . And methinks my Interpretation is not improper; for He may lawfully be said, in the Greek Tongue, to be Pan, since He is our All. For all that we are, all that we live, all that we have, all that we hope, is Him, by Him, from Him, and in Him; He is the Good Pan, the Great Shepherd; who, as the loving Shepherd Corydon affirms, hath not only a tender Love and Affection for his Sheep, but also for their Shepherds. At his Death, Complaints, Sighs, Fears and Lamentations were spread through the whole Fabrick of the Universe, whether Heaven, Land, Sea, or Hell."[15]

A host of other commentators assented. "Who is *the great* Pan," they were wont to insist, "but hee who is all in all, our Lord Iesus Christ?"[16] Milton, who specifically designates Jesus "the mighty Pan," concurred—and so did Marvell and Dryden.[17]

[15] *Gargantua and Pantagruel*, IV, 28; trans. Peter le Motteux (1694), ed. Charles Whibley (1900), III, 130. The original French is quoted by A. S. Cook (as above, note 1), and in the Variorum edition of Spenser's *Minor Poems* (Baltimore, 1943), I, 299. See further Jean Plattard, *L'Œuvre de Rabelais* (Paris, 1910), pp. 243 f., but especially M. A. Screech, "The Death of Pan and the Death of Heroes in the Fourth Book of Rabelais," *BHR*, XVII (1955), pp. 36-55; and three studies by A. J. Krailsheimer: "Rabelais and the Pan Legend," *French Studies*, II (1948), pp. 159-61; "Rabelais et Postel," *BHR*, XIII (1951), pp. 187-90; and "The Significance of the Pan Legend in Rabelais' Thought," *MLR*, LVI (1961), 13-23 (reprinted in his *Rabelais and the Franciscans* [Oxford, 1963], pp. 125-43).

[16] Gilbert Primrose, *The Christian Mans Teares* (1625), I, 132. Thus also Bovet and Marsus (as above, note 8), and Perkins (note 9).

[17] Milton, *Nativity Ode*, l. 34; Marvell, "Clorinda and Damon," l. 20; and Dryden, *The Hind and the Panther*, II, 711. The relationship of Marvell's reference to Spenser's is noted by John D. Rosenberg, "Marvell and the Christian Idiom," *BUSE*, IV (1960), p. 157. On Milton, see further Kathleen M. Swain, " 'Mighty Pan': Tradition and an Image in Milton's Nativity *Hymn*," *SP*, LXVIII (1971), pp. 484-95.

Yet we should not assume that there was unanimity in this seemingly ready identification of Pan with Christ. Far from it; for there were also those who inclined to the contrary view that Pan was Satan, and these, moreover, had the formidable support of Eusebius, who had concluded that the lament heard by Thamus and his fellow-travellers came from the devils who were then mourning the overthrow of Satan by Christ.[18] Thomas Milles deferred to the Eusebian thesis: ". . . it is plaine and manifest," he wrote, "that (euen in all parts) the Deuils complained on the Nativity of our Lord, because it was their vtter destruction." Henry Howard professed as much, pointedly asserting that those who "assure themselues, that this great *Pan* was the great fiend of Hell" constitute (together with Howard, of course) the "better sort" of commentators on Plutarch's story.[19] Later in the seventeenth century Ralph Cudworth offered his cautious consent, persuaded that it is "much more probably concluded" that the chorus of lamentation "was no other than a Lamentation of Evil Demons (not without a mixture of Admiration) upon account of our Saviours Death, happening at that very time. They not mourning out of Love for him that was dead, but as sadly presaging evil to themselves from thence, as that which would

[18] As above, note 10. At least one modern theologian agrees with Eusebius. According to Evgueny Lampert, upon Christ's death "there took place a shattering and mighty exorcism of the cosmos and of Nature from within: 'Great Pan has died,' the demonic possession of Nature is forthwith broken, the Prince of this world is driven out" (*The Divine Realm* [1944], pp. 115-16).

[19] Milles, *The Treasurie* (as above, note 7), p. 642, and Howard (note 8), fol. 50. Ralegh (quoted earlier) also equates Pan with Satan. But it is difficult to decide what Pascal meant us to make of his bare statement "Le grand Pan est mort" (*Pensées*, with the translation by H. F. Stewart [1950], p. 242).

threaten danger to their Kingdom of Darkness, and a Period to that Tyranny and Domination which they had so long exercised over Mankind."[20]

One other theory may safely be sidestepped: Ben Jonson's juxtaposition of Pan and James I, made all the more improbable by distinct echoes of a statement St. Paul had applied to Christ (Acts 17.28). Jonson urged his analogy on the grounds that the Stuart monarch is, like Pan, "our All, by him we breathe, we live, / We move, we are"![21]

Within the tradition proper, however contradictory the views on Pan's identity may have been, on one point at least there was remarkable agreement: the death of the "great god" had marked the death of the pagan oracles as well. This idea is directly related to the widespread Christian belief that the pagan gods were fallen angels, and the oracles their instruments of delusion. Justin Martyr was the first, but certainly not the last, to admit this theory; thereafter the notion appears in such diverse thinkers as Tertullian, Origen, and Lactantius,[22] and continues uninterruptedly until the Renaissance. Perhaps the most reputable sixteenth-century at-

[20] *The True Intellectual System of the Universe* (1678), p. 345. For the views of other Cambridge Platonists, see Benjamin Whichcote, *Select Sermons* (1698), p. 12, and John Smith (as below, note 30). Cf. Peter Sterry, *A Discourse of the Freedom of the Will* (1675), p. 237.

[21] *Pan's Anniversary*, ll. 191-92; *apud* Douglas Bush, *Pagan Myth and Christian Tradition in English Poetry* (Philadelphia, 1968), p. 7. The same poem was in part reworked as *A New Year's Song to King Charles* (1635): see Evelyn Simpson's remarks in *RES*, XIV (1938), pp. 175-78.

[22] Justin, *Apologia*, I, 5, 21, 25, 66, etc.; Tertullian, *De spectaculis*, XIX; Origen, *Contra Celsum*, VII, 3-4; Lactantius, *Divinæ institutiones*, II, 16; *et al*. Their view has distant Scriptural support in Psalm 96.5: "all the gods of the nations are idols" (A.V.), where "idols" translates the Septuagint's δαιμόνια and the Vulgate's *dæmonia*.

114

tempt to identify the Greek gods with Satan and his "feends" was Philippe de Mornay's exposition in *De la verité de la religion chrétienne* (1581), the English translation of which was begun by Sir Philip Sidney and completed by Arthur Golding.[23] But other substantial intellects argued just as categorically that "the gods of the gentiles were diuels": the Protestant theologians Rudolf Gwalter, Andreas Gerardus Hyperius, Niels Hemmingsen, and Lucas Trelcatius; the silver-tongued Henry Smith and the celebrated Lancelot Andrewes; the popular Joseph Mede; Milton himself; and others of far humbler stature.[24] Given this belief, Plutarch's story of the death of Pan was invoked yet again in support of the theory that the oracles ("the diuels mouth") ceased abruptly upon the sacrifice on the Cross. "Pans Death," in Cowley's elemental statement, "all Oracles broke."[25] In the

[23] *A Woorke concerning the Trewnesse of the Christian Religion* (1587), Ch. XXIII; the French original was also translated into Latin in 1583. The intellectual milieu of Mornay's exposition is set forth by D. P. Walker, "Orpheus the Theologian and Renaissance Platonism," *JWCI*, XVI (1953), pp. 100-20; reprinted in his *The Ancient Theology* (1972), Ch. I.

[24] Gwalter or Walther (Rudolphus Gualterus), *Homylyes or Sermons, vppon the Actes*, trans. John Bridges (1572), p. 364; Hyperius, *Two Common Places*, trans. R. Vaux (1581), pp. 92-94; Hemmingsen (Nicolas Hemmingius), *The Faith of the Chvrch Militant*, trans. Thomas Rogers (1581), p. 192; Trelcatius, *The Common Places of Sacred Divinitie*, trans. John Gaven (1610), pp. 3-4; Smith, *Gods Arrowe against Atheists* (1953), sigs. E4 ff.; Andrewes, *A Patterne of Catechisticall Doctrine* (1641), p. 73, and *The Morall Law Expounded* (1642), p. 45; Mede, *Diatribæ* (1642), p. 164; William Loe, *The Mysterie of Mankind* (1619), pp. 68-69; *et al.* Burton reports the common view in *The Anatomy of Melancholy*, 6th ed. (1652), p. 44 (Part. I, Sect. 2, Memb. I, Subs. 2). In *Paradise Regained* Jesus similarly tells Satan, "all Oracles / By thee are giv'n" (I, 430-31). Cf. Douglas Bush, *Mythology and the Renaissance Tradition in English Poetry*, rev. ed. (1963), p. 286, who also cites Milton and Burton as well as Hooker, Gosson and Prynne.

[25] "On the Death of Mr. Crashaw," l. 21.

excitement, however, the cessation of the oracles was most often said to have occurred not during the Passion but upon the Nativity. As we have seen, this was the case with Milton. But other poets agreed: Prudentius long since, and more recently Thomas Heywood ("at Christs birth all Oracles were mute, / And put to lasting silence") and Giles Fletcher ("The Angels caroll'd loud their song of peace, / The cursed Oracles were strucken dumbe").[26] A similar confusion in dating the end of the oracles appears among prosewriters. Thus Peter Martyr was convinced that "immediatlie vpon the birth of Christ, all the oracles of the gods were put to silence," yet George Sandys was equally persuaded that their cessation "doubtlesse was vpon the passion of our Sauiour."[27] It would seem, however, that the prosewriters, like the poets, generally favored the Nativity as marking the death of the oracles.[28]

[26] Prudentius, *Apotheosis*, ll. 435-40 (quoted in the headnote, above); Heywood, *The Hierarchie of the Blessed Angells* (1635), p. 24; and Fletcher, *Christs Victory and Triumph* (Cambridge, 1640), p. 24 (Part I, St. 82), as well as his prose treatise *The Reward of the Faithfull* (1623), pp. 321 ff. See also Crashaw's account—not indeed in his Nativity hymn which is often compared with Milton's, but in his hymn "In the glorious Epiphanie of our Lord" (1625), ll. 85 ff.

[27] Martyr (Pietro Martire Vermigli), *Common Places*, trans. Anthony Marten (1574), I, 92, and Sandys, *A Relation of a Iourney begun An: Dom: 1610* (1615), p. 11. Others in agreement with Sandys include Richard Carpenter, *Experience, Historie, and Divinitie* (1642), I, 166; Cudworth (as above, note 20); Edward Sparke, Θυσιαστήριον, 3rd ed. (1663), p. 231; and [in verse] William Vaughan, *The Chvrch Militant* (1640), p. 351.

[28] Thus John Stoughton, *XI. Choice Sermons* (1640), II, 55; Anthony Maxey, *Certaine Sermons*, 7th ed. (1634), p. 195; Perkins (as above, note 9); Smith (note 24), sig. F4; Theodorus Buchmann (Bibliander), *De ratione communi* etc. (Zurich, 1548), p. 212; Lancelot Andrewes, *The Morall Law* (1642), pp. 61-62; *et al.* Joseph Mede's statement is quoted in M. Y. Hughes's edition of Milton (1957), p. 42.

Of the major figures of the English Renaissance, I am aware of only one whose views on the legend were both positive and negative. He is Sir Thomas Browne, whose initial affirmation of "that great and indisputable miracle, the cessation of Oracles" in *Religio Medici*, was inverted, within a decade, by the following statement in his *Pseudodoxia Epidemica*:

"That Oracles ceased or grew mute at the comming of Christ, is best understood in a qualified sense and not without all latitude; as though precisely there were none after, nor any decay before. For (what we must confesse unto relations of Antiquity) some pre-decay is observable from that of Cicero urged by Baronius, *Cur isto modo jam oracula Delphis non eduntur, non modo nostra ætate, sed jam diu, ut nihil possit esse contemptius*. . . . In briefe, histories are frequent in examples, and there want not some even to the reign of Julian.

"What therefore may consist with history; by cessation of Oracles with Montacutius we may understand their intercision, not absission or consummate desolation; their rare delivery, not totall dereliction: and yet in regard of divers Oracles, we speak strictly, and say there was a proper Cessation."[29]

Whether or not we attribute the affirmation in *Religio Medici* to the dramatic nature of that work, we must certainly ascribe the axiomatic statement in *Pseudodoxia Epidemica* to Browne's awareness that the "indisputable

[29] *Rel. Medici*, I, 29, and *Ps. Epidemica*, VII, 12; in *BMP*, pp. 97 and 253. The references in the second quotation are to Cicero, *De divinatione*, I, 19 (cf. II, 56); Baronius (as above, note 8); and Montacutius [Richard Montagu], Θεανθρωπικòν: *seu . . . originum ecclesiasticarum libri duo* (1640), II, 421-22. It may be noted that Montagu, Bishop of Norwich from 1638, was personally known to Browne who had settled in the same city in 1636.

miracle" had been disputed in some quarters after all. As this realization slowly affected the attitude of other thinkers, we find John Smith the Cambridge Platonist cautiously and reasonably maintaining that the oracles ceased only after the advent of Christianity in their several regions,[30] while that seductive writer, Dr. Walter Charleton, just as carefully averred that ". . . by the *Cessation of Oracles*, I may not intend a *total and absolute expulsion* of that grand *Impostor* from all his Fanes, Tripods, and other shops wherein he professed his delusions, at once; as if the *Incarnation of Truth* had strook him dumb at one blow: but an extermination of him from his metropolitan Temple at Delphos, and an *Intercision, Diminution*, or *sensible Decay* of his Amphibologies, Predictions and other Collusions in all other places."[31] Less eloquently and far more bluntly, John Selden— "What fables have you vexed!" Jonson exclaimed in his epistle on him—dismissed both the "miracle" of the oracles' abrupt cessation and the traditional view that they were "the diuels mouth": "Oracles ceas'd presently after Christ, as soon as no body believ'd them. Just as we have no Fortune-Tellers, nor wise Men, when no body cares for them. Sometime you have a Season for them, when People believe them, and neither of these, I conceive, wrought by the Devil."[32]

---

[30] *Select Discourses* (1660; facsimile ed. C. A. Patrides, Delmar, N.Y., 1979); p. 458. Ralegh was just as cautious: the oracles declined, he wrote with intentional vagueness, "after the Gospell beganne to be preached in the World" (*HW*, p. 271 [IV, ii, 7]).

[31] *The Darknes of Atheism* (1652), p. 139; see further Ch. IV, Sect. V, Art. 12. Charleton displays Browne's influence, in ideas as in style, both here and in the instance noted above, Ch. V, §2.

[32] *Table-Talk*, 2nd ed. (1696), pp. 113-14. This is a posthumous work (1st ed., 1689); Selden died in 1654.

A storm was about to break, for the dark clouds had already gathered and flashes of lightning could be seen in the horizon. At last the storm broke—first in Holland, but soon involving France, and finally affecting the rest of Western Europe.

III

The first considerable attack on the "indisputable miracle" was undertaken by the Dutch scholar Antonius van Dale in *De oraculis ethnicorum* (1683). Within two years Georg Moebius, professor of theology at Leipzig, endeavored an equally lengthy confutation[33]—but to no avail, as it turned out, since Fontenelle was about to join the contest and deal the decisive blow in his celebrated *Histoire des oracles* (1687).[34]

Notwithstanding his own admission, Fontenelle was only nominally indebted to van Dale; actually he produced an entirely original work, distinguished—as van Dale's treatise was not—by its literary merit, sparkling good sense, and devastating humor. The work begins with a declaration of Fontenelle's surprise that "this Article of Oracles," which was "a Point of Religion" among the pagans, should have "become so without any Neces-

[33] *Tractatus philologico-theologicus de oraculorum ethnicorum origine, propagatione, et duratione . . . adversus D. Anton. van Dale* (Leipzig, 1685). Moebius' arguments were reported in *Nouvelles de la republique des letters* (Amsterdam, June 1686), Art. IV, pp. 673-80.

[34] Translated into English by Aphra Behn (1688) as well as by Stephen Whatley (1750). The work is discussed within the context of the war on tradition by J. B. Bury, *The Idea of Progress* (1932, repr. 1955), Ch. V, especially p. 117, and Paul Hazard, *The European Mind*, trans. J. Lewis May (1953), Part II, Ch. II, especially pp. 162 ff.

sity among Christians" as well.[35] To demonstrate the absurdity of the traditionalists' credulity, Fontenelle attempted two tasks at once: "to prove that Oracles, were they of what nature soever, were not delivered by Dæmons, and that they did not cease at the coming of Jesus Christ." The rejection of the one idea, Fontenelle argued, automatically eliminated the other: for if the devils were not involved in any way with the pagan oracles, their reported cessation at the time of Jesus did not in the least concern the Christian faith. Nonetheless, reviewing the evidence carefully, he concluded that the gradual decline of the oracles during the four centuries after the advent of Christ merely "proves the Cessation of some *Oracles* and the Diminution of others; but not the intire Cessation of all." The story of Pan's death, furthermore, was dismissed as of no consequence whatsoever, though not before Fontenelle expressed his astonishment that it had been so widely accepted; for the story, within its context in Plutarch's treatise, is followed by a totally absurd tale, yet "great Authors" have curiously accepted the one but as readily dismissed the other. Finally, concerning the identification of Pan with Christ, Fontenelle merely smiled to remember that Pan had also been identified with Satan. "Thus," he wrote, "a Way has been found out to give two Faces very different to this great Pan."[36]

As was to be expected, Fontenelle's work was not received without violent opposition.[37] However, as its merits

[35] From Whatley's version (1750), p. 3.

[36] *Seriatim: ibid.*, pp. 4, 153, 26, 11-12.

[37] The most significant reply to Fontenelle was by Jean-François Baltus, S.J., *Réponse à l'histoire des oracles* (Paris, 1707, with another volume added in 1708; both translated into English as *An Answer to Mr de Fontenelle's*

gradually became apparent, the common judgment of posterity was anticipated by Conyers Middleton when he declared in 1750 that the "fatal blow" to the legend of the ceasing of the oracles had been dealt by Fontenelle.[38] And so died a tradition that had entranced so many Christian apologists from Eusebius to Milton and beyond—impressive minds all, who nonetheless (together with Milton's admirer, Sir Henry Wotton) were "stupefied" that upon the advent of Christ the "false *Oracles* and *Delusions* [should be] strucken mute, and nothing to be heard at *Delphos* or *Hammon*."[39]

The passing of the legend did not mean the death of the great Pan as well. Quite the contrary, since the durable demigod has reappeared in Victorian literature, notably in Elizabeth Barrett Browning's poem *The Dead Pan*. In no fewer than thirty-nine stanzas, this uneven performance invokes the legend of the "dismal cry" heard by Thamus at Palodes, and dutifully associates it with the Passion of Christ. Yet the burden of the poem is

---

History of Oracles. In which Mr Van-Dale's System . . . is confuted [1709-10], 2 vols.). Baltus' first volume was reported at length by Jean le Clerk in *Bibliothèque choisie* (Amsterdam, 1707), XIII, 178-282. But it was soon possible to bypass this controversy altogether in pursuit of a sophisticated enquiry into the legend, witness John Beaumont's "A Discourse of the Oracles Deliver'd at Delphos, and the other Temples of the *Gentiles*; and of the Cessation of them," in his *Gleanings of Antiquities* (1724), pp. 131-87.

[38] *An Examination of . . . Discourses concerning the Use and Intent of Prophecy* (1750), p. 111. On Middleton's view of the pagan oracles ("wholly invented and supported by human craft, without any supernatural aid or interposition whatsoever"), see pp. 107 ff. Voltaire's admiration for the *Histoire des oracles* was, inevitably, "unfeigned and enduring" (H. Linn Edsall, "The Idea of History and Progress in Fontenelle and Voltaire," *Yale Romanic Studies*, XVIII [1941], p. 165).

[39] *Reliquiæ Wottonianæ*, 2nd ed. (1654), pp. 321-22.

distinctly in favor of the "discrowned and desecrated" gods of Hellas, whose passing Mrs. Browning lamented in a number of purgatorial lines:

> a darkness and a silence,
> Quenched the light of every shrine. . . .[40]

A similar pain was later to overflow the banks of A. E. Housman's "The Oracles" (1922):

> 'Tis mute, the word they went to hear
>   on high Dodona mountain
> When winds were in the oakenshaws
>   and all the cauldrons tolled,
> And mute's the midland navel-stone
>   beside the singing fountain,
> And echoes list to silence now
>   where gods told lies of old. . . .[41]

Pan figures in other contexts as well, notably in the disguises provided for him by D. H. Lawrence; but his persistent survival, no longer bearing any resemblance to the tradition outlined here, properly forms part of another story.[42] Only in modern Greek literature, it would appear, is it still possible to approximate to the life gen-

---

[40] *Poetical Works* (1904), pp. 303-06. This and other instances of the legend's treatment in nineteenth-century literature are noted by Patricia Merivale, *Pan the Goat-God: his Myth in Modern Times* (Cambridge, Mass., 1969).

[41] *Collected Poems* (1939), p. 127.

[42] See W. R. Irwin, "The Survival of Pan," *PMLA*, LXXVI (1961), pp. 159-67; Merivale (as above, note 40); Joseph Baim, "The Second Coming of Pan: A Note on D. H. Lawrence's 'The Last Laugh,' " *Studies in Short Fiction*, VI (1968), pp. 98-100.

erated during the Renaissance by the confluence of Pan
and Jesus, paganism and Christianity:

Στὰ ἐντάφια λευκὰ σάβανα
γυρτὸς ὁ Ἐσταυρωμένος
εἶν' ὁλόμορφος Ἄδωνης
ῥοδοπεριχυμένος.

Ἡ ἀρχαία ψυχὴ ζῆ μέσα μας
ἀθέλητα κρυμμένη·
ὁ Μέγας Πὰν δὲν πέθανεν. . . .[43]

[43] "Christ crucified, lying in his white winding-sheet, is beautiful Adonis
covered with roses. The soul of ancient Greece lives hidden unwillingly
within us. Great Pan is not dead . . ." (Kostis Palamas [d. 1943], trans.
Constantine A. Trypanis, *The Penguin Book of Greek Verse* [1971], p. 537).

"The beast with many heads":
Views on the Multitude

. . . what is the applause of the Multitude, but as the outcrie of an Heard of *Animals*, who without the knowledge of any true cause, please them-selves with the noyse they make? For seeing it is a thing exceeding rare, to distinguish Vertue and Fortune: the most impious (if prosperous) have ever beene applauded; the most vertuous (if unprosperous) have ever beene despised.—Sir Walter Ralegh

I

Smollett's epistolary account of the peregrinations of Humphry Clinker and company (1770) individualizes the participants largely by contrasting their responses to a variety of experiences. On one occasion, the splenetic Matthew Bramble remarks that "the mob is a monster I could never abide, either in its head, tail, midriff, or members; I detest the whole of it, as a mass of ignorance, presumption, malice, and brutality." But his young nephew Jery is of the opposite persuasion. Delighted by the behavior of amassed people, he confesses that "this chaos is to me a source of infinite amusement."[1] Jery would have had some difficulty in obtaining an endorsement of his attitude from any self-respecting spokesman during the Renaissance. None of them appears to have

[1] *The Expedition of Humphry Clinker* (1929), pp. 41 and 55.

been amused by the multitude, even if the reasons for their lack of response cannot be attributed solely to their spleen.

Shakespeare's Coriolanus is certainly not very partial to "the beast / With many heads" (IV, i, 1-2). The play over which he presides abounds in vitriolic denunciations of the multitude. For example:

He that will give good words to thee, will flatter
Beneath abhorring. What would you have, you
    curs,
That like nor peace nor war? The one affrights
    you,
The other makes you proud. He that trusts to
    you,
Where he should find you lions, finds you hares;
Where foxes, geese: you are no surer, no,
Than is the coal of fire upon the ice,
Or hailstone in the sun. Your virtue is,
To make him worthy whose offence subdues him,
And curse that justice did it. Who deserves
    greatness,
Deserves your hate; and your affections are
A sick man's appetite, who desires most that
Which would increase his evil. He that depends
Upon your favours, swims with fins of lead,
And hews down oaks with rushes. Hang ye! Trust
    ye?
With every minute you do change a mind,
And call him noble that was now your hate,
Him vile that was your garland.
                         (I, i, 166-82)

The dramatic context of this as of similar attacks[2] should oblige us to pause before equating the violent outbursts of Coriolanus with Shakespeare's own convictions. Yet some critics have not hesitated to accept, and on occasion to press further, Hazlitt's considered opinion that in Coriolanus "Shakespeare himself seems to have had a leaning to the arbitrary side of the question"[3]—or, in blunter terms, that he "hated" the multitude, that indeed he "despised" the masses.[4] True, Shakespeare has often been defended valiantly, and sometimes even persuasively;[5] but there is still some support for the proposition that, even if he was not in favor of Coriolanus' brutal phraseology, he appears to have inclined in the general direction of his protagonist's sentiments. The play's clusters of images, for one, suggest "very subtly" that Shakespeare's attitude toward the populace does not—as it necessarily cannot—be said to coincide with our own democratic principles.[6] There is moreover the peculiar enthusiasm with which Shakespeare went out of his way to "blacken" the multitude without warrant from Plutarch, his capital source,[7] so that the views expressed

---

[2] See further I, iv, 30-42; III, i, 33-161; III, iii, 68-133; etc. (ed. Philip Brockbank, The Arden Shakespeare, 1976).

[3] *Characters of Shakespeare's Plays* (1952), p. 56; first published in 1817.

[4] For a number of such statements see the quotations in H. H. Furness, ed., *Coriolanus*, Variorum edition (1928), pp. 701 ff. *passim*, and Tupper (as below, note 10), pp. 487 ff.

[5] Especially by John Palmer, *Political Characters of Shakespeare* (1945), pp. 313 ff.

[6] W. H. Clemen, *The Development of Shakespeare's Imagery* (Cambridge, Mass., 1951), Ch. XV. Other relevant studies of Shakespearean imagery are cited by G. Thomas Tanselle and Florence W. Dunbar, "Legal Language in *Coriolanus*," *SQ*, XIII (1962), pp. 230-38.

[7] John Dover Wilson, "Introduction" to *Coriolanus* (Cambridge, 1960), p. xxi, who nevertheless denies that Shakespeare was antipathetic to "the

by Coriolanus are far more extreme than was common among any of the *dramatis personae* in other Elizabethan plays.[8] The unreliability of the Shakespearean multitude, finally, appears at times to be elevated to the status of a doctrine shared by diverse characters beyond Coriolanus. Thus the premise in Jack Cade's strictly rhetorical question in *2 Henry VI*—"Was ever feather so lightly blown to and fro as this multitude?" (IV, viii, 56)—reappears in *3 Henry VI* where the royal protagonist pointedly deploys the same metaphor:

> Look, as I blow this feather from my face,
> And as the air blows it to me again,
> Obeying with my wind when I do blow,
> And yielding to another when it blows,
> Commanded always by the greater gust;
> Such is the lightness of you common men.
>
> (III, i, 84-89)

There is possibly a more balanced view, however. For so long as Shakespeare was concerned with the preservation of order in the State—assuredly an omnipresent dimension of his plays—it may be that he meant sharply to discriminate after the fashion urged by one critic, that "towards the common people acting in their appointed vocations, Shakespeare shows tolerance and sympathy,"

common people." The best attempt to contrast Plutarch's account and Shakespeare's version is by M. W. MacCallum, *Shakespeare's Roman Plays* (1910), pp. 484 ff. Plutarch's text, in North's version from Amyot, is available in Furness (as above, note 4), pp. 621 ff.; E. K. Chambers, ed., *Coriolanus* (Boston ed., n.d.), App. A; C. F. Tucker Brooke, ed., *Shakespeare's Plutarch* (1909), II, 137-207; T.J.B. Spencer, ed., *Shakespeare's Plutarch* (1964), pp. 296-363; and Geoffrey Bullough, ed., *Narrative and Dramatic Sources of Shakespeare* (1964), V, 505-49.

[8] See Brents Stirling, *The Populace in Shakespeare* (1949).

but "when a commoner, alone or in a mob, seeks to meddle in politics and government, he becomes the object of some of the dramatist's fiercest scorn."[9]

The dramatic context of Shakespeare's plays may never be disregarded, certainly. On the other hand, it is an error forcefully to extract Shakespeare from his age and endow him with ideas foreign to that age, in this instance democratic attitudes. We are already cognizant that during the Renaissance the scales inclined heavily toward "the arbitrary side of the question," notably among the period's political thinkers;[10] and we noted earlier how Joseph Hall, in arguing the existence of celestial "degrees," observed with a tellingly casual manner that "Equality hath no place, either in earth or in hell; we have no reason to seek it in heaven" (above, Ch. I, §3). But we also need to know more fully the rationale that informs the extensions of the same frame of mind, for instance the denunciation of the multitude in *Religio Medici* as "a monstrosity more prodigious than Hydra," or the ascription to Jesus in *Paradise Regained* of a contemptuous reference to the people as "a herd confused, / A miscellaneous rabble."[11]

---

[9] James E. Phillips, Jr., *The State in Shakespeare's Greek and Roman Plays* (1940), p. 154.

[10] See Christopher Hill, "The Many-Headed Monster in late Tudor and early Stuart Political Thinking," in *From the Renaissance to the Counter-Reformation*, ed. C. H. Carter (1965), pp. 296-324. An impressive series of other references was cited long ago by Frederick Tupper, Jr., "The Shakesperean Mob," *PMLA*, XXVII (1922), pp. 486-523, *passim*. See also above, note 8, and Kenneth Muir, "The Background of *Coriolanus*," *SQ*, X (1959), especially pp. 144-45.

[11] *Religio Medici*, II, 1 (in *BMP*, p. 134), and *Paradise Regained*, III, 49-50. See also the pertinent passages quoted by Mario Praz, "Sir Thomas Browne," *ES*, XI (1929), p. 162.

II

The rebuke of the multitude in *Religio Medici* encompasses the remarkable claim that it is "no breach of Charity" to regard the multitude as "fooles"; in fact, we are told, "it is the stile all holy Writers have afforded them, set downe by *Solomon* in canonicall Scripture, and a point of our faith to beleeve so." Milton in *Paradise Regained* also invokes a Biblical context in that he has Jesus upraid the multitude for extolling "things vulgar, and well weighd, scarce worth the praise," in order promptly to emphasize that "true glory and renown" consist in God's approbation of the faithful few who seek to further the divine purpose (III, 60-64). Is there any warrant for these large claims in the Scriptures and in theological literature generally?

We assume that the historic Jesus never conducted himself quite in the manner he does in *Paradise Regained*. Yet he often displayed wrath, the ὀργή which the New Testament frequently attributes to him in order to affirm God's violent opposition to disobedience;[12] nor is it difficult to establish the *locus classicus* of this attitude since all four gospels detail it at some length in their account of Christ's angry cleaning of the Temple,[13] not to mention the apocalyptic "wrath of the Lamb" so clearly upheld in the Book of Revelation (6.16). So far as the

[12] See Gustav Stahlin, 'Οργή, *Theological Dictionary of the New Testament*, ed. Gerhard Kittel, trans. G. W. Bromiley (Grand Rapids, Mich., 1967), V, 382-447; R.V.G. Tasker, *The Biblical Doctrine of the Wrath of God* (1951, repr. 1957); A. T. Hanson, *The Wrath of the Lamb* (1957); George A. F. Knight, *A Christian Theology of the Old Testament* (1959), Ch. XII; *et al.*

[13] Matthew 21.12-13, Mark 11. 15-19, Luke 19.45-46, and John 2.13-16; cf. Matthew 18.15 ff. and 23.2 ff., and Mark 12.38 ff. One of the best commentaries on these Biblical accounts is visual: Rembrandt's *Christ driving the Money-changers from the Temple* (1626).

orthodox thinkers of the Renaissance were concerned, however, the ὀργὴ of Jesus was justified especially in the light of the multitude's direct responsibility for his execution. As the popular writer Arthur Warwick observed in the 1630s:

"That *the voice of the common people is the voice of GOD*, is the common voice of the people; yet it is as full of falshood, as commonesse. For who sees not that those blacke-mouthed hounds, upon the meere scent of opinion, as freely spend their mouthes in hunting counter, or like Actaeon's doggs in chasing an innocent man to death, as if they followed the chase of truth itselfe, in a fresh scent. Who observes not that the voice of the people, yea of that people that voiced themselves the people of GOD, did prosecute the GOD of all people, with one common voice, *hee is worthy to die.*"[14]

John Batt in considering the same issue in 1605 pontificated that "multitude is rather a mark of the false then of the true church"[15]—a conviction possibly echoing Calvin's attack on "the common herd, whose madness in profaning the truth of God exceeds all bounds."[16]

[14] *Spare-Minutes* (1821), pp. 81-82; the text is of the 6th edition (1637).

[15] *The Royall Priesthood of Christians* (1605), fol. 40v. Protestant thinkers repeatedly asserted as much: e.g. Rudolf Gwalter (Gualterus), *Homelyes . . . vppon the Actes*, trans. John Bridges (1572), p. 574; Calvin, *Sermons . . . vpon . . . the Galatians*, trans. Arthur Golding (1574), fols. 225v-226; Marlorat (as below, note 20), fol. 137; Thomas Scott, *The high-waies of God and the King* (1623), p. 38; Griffith Williams, *The Trve Church* (1629), p. 107; Edward Reynolds, *An Explication of the Hundreth and Tenth Psalme* (1632), p. 101; Richard Carpenter, *Experience, Historie, and Divinitie* (1642), I, 128 f.; *et al.*

[16] *Institutes*, I, v, 11. Calvin, we are assured by an authority, "always mistrusted and feared the multitude" (J. S. Whale, *The Protestant Tradition* [Cambridge, 1959], p. 158n). So did Luther, not without reason (Heinrich Bornkamm, *Luther's World of Thought*, trans. Martin H. Bertram [St. Louis, Mo., 1958], p. 197).

But for a fuller statement we must turn to the saintly Lancelot Andrewes, who incidentally supplies some of the passages in "canonicall Scripture" invoked in *Religio Medici*:

". . . what is the *people?* Let *Moses* speak (for, he knew them) *Siccine popule stulte & insipiens?* [Exodus 34.9, Deuteronomy 9.6, 31.27] And *Aaron* too (for, he had occasion to trie them) *This people is even set on mischiefe* [Exodus 32.22]. And (if you will) *David* also, *Inter Belluas populorum* [Psalm 68.30]. And to conclude, GOD himself, *Populus iste durae cervicis est* [Exodus 32.9, 33.3, Deuteronomy 9.13]. This is the *people*. We may briefly take a view of all these.

"Will you see the folly and giddinesse of this multitude? ye may, *Acts* 19. there, *they be at the Towne-house, some crying one thing, some another; and the more part knew not why they were come together* [Acts 19.32]. Therefore *Moses* truly said, it was *a fond and giddy-headed people.*

"Will you see the brutishnesse of the *people?* In the 22, *Acts*, you shall see them taking up a crie, upon a word spoken by S. *Paul, and casting off their cloaths and throwing dust into the aire* [Acts 22.23], as if they were quite decayed of reason; that *David* truly might say *inter belluas populorum.*

"Will ye see the spight and malice of the people? In the sixteenth of *Numbers*, for *Corehs* death they challenge *Moses* and *Aaron, ye have persecuted and killed the people of the Lord* [Numbers 16.41]. Yet neither did *Moses* once touch them, but *GOD* Himself from heaven, by visible judgement, shewed them to be as they were. . . . That *Aaron* said truly of them, *This people is even set on mischiefe.*

"Lastly, if ye will see their head-strongnesse, looke upon them in the *eight* of the *first* of *Samuel*, where having phansied to themselves an alteration of estate, though they were shewed plainly by Samuel, the sundry inconveniences of the government, they so affected, they answer him with; *No* (for that is their *Logick*, to *deny the conclusion*) *but we will be like other countries about us, and be guided as we thinke good our owne selves* [I Samuel 8.19-20]. That (of all other) GODs saying is most true, *It is a stiffe-necked and head-strong generation* . . .

"And this is the people, *Populus*. And surely, no evill can be said too much of this word *people*. . . ."[17]

The countless denunciations of the multitude during the Renaissance are distinguished by their severely circumscribed literary dimension. The metaphor deployed as we have seen by Shakespeare's Jack Cade and Henry VI is common to the point of vulgarity; and, reiterated *ad nauseam*, it was to appear yet again in the proclamation of Benjamin Whichcote, the founding father of Cambridge Platonism, that "the Wind doth not change so often as the giddy Multitude."[18] At most, indeed, such statements were likely to deploy the equally predictable metaphors mentioned by the great Swiss theologian Heinrich Bullinger when he asserted that "the cōmon folke or people are rightly compared to waters, whiche are also for their vnstablenes called mouable or vnconstaunt, and for their rage both furiouse and madde."[19]

Similarly hostile comments on the people as "una bestia varia e grossa"—to quote Tommaso Campanella—came, and continued to come, from many quarters: the highly esteemed French Protestant exegete Augustin

---

[17] *XCVI. Sermons*, 4th ed. (1641), pp. 278-79. Thereafter Andrewes advances to an exposition of Christ's transformation of the populace into God's people "capable of any blessing or benefit."

[18] *Several Discourses*, ed. John Jeffery (1701-7), IV, 249.

[19] *A Hundred Sermons vpon the Apocalips*, trans. John Daws (1561), p. 524.

Marlorat, the celebrated German jurisconsult Philipp Camerarius, the French philosopher Guillaume du Vair, Sir Walter Ralegh as well as his predecessor the Italian historian Guicciardini, the "singularly well skyled" George Whetstone and that prolific "gentleman" Barnaby Rich, the Puritan divine Charles Herle and Bishop Miles Smith, Ben Jonson and the "ever-memorable" John Hales of Eton, Herrick and Vaughan, the minor versifier John Abbot[20]—and numerous poets of the first magnitude who consciously cultivated the "haughty obscure style" in an attempt to escape the unwanted commendation of the "profane multitude."[21] But the most violent rebuke, worthy of a Coriolanus, was penned by Pierre Charron

---

[20] Marlorat, *A Catholike Exposition vpon the Reuelation*, trans. Arthur Golding (1574), fol. 232v; Camerarius, *The Living Library*, trans. John Molle (1621), Bl. II, Ch. XX; Du Vair, *The Moral Philosophie of the Stoicks*, trans. Thomas James (1598), ed. Rudolf Kirk (New Brunswick, N.J., 1951), p. 124; Ralegh, pp. 63-64 [quoted in the headnote, above]; Guicciardini, *Ricordi*, trans. N. H. Thomson (1949), p. 226; Whetstone, *The English Myrror* (1586), pp. 20 ff.; Rich, *Faultes Faults and Nothing else but Faults* (1606), fols. 42v ff., and *Opinion Diefied* (1613), ch. XXIV; Herle, *Contemplations and Devotions* (1631), pp. 187 ff.; Smith, *Sermons* (1632), p. 23; Jonson, *Timber*, in *Ben Jonson*, edd. C. H. Herford *et al.* (Oxford, 1947), VIII, 593-94; Hales, *Sermons preach'd at Eton* (1660), p. 12; Herrick, "Good Friday," ll. 5-6; Vaughan, "Jacobs Pillow, and Pillar," ll. 5-6; and Abbot [Rivers], *Devout Rhapsodies* (1648), pp. 44 f. Thus also John King, *The Fovrth Sermon preached at Hampton Covrt* (Oxford, 1607), p. 22; Richard Webb, *Christs Kingdome* (1611), p. 32; John Norden, *The Labyrinth of Mans Life* (1614) sig. E3v; John Spencer, Καινὰ καὶ παλαιὰ (1658), p. 629; etc. It may be that Copernicus is the exception to the rule (see Edward Rosen, "Copernicus' Attitude toward the Common People," *JHI*, XXXII [1971], pp. 281-88); but other major scientists, notably Galileo, conform to the usual pattern: see his letter to Kepler (August 19, 1610) on "the extraordinary stupidity of the crowd" etc. (quoted by Carola Baumgardt, *Johannes Kepler* [1952], p. 86).

[21] Consult the extensive evidence presented by Arnold Stein, "Donne's Obscurity and the Elizabethan Tradition," *ELH*, XIII (1946), especially pp. 109 ff.

in *De la sagesse* (1601), which Samson Lennard translated shortly thereafter (1606 ff.). Charron's attack, extended to the length of a chapter, begins with the Horatian allusion present in nearly all references to "the beast with many heads,"[22] and ends with the word we have already encountered in *Religio Medici*. The following excerpts adequately suggest the burden of the argument as well as the narrow circumference of the metaphors noted earlier:

"The people . . . are a strange beast with many heads, and which in few words cannot be described, inconstant and variable, without stay, like the waves of the sea; they are moved and appeased, they allow and disallow one and the same thing at one and the same instant: there is nothing more easie than to drive them into what passion he will; they love not wars for the true end thereof, nor peace for rest and quietnesse, but for varieties sake, and the change that there is from the one to the other: confusion makes them desire order, and when they have it, they like it not: they runne alwaies one contrary to another, and there is no time pleaseth, but what is to come. . . . To conclude, the people are a savage beast, all they thinke, is vanitie; all they say, is false and erronious; that they reprove, is good; that they approve, is naught; that which they praise, is infamous, that which they doe and undertake is follie . . . The Vulgar multitude is the mother of ignorance, injustice, inconstancie, idolatrie, vanitie, which never yet could be pleased: their mot is, *Vox populi, vox Dei; The voyce of the people is*

[22] "Belua multorum es capitum" (*Epistolae*, I, i, 76). The allusion is cited, of course, by nearly all editors of *Coriolanus*. Its context—the sustained prejudice against the populace in ancient Rome—is studied by Z. Yavetz, *Plebs and Princeps* (Oxford, 1969).

the voyce of God: but we may say, *Vox populi, vox stultorum; The Voyce of the people is the voyce of fooles.*"[23]

It was not without some accuracy that when one of Shakespeare's citizens complains because Coriolanus reproved the multitude as "many-headed," another citizen replies, "We have been called so of many" (II, iii, 16-17).

Our enlightened era, we like to think, has overcome the prejudices of the past inclusive of the extreme disapprobation of "the people" so common during the Renaissance. Yet those attitudes did not fail to inform even, say, the debates that in the 1780s were to result in the Constitution of the United States. James Madison, for instance, warned that an ever-increasing membership of the House of Representatives could, and possibly would, result in a decrease of its representative nature. His actual statement is intriguing:

". . . in all legislative assemblies, the greater the number composing them may be, the fewer will be the men who will in fact direct their proceedings. . . . [T]he more multitudinous a representative assemby may be rendered, the more it will partake of the infirmities incident to collective meetings of the people. Ignorance will be the dupe of cunning; and passion the slave of sophistry and declamation. The people can never err more than in supposing that by multiplying their representatives, beyond a certain limit, they strengthen the barrier against the government of a few. . . . The countenance

---

[23] *Of Wisdome* (1640), pp. 208, 211 [Book I, Ch. LII]. It should be noted that Lennard's translation of Charron formed part of Browne's library (Frank L. Huntley, *Sir Thomas Browne* [Ann Arbor, 1962], p. 175).

of the government may become more democratic; but the soul that animates it will be more oligarchic."[24]

Even more relevantly, Alexander Hamilton was inclined toward a government of the elite—at the very least analogous, it should be noted, to Milton's proposals in *The Readie and Easie Way to Establish a Free Commonwealth* (1660)—because his faith in "the people" was evidently minimal. According to a report by a witness—not, admittedly, an entirely friendly witness—Hamilton is said to have spoken during the Constitutional Convention thus:

"All communities divide themselves into the few and the many. The first are the rich and well born, the other the mass of the people. The voice of the people has been said to be the voice of God; and however generally this maxim has been quoted and believed, it is not true in fact. The people are turbulent and changing; they seldom judge or determine right. Give therefore to the first class a distinct, permanent share in the government. They will check the unsteadiness of the second. . . ."[25]

It appears that one need not possess the splenetic nature of Smollett's Matthew Bramble to be weary of the "miscellaneous rabble" as "a monstrosity more prodigious than Hydra."

[24] *The Federalist*, ed. Jacob E. Cooke (Middletown, Conn., 1961), pp. 395-96 [No. 58 (57), February 20, 1788].

[25] From the report by Robert Yates, June 18, 1787; in *The Papers of Alexander Hamilton*, ed. Harold C. Syrett (1962), IV, 200. See further Gerald Stourzh, *Alexander Hamilton and the Idea of Republican Government* (Stanford, 1970), pp. 46 ff. I am grateful for both references to Professor John W. Shy.

🎋 9 🎋
"*The bloody and cruell Turke*":
The Judgments of God
in History

God presses the Devill, and makes the Devill his Soldier, to fight his battles, and directs his arrowes, and his bullets . . . so that God, and the Devill, and we, are all in one Army, and all for our destruction; we have a warre, and yet there is but one Army, and we onely are the Countrey that is fed upon, and wasted.—John Donne

I

History is like Milton's *Lycidas*, fraught with apparent digressions which upon consideration form part of the design at the center of the one as of the other. In the words of John Smith the Cambridge Platonist, "a wise man that looks from the Beginning to the End of things, beholds them all in their due place and method acting that part which the Supreme Mind and Wisedome that governs all things hath appointed them, and to carry on one and the same Eternal designe."[1]

The claim summarizes the view of history which, initiated by Judaism, was adopted by Christianity in the form developed in the first instance by St. Paul and thereafter by Eusebius of Caesarea, St. Augustine, Paulus Orosius, and numerous theologians to the Renais-

---

[1] *Select Discourses* (1660); in *CP*, p. 190.

sance.[2] The formidable tradition emanates from the Hebrew prophets, whose ideas, destined to become commonplaces, were forged on the anvil of their strict and often militant monotheism. Amos in the ninth century B.C. first tried to expand the restricted concept of Yahweh as a purely national deity by maintaining that the same God who brought Israel out of Egypt also delivered the Philistines from Caphtor and the Syrians from Kir (Amos 9.7). The universal jurisdiction of God proclaimed by Amos was soon after reaffirmed by Isaiah, who pronounced on behalf of God, "Blessed by Egypt my people, and Assyria the work of my hands, and Israel mine inheritance" (Is. 19.25). Isaiah also advanced the theory that God directly manipulates temporal states as instruments to the purposes of divine justice, affirming unhesitatingly that God used the despised Assyrians as the rod of the divine wrath against Israel (Is. 10.5). Jeremiah, by altering details of the theory so that it should include the Babylonians, concurred (Jer. 51.7). In the sixth century, the second Isaiah complemented the theory of his great predecessor by presenting another nation not now as the instrument of divine wrath but of divine mercy: Persia, then under the sway of Cyrus the Great, the Lord's "anointed" (Is. 45.1). Underlying this family of ideas was the conviction, summarily stated in the Book of Daniel, that "the Most High ruleth in the kingdom of men, and giveth it to whomsoever he will" (4.17).

The continuity of tradition to the Renaissance is attested by the similar claim of William Covell, in 1595, that "GOD giveth the Scepter of realmes as it pleaseth

[2] See my account in *"The Grand Design of God": The Literary Form of the Christian View of History* (1972).

him, and taketh them away as his pleasure is."[3] The Biblical orientation of this and similar claims is patently clear. As James Rowlandson maintained in 1623, ". . . there is no publique calamitie inflicted on man, or other creatures of which wee may not say as the Prophet of the *Assyrian* tyrant, that it is *the rod of Gods anger*."[4] George Petter in summarizing the common viewpoint in 1661 provided also its standard extensions:

". . . in the times of the Old Testament, God punished the wicked Jews by the *Chaldeans* or *Assyrians*, and therefore the King of *Assyria* is called the rod of Gods anger, *Esay* 10.5. Afterward he punished the *Chaldeans* or Assyrians, by the *Persians*; the *Persians*, by the *Grecians*; the *Grecians*, by the *Romans*; . . . the *Romans* by other Nations, as by the *Goths* and *Vandalls*. . . . And of later times, how God hath scourged one Nation by another for their sins, and doth at this day, is well known unto all."[5]

One other extension was no less inevitable, namely, that God's absolute control of the created order encompasses Satan and his disciples. However Calvinistic in appearance, this belief is in fact broadly traditional, since any other possibility would result in the pernicious heresy of dualism. A Renaissance apologist's statement, necessarily uncompromising, may be taken as represent-

---

[3] *Polimanteia* (1595), sig. E2.

[4] *Gods Blessing in Blasting* (1623), pp. 11-12.

[5] *Commentary upon . . . Mark* (1611), II, 1077. There is a parallel summary statement by Richard Eburne, *The Two-folde Tribvte* (1613), I, 18. For similar surveys of history, see George Whetstone, *The English Myrror* (1586), pp. 54 f.; Thomas Ireland, *The Oath of Allegiance* (1610), sig. B4v; Martin Fotherby, *Atheomastix* (1622), pp. 260 ff.; Thomas Barnes, *Vox belli* (1626), pp. 9 ff.; *et al.* Cf. Calvin's commentary on Isaiah 10.5, in *Calvin: Commentaries*, trans. Joseph Haroutunian, *LCC* (1958), XXIII, 270-72.

ative of the Christian view: "Evil spirites are sayd to be oure Lords, because they are in Gods power, and what so euer they do, they do it by God."[6] Only another step and we are at the conclusion that Satan is "the whippe of God,"[7] an active servant of the divine purpose.

The implications of such a concept trouble us. But the thinkers of the Renaissance were equally troubled, at least implicitly, since Théodore de Bèze felt obliged to comment on the manner in which the devils may be said to do the will of God. In his words:

"If you take will in his generall signification, that is to wyt, for that thinge whyche god hath willingly determyned too haue come to passe, and refer the woord *Doo*, not too the intent and purpose of the wicked, but too the falling out of the matter: then surely God executeth his will (that is to saye the thinge that he hath determined from euerlastinge) euen by the wicked also: according too this saying, who shal resist gods will [Romans 9.19]? But if that by the name of *Will*, yee meene the thinge that of it selfe is acceptable vntoo God, and will haue the woord Doo, too importe a ryght affection of obeying: then truely I aunswer, that the wicked sort, not onely doo not Gods will, but also are caryed wholly to the contrary part."[8]

After some such manner, it was conjectured, God uses as "agents and instruments" of his justice Satan and even

---

[6] Nicolaus Hanapus, *The Ensamples of Vertue and Vice*, trans. Thomas Paynell (1564), sig. N5v.

[7] John Done, *Polydoron* (1631), p. 188. Cf. John Donne: "The Devill himselfe is but a *slave* of God" (*Sermons*, X, 135).

[8] *A Booke of Christian Questions and Answers*, trans. Arthur Golding (1574), fols. 65-65v. For similar arguments, see Calvin, *Commentaries . . . vpon the Prophet Daniell*, trans. Arthur Golding (1570), fols. 65 f.; Jacobus Kimedoncius, *Of the Redemption of Mankind*, trans. Hugh Ince (1598), pp. 315 f.; William Hampton, *A Proclamation of Warre* (1627), pp. 5 f.; *et al.*

the sum total of the created order which, according to Heinrich Bullinger's roll call, includes "Aungels, diuels: and men: as Kinges and Princes &c. Sometimes the Elements, or things that come of the Elements, as winds, lightnings, thunder, hayle, raine, frostes, &c. sometimes beastes."[9] The common end to which God manipulated these agents was agreed upon readily: it is to scourge "sinne with sinne,"[10] to "try vs in the furnace of aduersity, that the drosse of our sinnes may be purged from vs."[11] An old theory assuredly, expounded long ago by Job's "friends," yet despite his vehement protests surviving until the Renaissance.

But one part of Bullinger's catalogue interests us here especially. This is God's use of "Kinges and Princes"— the "cruell Kinges, and Blouddy tyrannes" of Pedro Mexía's popular exposition of all such "Ministers of God."[12] Few theories of the Renaissance were so widely used or so violently abused. Catholic surveys of history,

[9] *Common Places of Christian Religion*, trans. John Stockwood (1572), fol. 59v. Thus also Calvin (below, note 14), p. 53; Zacharias Ursinus, *The Summe of Christian Religion*, trans. Henry Parry (Oxford, 1587), p. 198; Thomas Bilson, *The Survey of Christs Sufferings* (1604), p. 33; John Gaule, *Practiqve Theories* (1629), pp. 157 f.; Cristóbal de Fonseca, *Devovt Contemplations*, trans. Henry Mabbe (1629), p. 380; Richard Clerke, *Sermons* (1637), p. 180; John Trapp, *Gods Love-Tokens* (1637), *passim*; Richard Sibbes, *The Christians Portion* (1638), p. 17; Henry Ainsworth, *The Orthodox Foundation of Religion* (1641), p. 26; Donne, *Sermons*, VI, 349, VII, 81, VIII, 359, etc.; *et al.* See further Ariosto's fine exposition in *Orlando furioso*, XVII, i, 1 ff., and the discussion of the Italian humanists' parallel attitude by Charles E. Trinkaus, *Adversity's Noblemen* (1940), pp. 128 ff.

[10] Nicholas Byfield, *The Paterne of Wholsome Words* (1618), p. 121, and John Dod and Robert Cleaver, *Exposition of the Ten Commandements*, 19th ed. (1635), p. 264. Thus also Donne: "God punishes sin by sin" (*Sermons*, IX, 381).

[11] William Whately, *Sinne no More*, 3rd ed. (1630), pp. 22-23.

[12] *Silua de varia lection* (Valladolid, 1551), Part I, Ch. XXXV; trans. Thomas Fortescue, *The Foreste* (1571), Part I, Ch. XV.

for example, inevitably citing the Ottoman conquest of "proud Bizantium" as capital proof of God's vengeance against schismatics, hinted darkly that a worse fate was in store for Protestant heretics.[13] Among constant admonitions to preserve order in the state, we often find the argument that even tyrants, being scourges of the divine wrath, must be tolerated patiently. No man has the right, it was claimed, "with the dog to snarle at the staffe wherewith he is beaten."[14] Not surprisingly, sovereigns welcomed this theory with marked enthusiasm. James I might have been preparing for the worst when he maintained: "Although a wicked King is sent by God for a curse to his people, and plague for their sins; yet it is not lawfull for them to shake off that curse at their own pleasures, that God hath laid upon them."[15] It may be added that Renaissance writers managed to detect scourges of God everywhere, from Timur, particularly under his Marlovian guise as Tamburlaine,[16] to—least

---

[13] John Abbot, *Iesus Praefigured* (Antwerp, 1623), pp. 12-13; John Colleton, *The Theatre of . . . Religion* (St. Omer, 1620), Bk. I, Ch. VI.

[14] George Downame, *The Christians Sacrifice* (1604), p. 75. For Calvin's view, see *Sermons . . . vpon the Booke of Iob*, trans. Arthur Golding (1574), p. 617.

[15] *Regales aphorismi* (1650), p. 89.

[16] While we must accept the verdict that Marlowe's hero claims to be the scourge of God "not reverentially but arrogantly and blasphemously for his own aggrandisement" (Paul H. Kocher, *UTQ*, XVII [1948], p. 114), the claim itself loomed large in nearly every Renaissance account of Tamburlaine. For discussions of the works which Marlowe might have consulted, see Leslie Spence in *MP*, XXIV (1929), pp. 181-99; Ethel Seaton in *RES*, V (1929), pp. 385-401; U. M. Ellis Fermor, ed., *Tamburlaine the Great* (1930), pp. 17-61; S. C. Chew, *The Crescent and the Rose* (1937), pp. 469 ff.; Roy W. Battenhouse, *Marlowe's "Tamburlaine"* (Nashville, 1941), pp. 129-49, and *PMLA*, LVI (1941), pp. 337-48; John Bakeless, *The Tragicall History of Christopher Marlowe* (Cambridge, Mass., 1942), I, 204 ff., 214 ff.; Thomas C. Izard in *MLN*, LVIII (1943), pp. 411-17; Hallett

probable of all—lawyers ("Corrupt Lawyers are no doubt a scourge of God").[17]

II

The traditional theory was most consistently deployed in connection with the Ottoman Empire. By the sixteenth century Turkish power had reached its zenith. During the reign of Suleiman the Magnificent (1520-1566), the Turks had knocked boldly at the gates of Europe, seized Rhodes, besieged Malta and Vienna, conquered Belgrade, and overrun the better part of Hungary. Europeans could not, and did not, respond to the Turkish menace after the fashion of the Flemish diplomat Busbecq, who endeavored to humanize the Turks by reporting *inter alia* that they are "passionately fond of flowers." Rather, awe-stricken, most agreed all too readily with René de Lucinge that the Turks were "the scourge of the East and the Terror of the West"[18]—in short, as

Smith, in *Elizabethan Studies . . . in Honor of G. F. Reynolds* (Boulder, Colo., 1945), pp. 126-31; Paul H. Kocher, *Christopher Marlowe* (Chapel Hill, 1946), pp. 180-83; Hugh G. Dick in *SP*, XLVI (1949), pp. 154-66; and Irving Ribner in *CL*, VI (1954), pp. 349-56. For the remarkable change in the attitude toward Timur that set in by the nineteenth century, see Dorothee M. Finkelstein, *Melville's Orienda* (New Haven, 1961), pp. 175 ff.

[17] Leonard Wright, *A Summons for Sleepers* (1589), p. 12.

[18] See *The Life and Letters of Ogier Ghiselin de Busberg*, trans. Charles T. Foster and F. H. Blackburne Daniell (1881), I, 108; and on Lucinge: *The Beginning, Continuance, and Decay of Estates*, trans. John Finet (1606), sig. bᵛ. On the contemporary situation, consult Sir Charles Oman, *The Sixteenth Century* (1936), Ch. III; Stephen A. Fischer-Galati, *Ottoman Imperialism and German Protestantism 1521-1555* (Cambridge, Mass., 1959); Roger B. Merriman, *Suleiman the Magnificent* (Cambridge, Mass., 1944); Myron P. Gilmore, *The World of Humanism* (1952), pp. 6 ff., 273 ff.; Paul Coles, *The Ottoman Impact on Europe* (1968); and Carl M. Kortepeter, *Ottoman Imperi-*

King James maintained, "ye awowed enemie of God," that is to say, Antichrist.[19] Worse still, fact was confounded with legend, and the menace of the seemingly invincible Ottoman armies exaggerated by lurid accounts of what Henry More later described as "the tearing Cruelty and Savageness" of the Turks.[20] Christians in the West, their own security now threatened, began to appreciate the plight of their Orthodox brethren in the East who had been captive since the mid-fifteenth century. William Habington, more eloquent than most, was one of a number who penned an imaginative account of Constantinople's hour of doom, when the Mistress of the East "like a ship overcome by tempests, yeelded at length to a Sea of enemies which enter'd through the breaches, and suncke it for ever."[21] And then, with surging emotion, an account of the rape:

---

alism during the Reformation: Europe and the Caucasus (1972). On the attitude of "extreme prejudice" against the Turks that the Renaissance inherited from the Middle Ages, see P. Alphandéry, "Mahomet-Antichrist dans le Moyen Age Latin," in *Mélanges Hartwig Derenbourg* (Paris, 1909), pp. 261-77; Norman Daniel, *Islam and the West* (Edinburgh, 1958), especially Ch. X; R. W. Southern, *Western Views of Islam in the Middle Ages* (Cambridge, Mass., 1962); and Robert Schwoebel, *The Shadow of the Crescent: The Renaissance Image of the Turk 1453-1517* (Nieuwkoop, 1967). On the reflection of that prejudice in Renaissance literature see Franklin L. Baumer, "England, the Turk, and the Common Corps of Christendom," *American Historical Review*, L (1944), pp. 26-48, and especially the admirable survey by Samuel C. Chew, *The Crescent and the Rose* (1937), Ch. III, " 'The Present Terror of the World.' " For some more favorable views consult Terence Spencer, "Turks and Trojans in the Renaissance," *MLR*, XLVII (1952), pp. 330-33.

[19] *Ane frvitfull Meditatioun . . . {on} Reuelatioun* (Edinburgh, 1588), sig. B2. For a summary of the usual arguments "proving" this notion, see Griffith Williams, 'Ο Ἀντίχριστος (1660), pp. 9-12. Consult also Christopher Hill, *Antichrist in Seventeenth-Century England* (1971), pp. 181-82; and below: Firth in note 26 and Ball in note 36.

[20] *Divine Dialogues* (1668), p. 60.

[21] *Observations upon Historie* (1641), p. 107.

"The Citie three dayes lay prostitute to the licence of the conquerours: who were wittie to invent new mischiefes to please their barbarous wantonnesse. And well might they congratulate the fortunes of their victories; for never did so much treasure become a prey to so much rapine: and never did such ancient greatnesse fall to so low a slavery; honour became a contumely, former wealth serv'd onely to aggravate future poverty: and beautie farre more cruell than wrinkles, betray'd it selfe to the most loathed deformitie."[22]

But the apologists of the faith refused to be distracted by such emotionalism. Their concern was to trace God's hand in history, and, viewing the case of "the bloody and cruell Turke" as parallel to the Assyrian menace in Isaiah's time and to the Babylonian terror in Jeremiah's, they reacted in a manner identical to that of the great prophets. "The puisant kingdome of the *Turkes*," wrote George Whetstone in 1586, is "a scourge sent and suffered by God, for the sins and iniquities of the Christians."[23] Sinful man, Roger Ley thundered from his pulpit later, "hath so exasperated the Iudge of the earth, that Turkish cruelty hath cut of the goodliest branches of this Vine, and that Citty which the Tartarian conquerour iudged fit to command the world, is become

---

[22] *Ibid.*, pp. 109-10. Behind Habington's account hover the frequent pleas for the recognition of Eastern Christendom's plight, witness on behalf of humanists the representative work by Vives, *De Europae dissidiis et bello turcico dialogus* (1526; consult Robert P. Adams, *The Better Part of Valor* [Seattle, 1962], Ch. XV); and on behalf of more directly committed individuals: the propagandistic efforts of Greeks like Cardinal Bessarion, who invariably denounced the Turks as "most inhuman barbarians" and longingly commended Constantinople as "the splendor and glory of the East, the school of the best arts, the refuge of all good things" (letter to Francesco Foscari, Doge of Venice, July 13, 1453, in *The Portable Renaissance Reader*, ed. James B. Ross and Mary M. McLaughlin [repr. 1978], p. 71).

[23] *The English Myrror* (1586), p. 69.

the chiefe seate of this Mahometant tyrant."[24] No man should wonder, added Thomas Fuller, why the infidels have advanced so far: " . . . the cause of causes was the justice of God," which has permitted "this unregarded people to grow into the terrour of the world for the punishment of Christians."[25] Some Protestants, not quite prepared to concede that God was angry at their sins, enthusiastically transferred all responsibility for the Turkish terror upon the Catholic Church. "With these horrible sinnes of thine," Thomas Brightman maintained in a direct address to the Pope, "[thou dost] bring this most fell and fierce Furye, this cruell Turke vppon the Christian world, and keepest him in so long."[26] Catholics for their part were just as ready to blame Protestants.[27]

The English attitude toward the Ottoman Empire was conditioned by the views of authorities on the Continent. Among Reformers, Luther was the principal ex-

[24] *The Bruising of the Serpents Head* (1622), p. 8.

[25] *The History of the Holy Warre* (Cambridge, 1639), p. 10. Thus also Meredith Hanmer, *The Baptizing of a Turke* (1586?), sig. B7; Sir John Stradling, *Beati pacifici* (1623), p. 34; David Pareus, *A Commentary upon the Revelation*, trans. Elias Arnold (Amsterdam, 1644), p. 188; Richard Byfield, *The Power of the Christ* (1641), pp. 21, 44; John Trapp, *A Commentary . . . upon all the Epistles* (1647), p. 615; *et al.*

[26] *A Revelation of Revelation* (1615), p. 332. On the standard Protestant attitude toward the Turks—an attitude invariably delineated in interpretations of the Book of Revelation—see Katherine R. Firth, *The Apocalyptic Tradition in Reformation Britain 1530-1645* (Oxford, 1979), Ch. I.

[27] Specifically, Protestants were accused of being "verelye the sect of Mahumete, preparing the waye for the Turke to overrunne all Christendome." According to a Catholic prelate's report, "wryters at thys daye, call thys heresye . . . which Luther first began and most manteyned, by this name *Secta Mahumetica*" (Thomas Watson, *Twoo Notable Sermons, made . . . before the Quenes Highnes* [1554], sigs. B5v, B6).

ponent of the theory that Islam was the scourge of God.[28] But others, as influential, shared this view, for example the respected Swiss theologian Theodor Buchmann or Bibliander, whose detailed treatise *Ad nominis Christiani socios consultatio, qua nam ratione Turcarum dira potentia repelli possit ac debeat a populo Christiano*, published in 1542, was translated into English the same year. Bibliander makes clear in his epistle to the reader his traditionalist approach by reasserting the fundamental tenet that "it is God the gouernoure of heauē and erth / which by iudgement & sure reason giueth vnto some mē merye victorye / & turneth an other sorte vnto flyght." Since God exercises such control, he further asserted, to punitive ends, it follows that "the monarchy of Mahumet wyth hys superstytyous and damnable lawe" is currently directed against Christians for "oure vyces whyche bragge and cracke in vayne the moste worthy name of Christe / and haue no dedes of holy lyuinge agreable to the same."[29] In his more detailed statement, felicitously interspersed with telling images, he added:

"It is not the crueltye and tyrānye of the Turkes that fyghteth agaynste vs: but the wrath of god from aboue is sore kyndeled and waxeth cruell vpon vs by a cruell people. The Turkes brynge not in warres vpon vs so

---

[28] See G. Simon, "Luther's Attitude toward Islam," *Moslem World*, XXI (1931), pp. 257-62; George W. Forell, "Luther and the War against the Turks," *CH*, XIV (1945), pp. 256-71; Dorothy M. Vaughan, *Europe and the Turk* (Liverpool, 1954), pp. 135 ff.; Harvey Buchanan, "Luther and the Turks 1519-1529," *Archiv für Reformationsgeschichte*, XLVIII (1956), pp. 145-60; and Heinrich Bornkamm, *Luther's World of Thought*, trans. M. H. Bertram (St. Louis, 1958), pp. 195-217.

[29] *A Godly consultation vnto the brethren and companyons of the Christen religyon. By what meanes the cruell power of the Turks both may and ought for to be repelled of the Christen people* (1542), fol. 6v.

that ower garisons of men and coūcell may not turne them awaye: but god the Lorde of powers and the maker and gowernoure of heauen and erth fyghteth agaynste vs. The hand of god / the plages of god are strycken into vs. Solimanne is onely the whyppe with the whych the holy and ryghteous Lorde dothe beate and scourge vs for owre vicious lyuynge. He is the rasoure wyth the whych he hath determyned to pare vs to the quycke. He is the swoorde wherewith all the transgressors of Gods lawes be slayne. He is the fell and vengeable instrument wherwith we muste ether be amended / or els be vtterly destroyed."[30]

To this exposition Bibliander adjoined the common enough plea "to trāsfourme ower lyuynge & to put awaye the bourdē of iniquity / for the whiche the vēgeaūce of god both wyth other instrumētes / & also wyth the weapons of the turkes inuadith christēdome with ragynge violence."[31]

The diminishing menace of the Ottoman Empire was not necessarily due to any marked decrease in Western Europe's "burdē of iniquity." But Christian apologists of the Renaissance were never dismayed, and rose to fresh occasion by employing their ingenuity. If the theories of Isaiah and Jeremiah failed them, they could fall back confidently on the Book of Daniel, perennially capable to bolster up any theory, conceivable and inconceiva-

---

[30] *Ibid.*, fol. 117.

[31] *Ibid.*, fol. 76. Behind such pleas stands the common belief that a sincere reformation of "ower lyuynge" would automatically result in the withdrawal of God's scourges. Cf. Arthur Lake, *Ten Sermons* (1640), p. 2: "If man sinne, God striketh; if man repent of his sinne, God relenteth from his wrath." For two typical applications of this belief, cf. John Udall, *The True Remedie against Famine and Warres* (1587?), and Lancelot Andrewes, *A Sermon of the Pestilence . . . 1603* (1636).

ble.[32] Johann Philippson surnamed Sleidanus, the historiographer of the Reformation, was one of the first to trace a relationship between Daniel and the Turkish "terror":

"A few yeres past $\overset{e}{y}$ Turkes passed $\overset{e}{y}$ straight of Thracia, and proyed and spoyled al ouer Europa: and at this present haue so enlarged them selues that theyr dominion bordereth vpon Germanye. Wherethrough she is in great daunger as well as Italy, for the nearenes. Howbeit if we marke Daniel more narowly, it is to be hoped that their strength & power is come euer to the vttermost steppe. For Daniel attributeth vnto them but only thre hornes, . . .[33] the which they now obtain, first of al in possessing the dominion of Asia, afterwards of Grecia & of Egypt."[34]

Whatever our view of such exegetes, they teach us to appreciate the emotional response that Renaissance writers expected even in their casual references to the Turks. In the first book of *Paradise Lost*, for example, Milton terms Satan a "great Sultan" (I, 348). Today the descrip-

[32] One of the most abused parts of the Book was its reference to the "little horn" (7.8, 8.9). During the interregnum, for example, William Aspinwall identified it with Charles I, even as John More of Barnelms claimed that it stood for Cromwell. See, respectively: *An Explication . . . of the Seuenth Chapter of Daniel* (1654), and *A Trumpet Sounded: or, The Great Mystery of the Two Little Horns* (1654).

[33] The reference is to Daniel's vision (8.3-8) of the two-horned goat and the one-horned he-ram. But Sleidanus, notwithstanding this interpretation, was fully aware that in fact "the Ramme with two hornes signifieth the kings of the Medes & Perses, but the Goate the Greke empyre" (next note, fol. 102v).

[34] *De quatuor summis imperiis* (Strassburg, 1556); trans. Stephen Wythers, *A Briefe Chronicle of the foure Principall Empyres* (1563), fol. 104. Cf. Luther, *Table-Talk*, trans. Henry Bell in *Colloquia mensalia* (1652), p. 540. For a parallel argument originating in England, see Sir Henry Finch, *The Worlds Great Restauration* (1621), pp. 54 ff.

tion is unlikely to convey more than a vague notion of extreme luxury. Only in modern Greece might it have richer connotations, since Greek mothers still extract obedience from their children by threatening to call in a Turk! During the Renaissance, however, the reaction would have been vastly different and in keeping with the prevailing climate of opinion. Certainly no seventeenth-century reader of *Paradise Lost* would have failed to see the more obvious implications in Milton's analogy between Sultan and Satan: their seemingly invincible power, their tyranny, their calculated cruelty and legendary guile, the fear and terror inspired by both.[35] Nor did it require a reader of special perception to see further. Traditional points of view were widely disseminated during the Renaissance, and it is therefore reasonable to expect that most of Milton's readers would have noted his reference to two "Ministers of God": Satan, traditionally regarded as "the whippe of God," and Suleiman, become of late—in Bibliander's words—"the whyppe" of "the holy and rygheous Lorde."[36] Finally, anyone wishing to press the matter even further might have recollected that whatsoever Turks or devils do, "they do it by God." Divine Providence uses them as instru-

[35] Cf. Urbanus Rhegius, *An Homely or Sermon of good and Euill Angels*, trans. Richard Robinson (1590), fols. 6 ff.: "A man may see a certaine image of sathan in the *Turkes*, which are the most deerest and moste diligentest vessels and instruments of sathan. . . ." Thus also Meredith Hanmer, in the sermon cited above, note 25. The reference most pertinent to Milton's, however, is Richard Clerke's description of sin as "the great *Sultan* of Sathan" (*Sermons* [1637], p. 283.

[36] As above, note 30. The parallelism between Satan and Sultan was further reinforced by the frequent identification of the Ottoman Empire with the Antichrist: see Bryan W. Ball, *A Great Expectation: Eschatological Thought in English Protestantism to 1660* (Leiden, 1975), *passim* but especially pp. 141 ff. Cf. above, note 19.

ments largely by allowing them unrestrained progress even while their power is "suffered by God," as Whetstone said of the Turks. In Milton's epic, Gabriel's statement to the fallen archangel is equally clear:

> *Satan*, I know thy strength, and thou knowst
>   mine,
> Neither our own but giv'n; what follie then
> To boast what Arms can doe, since thine no more
> Then Heav'n permits, nor mine. . . .
>
> (IV, 1006-9)

But since power that is "giv'n" can also be taken away, Renaissance apologists could justly hope—without even running for the Book of Daniel—that the Turkish terror was sooner or later bound to reach its "vttermost steppe." And as with the Turks, so with the devils. Milton's Satan, whatever his other imprudences, is certainly not so foolish as to persist when he recognizes the futility of further action. After listening to Gabriel, he glances aloft. A sign in the heavens appraises him that, for the moment anyhow, license to do as he pleases has been withdrawn. Whereupon he flees murmuring; and with him flee the shades of night.

❧ 10 ❧
"A palpable hieroglyphick":
The Fable of Pope Joan

Truely, there are some passages in the Legend of Pope *Joan*, which I am not very apt to believe; yet, it is shrewd evidence, that in so many hundreds of years, six or seven, no man in that Church should say any thing against it: I would they had been pleas'd to have said something, somewhat sooner: for if there were slander mingled in the story, (and if there be, it must be their own Authors that have mingled it) yet slander it self should not be neglected.—John Donne

I

Pope Joan is not a historical figure. But she is part of history in that her existence has been so persistently believed in that at times belief threatened to create the thing it contemplated.

To meander through the vast literature devoted to Pope Joan might readily make us suspect that judgment had fled to brutish beasts, and men had lost their reason. On the other hand, her frequent appearance during the Middle Ages and the Renaissance shows, it could be said, "the very age and body of the time his form and pressure." So far, indeed, a study of Pope Joan's advent and progress through history is justified; for, even if our sense of the suspension of men's reason is thereby confirmed, the motives to this particular lunacy might delineate for us the nature of the ages under consideration. Though a byway in the popular literature of the Middle Ages and the Renaissance, the legend merged in due course with the highway traversed by illustrious authorities and obscure figures, enlightened humanists and "enthusiastic" partisans.[1]

The story of Pope Joan—"the stupid story of Pope Joan," as an irate scholar would have it[2]—involves details which, all too often mutually exclusive, have been

---

[1] The legend's primary sources—such as they are—will be mentioned selectively below. They were frequently cited during the Renaissance, for example by "H. S." (see note 4), "I. M." (note 24), Powel (note 37), White (note 38) *et al*. Modern studies of major importance include in particular: Johann J. I. von Döllinger, "Die Päpstin Johanna," in his *Die Papst-Fabeln des Mittelalters* (Munich, 1863), pp. 1-45, trans. Alfred Plummer, *Fables respecting the Popes of the Middle Ages* (1871), pp. 1-67; Félix Vernet, "Jeanne (la Papesse)," in *Dictionnaire apologétique de la foi catholique*, ed. A. d'Alès (Paris, 1911), II, 1254-70; Herbert Thurston, S.J., *Pope Joan* (1929; originally published in 1917); and Elphège Vacandard, "La Papesse Jean," in his *Études de critique et d'histoire religieuse*, 4th series (Paris, 1923), pp. 15-39. One should not neglect Pierre Bayle's entries in the *Dictionary Historical and Critical*, trans. Pierre Des Maizeaux, 2nd ed. (1735), II, 24-25 [apropos David Blondel], IV, 708-709 [apropos Martinus Polonus] and 725-40 [on Pope Joan]. See also Otto Andreae, *Ein Weib auf dem Stuhle Petri oder das wieder geöffnete Grab de Päpstin Johanna* (Gütersloh, 1866), which quotes from most of the primary sources; and Francisco Mateos Gago y Fernandez, *Juana la Papisa* (Seville, 1878), as well as its French version, *La Fable de la Papesse Jeanne* (Geneva, 1880), which alike contain full bibliographies. More recent efforts include Cesare d'Onofrio, *Mille anni di leggenda: una donna sul trono di Pietro* (Rome, 1978), and Mario Praz, "La leggenda della papessa Giovanna," *Belfagor*, XXXIV (1979), pp. 435-42. There are any number of other studies, often lengthy but just as often of slight consequence, such as Aurelio Bianchi-Giovini, *Esame critico degli atti e documenti relativi alla favola della papessa Giovanna* (Milan, 1845). Still other efforts may safely be avoided, for example the "popular" account by Angelo S. Rappoport, *The Love Affairs of the Vatican or the Favourites of the Popes* (1918), Ch. III.

[2] Horace K. Mann, *The Lives of the Popes*, 2nd ed. (1925), II, 307.

debated at far greater length than they ever merited. Even the champions of her existence, for instance, were by no means agreed about her place of birth or her original name. Most frequently, it was alleged that she was born in Moguntia or Maguntia, the city of Mainz (Mayence) in Hesse, which in some accounts was confused with the city of Metz in Lorraine. Yet several writers also believed her to have been Dutch, while John Lydgate, displaying in *The Fall of Princes* a rather exceptional talent for the rearrangement of the map of Europe, asserted that she was a native of "Mayence, a cite stondyng in Itaille, / Vpon the Reen"! (IX, 979-80). Moreover, by virtue of Joan's common appellation as "Joannes Anglicus," it was often claimed that legitimately she can only be fathered upon the English. Such a claim—ventured, needless to say, solely by Continental writers—was not welcomed in England with any noticeable enthusiasm. The English normally argued, as did Bishop John Jewel, that ". . . shee was not called *Iohane Englishe* by the name of the Countrie, for that she was an English Wooman, borne in *England* . . . but onely by the Surname of her Father. So are there many knowen this daie by the names of *Scot, Irishe, Frenche,* . . . : and yet not borne in any of al these Countries, but only in *Englande.*"[3] Much the same disaccord pervades the claims about her name prior to the assumption of the papal crown. One possibility was, of course, Joan or Joanna;

[3] *A Defense of the Apologie of the Churche of Englande. Conteininge an Answeare to . . . M. Hardinge* (1570), p. 429. For a typical Continental claim, see the assertion by Philip of Bergamo (in the editions cited below, note 17) that Joan was of "natiõe anglicus"—or, as his Italian version more amply avers, "nato nella prouincia ouero Isola de Anglia." Pedro Mexía (below, note 23) just as firmly calls her "vna muger natural de Ingalaterra."

but most writers appear to have favored Gilberta, still others Agnes—perhaps an intentionally assonant echo of "Joannes Anglicus"—and a few others Margaret or Isabella, even Glaucia, and finally Tutta or Jutta. A characteristic feature of the legend is, clearly, its variety.

No surviving account disputes our heroine's formidable intellectual abilities, even where we are informed that "it is said"—by those who denounced her as satanic, no doubt—that "she writ a Booke of *Necromancie*, of the power and strenth of deuils."[4] From Western Europe, at any rate, she is reported to have pursued her studies all the way to Athens. But another controversy promptly arose. Was medieval Athens the proper place to have advanced one's knowledge? Thomas Harding, in opposition to Bishop Jewel's contention that Athens was still highly respectable, predictably argued that "at that time neither any Athenes stoode, neither was there any place of learninge there any lenger: but al the countrie of Attica became Barbarous, and vtterly void of learninge."[5] "This tale," Bishop Jewel responded impatiently, "is your owne." One is led to suppose that to have determined the state of medieval Athens was also to have determined the existence of Pope Joan. Another characteristic feature of the legend, in short, is its impressive lack of logic.

From Athens the future Pope proceeded to a confrontation with her destiny in Rome. The court of the Ro-

<hr>

[4] "H. S.," *Historia de donne famose. Or the Romaine Ivbile which happened in the yeare 855* (1599), sig. C2v. This work is the English version of the Latin tract attributed to Witekind (below, §3; also Pl. 3). A particular dimension of its diverse versions is discussed by Sarah Lawson, "From Latin Pun to English Puzzle: An Elizabethan Translation Problem," *Sixteenth-Century Journal*, IX (1978), iii, 27-34.

[5] *Op.cit.* (note 3), p. 428.

man pontiff must have been devoid no less of well-educated individuals than of perceptive ones, for, while the recognition of her intellectual abilities was immediate, that of her disguise was deferred until a more dramatic moment. In due course made a cardinal, Joan—to use one of her many aliases—was finally elected Pope. The actual date of her election, however, invited several hypotheses of scant relationship to each other. Pope Joan was diversely said to lurk behind one or the other of four "real" popes: John VII (705-707), John VIII (878-882), John IX (898-900), or John XIV (983-984). But according to a fifth theory of even greater popularity, she is said to have reigned as either John VII or John VIII for nearly two and a half years from 855, thereby intervening between the officially recognized reigns of Leo IV (847-855) and Benedict III (855-858). Once elected, at any rate, Joan gained a lover too. She was widely said to have had one earlier, a young monk from the Benedictine abbey of Fulda in Hesse-Nassau, who accompanied her to Athens and eventually died there, cruelly abandoned. In Rome her paramour was a servant or, according to authors more favorably disposed, a chamberlain and possibly even a cardinal. In the event, the Pope was big with child.

The end came swiftly and, it must be granted, most theatrically. Joan's child—the "popit or little Pope," as an aggressive Protestant rather unkindly called him[6]—was born at an embarrassingly inopportune moment, during a formal procession to the Lateran Basilica (the Pope's official residence until the Avignon interlude). Soon after this epiphany, evidently, Joan died; but her manner of death, like her place of birth, is reported in a number

---

[6] "H. S." (as above, note 4), sig. C4v.

of different ways. Most commentators simply record that she and her son died immediately; others claim that she was torn apart by the raging mob; still others rather nastily assert that she was tied to the tail of a wild horse and dragged to a most painful death. At least one generous soul, however, decided to spare her life; for it is also said that Pope Joan was merely deposed, that she retired to a monastery by way of penance, and that in time she died and was buried at Ostia where her "popit" had acceded to the bishopric.[7]

Partisans of the legend also add that, in acknowledgment of the Church's shame, the street that witnessed the revelation of Joan's secret was thereafter avoided by all papal processions; while opponents of the legend maintain that the diversion was in fact dictated by the street's inability to accommodate any substantial pageant. The spot where Joan died, moreover, is alleged to have been marked by a statue; but its reputed inscription was debated with such passion, and had such an impact on the course of the controversy, that the evidence—such as it is—must be considered later. So must the most nefarious detail of all, centered on a ceremony said to have been introduced in order to prevent a woman from ascending St. Peter's throne ever again.

II

The *Liber Pontificalis*, the unofficially official list of Popes compiled in the ninth century, reported the reign of Joan in no uncertain terms. Two centuries later, in the

[7] The episode involving the wild horse is mentioned by H. Daniel-Rops, *The Catholic Reformation*, trans. John Warrington (1962), p. 339; and the more auspicious turn of events, by Thurston (as above, note 1), p. 7n. The former is detailed in the Metz chronicle (as below, note 11).

eleventh, the frequently cited chronicler Marianus Scotus (d. 1082?) provided an entry under A.D. 854 to the effect that Leo IV was succeeded by Joan—"Joanna, mulier"—for two years, five months, and four days.[8] Early in the following century, a chronicler of a like reputation, Sigebert of Gembloux (d. 1112), ventured a fuller entry on "Ioānes papa Anglicus" and expressly reported the "rumor" that she was a woman.[9] Three sources—one of them contemporary—constitute sufficiently respectable proof, especially for a legend.

Unfortunately for the champions of the legend, however, all three entries are interpolations made sometime in the thirteenth century and, in the case of the item in the *Liber Pontificalis*, in the fourteenth.[10] The first authentic relations of the legend, in fact, do not occur much before the thirteenth century. They include the accounts by the Dominican Étienne de Bourbon (d. 1261), by an anonymous Franciscan friar at Erfurt, and especially by the official chronicler at Metz, who alike

[8] "Leo papa obiit cal. Aug. Huic successit Joanna, mulier, annis 2, mensibus 5, diebus 4" (*Chronicon*, in *Rerum Germanicarum Scriptores*, ed. Joannes Pistorius [Regensburg, 1726], I, 639).

[9] "Fama est hunc Ioannē fœminam fuisse: & vni soli familiari tantum cognitam: qui eā complexus est / et grauis facta peperit / papa existens. quare eam inter pontifices non numerant quidam: ideo nomini numerum nō facit" (Sigebertus Gemblacensis, *Chronicon*, ed. A. Rufus [Paris, 1513], fol. 66v).

[10] L. Duchesne, ed., *Le Liber Pontificalis* (Paris, 1892), II, p. xxvi, where the entry is cited and its authenticity disputed. Editions of the other chronicles no longer even bother to include the interpolations. In Sigebert's case, for example, the *Patrologia latina* sidesteps the "locus famosus de Johanna papissa" (CLX, 162n). Yet another early authority, Anastasius Bibliothecarius (fl. 869), was strictly silent: the edition I consulted of his *Historia, de vitis Romanorvm Pontificvm* (Mainz, 1602), expressly disclaims his mention of "Ioannes 8. Fœmina."

assign Joan's pontificate to the years 1099-1101.[11] As already noted, however, it was still another account that in time proved most popular; and here Joan's reign was assigned to the years 855-857. Its author was the chronicler Martin of Troppau—usually referred to as Martinus Polonus (d. 1278)—whose credentials include service first as penitentiary under Pope Nicholas III and later as Archbishop of Gniezno (Gnesen). His influential account deserves to be quoted in full:

"After this Leo [IV], John an Englishman by nation Margantinus, held the see two years, five months, and four days. And the pontificate was vacant one month. He died at Rome. He, it is asserted, was a woman [*hic, vt asseritur, fœmina fuit*]. And having been, in youth, taken by her lover to Athens in man's clothes, she made such progress in various sciences, that there was nobody equal to her. So that afterwards lecturing on the Trivium at Rome, she had great masters for her disciples and hearers. And forasmuch as she was in great esteem in the city, both for her life and her learning, she was unanimously elected pope. But while pope, she became pregnant by the person with whom she was intimate. But not knowing the time of her delivery, while going from St. Peter's to the Lateran, being taken in labour, she brought forth a child between the Coliseum and St. Clement's church. And afterwards dying, she was, it is said, buried in that place. And because the Lord Pope

---

[11] For Étienne's account, see: *Scriptores ordinis praedicatorum*, ed. J. Quetif and J. Echard (Paris, 1719), I, 367; and for the other two accounts: the anonymous *Chronica* and the *Chronica Universalis Mettensis*, alike in *Monumenta Germaniae Historiae: Scriptorum tomus XXIV* (Hannover, 1879), pp. 184 and 514, respectively. The first and the third of these are translated by Thurston (as above, note 1), pp. 3-4.

always turns aside from that way, there are some who are fully persuaded that it is done in detestation of the fact. Nor is she put in the Catalogue of the Holy Popes, as well on account of her female sex as on account of the foul nature of the transaction."[12]

The first chronicler promptly to adapt this account to his purposes was another Martin, a Minorite;[13] but interpolations also drew on the same source, witness the report on Pope Joan inaccurately attributed to the English Benedictine chronicler Ranulph Higden.[14] Thus at any rate began a tradition that was to extend over the centuries ahead, not exclusive of our own.

In time, Pope Joan passed from chronicles into literature. The most celebrated literary adaptation of the legend during the fourteenth century assuredly belongs if not to Petrarch then to Boccaccio, whose *De claris mulieribus* (Ch. 99) recounts Joan's rise—"spurred by the devil"—in an evident effort to convert her into an exemplar of lust.[15] John Lydgate's versification of Boccaccio's tales in the next century also related Joan's for-

---

[12] *Chronicon* (Antwerp, 1574), pp. 316-19; trans. S. R. Maitland in *The British Magazine*, XXII (1842), pp. 42-43.

[13] Martinus Minorita, *Flores temporum*, in *Monumenta Germaniae Historiae* (as above, note 11), p. 243. Another late thirteenth century adaptation from Martinus Polonus was made by Gaufridus de Collone: see *Monumenta* etc. (Hannover, 1882), XXVI, 614.

[14] *The Cronykles of Englonde with the dedes of popes and emperours*, trans. John Trevisa (1528), fol. 75. Higden's *Polycronicon* is also available in an anonymous fifteenth-century translation: see the edition by Joseph R. Lumby (Rolls Series, 1876), VI, 333, which also provides the original Latin and the version by Trevisa.

[15] Petrarch (attr.), *Chronica delle vite de Pontefici et Imperatori Romani* (Venice, 1507), fol. 55v, and Boccaccio, *Concerning Famous Women*, trans. Guido A. Guarino (1964), pp. 231-33. The latter work was written and revised in 1355-1359.

tunes, as we have noted. Given the outrages she committed, however, Lydgate vowed to restrain himself. "I wil," he wrote, "on hire spende no more labour"— and, amazingly for such a garrulous poet, he did not.[16] The chronicles, in the meantime, continued to reiterate the story. The most popular version during the fifteenth century formed part of the universal history by Philip of Bergamo (Jacobus Philippus Foresti), whose account in Latin and its translation into Italian were alike reprinted several times.[17] Of other important versions during the later half of the same century, five in particular deserve to be mentioned: the accounts in the highly respected chronicle of St. Antoninus, Archbishop of Florence (d. 1459), and in the enormously popular *Fasciculus temporum* of Wernerus Rolewinckius de Laer; the entry in the annals of the historian Palmieri (d. 1475); the relation in the popular collection of miscellanies by Battista Fregoso (Fulgosus), sometime Doge of Genoa (d. 1502); and especially the details provided by the German humanist Hartmann Schedel in his famous *Nuremberg Chronicle* of 1493.[18] It may be added that this same period also witnessed the advent of several eloquent il-

---

[16] *The Fall of Princes*, IX, 967-1015 ("Off pope Iohn a woman with a child and put doun"); ed. Henry Bergen (Washington, D.C., 1923), III, 946-47.

[17] The Latin is found in *Supplementvm* (Venice, 1513), fol. 193v-94, and the Italian in *Cronycha de tuto el mondo vulgare* (Venice, 1491), fol. 198v.

[18] St. Antoninus, *Chronicorvm secvnda pars* (Lyon, 1586), pp. 568-69; Rolewinckius, *Chronica* (Basle, 1482), fol. 66v; Matthias Palmerius, *Evsebii . . . Chronicō . . . Ad quē & Prosper & Matthaeus Palmerius . . . addidere* (Paris, 1518), fol. 126; Fulgosus, *Factorvm dictorvmqve memorabilivm libri IX* (Paris, 1587), fol. 254; and Schedel, *Registrum huius operis liber cronicarum* (Nuremberg, 1493), fol. 169v. Leonard E. Boyle, O.P., of the Pontifical Institute of Mediaeval Studies in Toronto, alerted me to the occurrence of the fable in an equally unexpected place, the *Sanctorale* of Bernard Gui, O.P., a copy of which was presented to Pope John XII in 1329.

lustrations. One occurs in the *Nuremburg Chronicle*, where Joan is designated John VII and depicted in the line of succession immediately after Leo IV, moreover clearly sporting not her predecessors' staff but the "popit" (Pl. 1). An even more sensational illustration, setting forth the moment of Joan's childbirth during the formal procession to the Lateran, was first provided by *Der kurcz sin von etlichen frowen* (Ulm, 1473), which is to say the German version of Boccaccio's *De claris mulieribus* (Pl. 2); but soon the plate began to be reproduced in editions of the original Latin—for example, *De claris mulieribus* (Berne, 1539), fol. 73v—and was eventually adapted by Protestants like "H.S." (Pl. 3). Well might one exclaim, as did St. Antoninus, "O the depth of the riches both of the wisdom and knowledge of God: how unsearchable are his judgments, and his ways past finding out!"[19]

We pause in astonishment, of course. Why was it that such a legend arose at all and, having arisen, how could it have been endorsed by reputable members of the Church's hierarchy like Martinus Polonus or St. Antoninus? Efforts to account for this phenomenon are not wanting, however inadequate each may be. It has been suggested, for instance, that the origins of the legend should be sought in the protests heard not infrequently during the Middle Ages that one or another of the popes was, as it were, weak "like a woman"; and that eventually the popular imagination endowed the given protest with flesh and bones. This interpretation usually focuses on the pontificate of the "real" John VIII (878-882), whose attitude toward the Patriarch Photius of

---

[19] *Ibid.*; quoting, of course, Romans 11.33.

1. The papal line of succession: Sergius II, Leo IV, and John VII with her child. From the *Nuremberg Chronicle* compiled by Hartmann Schedel: *Registrum huius operis libri cronicarum* (Nuremberg, 1493), fol. 169v.

2. Pope Joan giving birth to her son. From the German version of Boccaccio's *De claris mulieribus: Der kurcz sin von etlichen frowen* (Ulm, 1473), fol. 134.

3. A Protestant adaptation of the previous illustration. From the title page of "H. S.," *Iesvitas, Pontificvm, Romanorvm emissarios, falso et frvstra negare Papam Ioannem VIII. fvisse mvlierem* (n.p., 1588).

4. Pope Joan at the moment of revelation. From an adaptation of a tract by Alexander Cooke: *A Present for a Papist: or the Life and Death of Pope Joan* (London, 1675), opposite the title page.

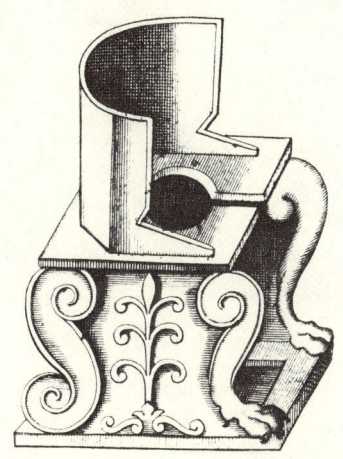

5. The *sedes stercorata*. From Jean Chifflet, *Ivdicivm de fabvla Ioannæ Papissæ* (Amsterdam, 1666), p. 7.

6. Pope Joan enthroned. From the French version of Friedrich Spanheim's *De Papa foemina*: *Histoire de la Papesse Jeanne* (Cologne, 1694), opposite the title page.

Constantinople was so conciliatory that "John" was by way of derision transmuted into "Joan."[20] The great Catholic historian Baronius, while endorsing this theory, endorsed also another one, according to which Pope Leo IX (1048-1054) protested to the Patriarch Michael Cerularius over a rumor that eunuchs had been elected to the See at Constantinople and that even a woman had been elevated to the priesthood; whereupon the Eastern Church is said to have retaliated by fabricating the legend of the female pope. However, no Eastern document even remotely confirms Baronius' dark suspicions. On the contrary, we are now in possession of a Western document, written in the tenth century, that purports to relate the election to the patriarchate at Constantinople of a woman who reigned for a year and a half—a deception, it is said, discovered through the intercession of an evil spirit in a dream.[21] Might it be that this unlikely report was in time transferred to the West by imaginative Western chroniclers? If so, however, the larger question of its endorsement by far more responsible historians lingers still. It lingers even where it is asserted, according to yet another theory, that the legend was first disseminated by Franciscans in revenge of Boniface VIII's adverse attitude toward them. And it lingers, too, when we are tempted to attribute the legend merely to the fondness of friars for a "spicy incident" by virtue of their

[20] The interpretation was later to be endorsed even by Lenglet du Fresnoy (as below, note 56). On the relations between John VIII and Photius, consult Francis Dvornik, *The Photian Schism: History and Legend* (Cambridge, 1948), *passim*.

[21] *Chronicon Salernitatum*, XVI; in *Monumenta Germaniae Historia: Scriptores* (Hannover, 1839), III, 481; trans. Thurston (as above, note 1), p. 16. This document was first noted by E. Bernheim, "Zur Sage von der Päpstin Johanna," *Deutsche Zeitschrift für Geschichtswissenschaft*, III (1890), 412.

"gossipy habit of mind."[22] No such habit, of course, is even remotely discernible in Martinus Polonus or St. Antoninus.

It is even less discernible in the authorities who in the sixteenth century likewise credited the existence of Pope Joan. These include, we should remind ourselves, the widely respected philologist and historian Marcantonio Coccio surnamed Sabellicus, "one of the famousest men in his time for all manner of good learning"; the poet Baptista Spagnuoli surnamed Mantuanus, whose ecclesiastical credentials include service as general of the Carmelites; the polymaths Joannes Nauclerus, Abbot Joannes Trithemius of Sponheim, Archbishop Bartolomé Carranza of Toledo, Paulus Constantinus Phrygio, and especially Raffaele Maffei surnamed Volaterranus, whose encyclopedic compilation was dedicated to Pope Julius II; the antiquary Richard de Wassebourg; the historians Giovanni Lucido, Christian Masseeuw, Marco Guazzo, and Francisco Vicente de Tornamira; and lastly the Spanish "universal man" Pedro Mexía, whose lengthy account of Pope Joan was translated into English as part of the vast compilation collected by Thomas Milles.[23] "I

[22] Thurston (as above, note 1), pp. 12, 13.

[23] *Seriatim*: Sabellicus, *Rhapsodiae historiarvm enneadvm* (Lyon, 1535), II, 325 [the quoted phrase is by Cooke (as below, note 37: *A Dialogve*, pp. 19-20]; Mantuanus, *Alfonsus* (Deventer, 1506), sig. G5; Nauclerus, *Chronica* (Cologne, 1579), pp. 712-13; Trithemius, *Chronicon* (Basle, 1559), p. 17; Carranza, *Svmma conciliorvm et pontificvm* (Salamanca, 1549), p. 529; Phrygio, *Chronicvm regvm* (Basle, 1534), p. 402; Volaterranus, *Commentariorvm vrbanorvm Raphaelis Volaterrani* (Basle, 1559), p. 503; Wassebourg, *Des antiquitez de la Gaule Belgicque* (Paris, 1549), fol. 162 and 167v; Lucidus, *Chronicon* (Venice, 1575), fol. 62 [also available in several earlier editions]: Massaeus, *Chronicorum . . . libri viginti* (Amsterdam, 1540), sig. flv; Guazzo, *Cronica* (Venice, 1553), fol. 176; Tornamira, *Chronographia, y Repertorio de los Tiempos* (Pamplona, 1585), p. 237; and Mexía, *Silua de varia*

make no doubt," wrote Mexía in a spectacular under-statement, "but that many have heard of a Woman, who was made Pope of *Rome*." So they had; and because they had, a militant Protestant could triumphantly yet justly remark of the legend: ". . . where I pray began the historie of her first? In Rome. From what place was it first published abroad into the world? Frō Rome. What be they that have written & declared it? The trustie friends of Rome: yea the great authenticall Doctors & commissioners of the Pope. . . ."[24] Somewhat less hysterically but much to the same purpose, John Donne maintained in 1626 that while he was "not very apt to believe" a number of the legend's aspects, it was rather odd that "no man" within the Catholic Church had ventured to correct the "slander."[25] In fact, however, Donne must have been fully aware that the counter-movement had begun well before his time, in the fifteenth century, by Platina.

One of Italy's great humanists, Bartolomeo de' Sacchi called Platina (1421-1481), was the means to the end eventually attained by an even more illustrious humanist. Platina completed his exhaustively researched biographies of the popes after his appointment by Sixtus IV as librarian of the Vatican. Published in 1479 as *Liber de vita Christi ac de vitis summorum pontificum omnium*, and thereafter translated into Italian and French as well as English, it includes an account of Pope Joan under the pontificate devoted to John VIII.[26] The basic details,

lection (Valladolid, 1551), fol. 9-9v [Part I, Ch. IX], trans. Milles, *The Treasvrie of Avncient and Moderne Times* (1613), I, 47-49 [Bk. I, Ch. XXI].

[24] "I. M.," *The Anatomie of Pope Ioane* (1624), sig. A8v.

[25] Quoted more fully in the headnote, above, from his *Sermons*, VII, 153.

[26] I consulted the Latin version in *Historia de Vitis Pontificum Romanorum*

duplicated largely from Martinus Polonus but encompassing the relations of other chroniclers too, were disposed after such a strictly scholarly fashion that the legend's glaring inconsistencies drew attention to themselves. Thus alerted, two scholars in the next century advanced to the only conclusion possible. One was the Bavarian historiographer Johann Turmair surnamed Aventinus (d. 1534), who in his *Annales* dismissed the "fabula de papa muliere" with utter contempt; the other was the Italian antiquary Onofrio Panvinio (d. 1568), who in his *Chronicon* bypassed Pope Joan silently even as in his annotations on Platina's *Lives of the Popes* argued his case against her authenticity with exemplary scholarship.[27] Without Panvinio, Platina could be made to appear what he may have been, the legend's defender; but with Panvinio, he was transformed into its opponent.

So effective were Panvinio's annotations, and so venomous the fury they aroused among the partisans of Joan's existence, that he was tellingly denounced by some of the more livid Protestants as "one of the Popes Parasites."[28] Panvinio's influence was certainly formidable; and thereafter the attacks on the authenticity of the legend proliferate greatly. On the Continent Florimond de Raemond, Georg Scherer, and Leone Allacci penned elaborately detailed treatises; Robert Cardinal Bellarmine and Caesar Cardinal Baronius argued against the

---

(Venice, 1562), fol. 101v-102. I also checked one of the editions in Italian (Venice, 1563), pp. 118 ff. ["Giovanni Femina"], as well as the translation into English by P. Rycault, *The Lives of the Popes* (1685), p. 165.

[27] Aventinus, *Annalivm Boiorvm libri septem* (Ingolstadt, 1554), p. 474; and Panvinio, *Chronicon ecclesiasticvm* (Cologne, 1568), sig. H4, and—for his annotations on Platina—the edition in Latin cited in the previous note: fol. 102-104v.

[28] "I. M." (as above, note 24), sig. A7.

legend more briefly but no less effectually; while still others—the French Jesuits Denis Pétau and Philippe Labbé among them—dismissed Pope Joan with eloquent brevity.[29] In England, at the same time, Thomas Harding was as we have seen controverting the legend with Bishop Jewel; and soon the ever-embattled Robert Parsons, S.J., endeavored to cope with John Foxe's lurid account of Pope Joan in the widely read *Book of Martyrs*. Parsons and Foxe were decidedly well matched in that both were journalists of the last order. Among the weapons in Parson's armory were shells fired indiscriminately on all exponents of the legend beginning with Martinus Polonus ("a very simple man"); a barrage of rhetoric intended to undermine confidence in a story replete with "incongruityes, simplicityes, absurdityes, varietyes and contrarietyes"; and a ruthless endeavor to deflect the enemy through the report, already noted, that a woman was elected not pope in Rome but patriarch in Constantinople ("so abhominable a thing, as the horror thereof doth not permitt vs to beleeue it").[30]

Thus spokesmen for the Catholic Church had—*pace*

---

[29] *Seriatim*: Raemond, *Errevr popvlaire de la Papesse Ieanne* (n.p., 1588), also available in several editions and in a Latin translation; Georg Scherer, *Ob es war sey Das auff ein zeit ein Papst zu Rom Schwanger gewesen vnd ein Kindt geboren babe* (Vienna, 1584); Allacci, *Confvtatio Fabvlæ de Ioanna Papissa* (Amsterdam? 1645); Bellarmine, *De Romano Pontifice*, Bk. III, Ch. XXIV, in *Bibliotheca Maxima Pontificia*, ed. J. T. Rocaberti (Rome, 1698), XVIII, 624-26; Baronius, *Annales ecclesiastici* (Mainz, 1603), X, 124 ff.; Pétau [Petavius], *Rationarivm temporum* (Mainz, 1646), I, 498; and Labbé, *Epitome historiæ sacræ ac profanæ* (Paris, 1654), p. 10.

[30] *A Treatise of the Three Conversions of England*, trans. from the Latin (n.p., 1603), I, 387-404 [Part II, Ch. V, §§ 17-36]. For another Catholic effort to establish that "Pope *Iohn* the Woman is a fable," see "Michael Christopherson"—i.e., Michael Walpole, S.J.—*A Treatise of Antichrist* ([St. Omer], 1613), pp. 415-20.

John Donne—argued extensively against the fable of Pope Joan. Frequently, indeed, they were joined by Protestants. As Parsons for once accurately maintained, "the very truth is, that this whole story of Pope Ioane is a meere fable, and so knowen to the learneder sort of Protestants themselues."[31]

III

As if by anticipation of the common Protestant response to the legend of Pope Joan, the Bohemian reformer John Huss both during the formal investigation of his opinions and in the course of his treatise on the Church accused the Catholic hierarchy of being "soiled with wicked, deceitful depravity and sin, as at the time of Pope Joanna, the Englishwoman, who was called Agnes."[32] The legend, clearly, seemed but to wait for the advent of Protestantism in order to become a powerful enough weapon to vex Catholics into nightmares. The tenor of predictable account after predictable account changed but slightly; only our heroine's name altered, as if to remind us that we had moved from one writer to another. Heinrich Bullinger's exceptionally brief remarks condense what others expanded into countless pages of abuse: "What will you saye that through the wonderfull prouidence of God it came to passe, that a woman fayning her selfe a manne, dyd clyme vp to the See of Rome, was created Bisshoppe, and called *Iohn* the 8. whyche was one *Gylberta*, a great whore, borne at *Mentz*. For thus woulde

[31] *Ibid.*, p. 391.

[32] *De Ecclesia*, Ch. VII and XIII; trans. David S. Schaff (1915), pp. 62, 127, 133-34. See also *John Hus at the Council of Constance*, trans. Matthew Spilka (1965), pp. 192 and 209.

God declare, that the Bysshoppe of Rome sitteth a whore vpon the beaste."[33]

In England there was in the first instance a play on Pope Joan ("poope Jone"), already old when Philip Henslowe first saw it in March 1591. We are not aware of the play's burden; but we are only too well aware of how another influential writer, John Foxe, treated its subject. "And here," Foxe proclaimed with evident glee after an account of several popes culminating in Leo IV:

"And here next now followeth & commeth in, the whore of Babylon (rightly in her true colours by the permission of God and manifestly without all tergiuersation) to appeare to the whole world: and that not onely after the spiritual sense, but after the very letter, and the right forme of an whore in deed. For after this *Leo* aboue mentioned, the Cardinals proceeding to their ordinary electiō (after a solemne Masse of the holy Ghost, to the perpetuall shame of them & of that sea) in stead of a mã Pope, elected an whore in deed to minister Sacraments, to say masses, to geue orders, to constitute Deacons, Priests, and bishops, to promote Prelates, to make Abbots, to consecrate Churches and altars, to haue the raigne and rule of Emperors and kings. . . ."[34]

The passage continues with an account of Pope Joan's pontificate and death, appropriately embellished to coincide with Foxe's usual tone of unmitigated sensationalism. True, Parsons protested that Foxe's details are "as follish and blasphemous, as they are wont [to be] in such

---

[33] *A Hvndred Sermons vpō the Apocalips*, trans. John Daws (1561), p. 507. Bullinger added, with the hyperbole characteristic of all partisans: "herein I follow the constant consent of al Historiographers."

[34] *Actes and Monuments*, rev. ed. (1583), p. 137. The lost play on "poope Jone" is recorded in *Henslowe's Diary*, ed. Walter W. Greg (1904), I, 13.

cases";[35] but, considering the source, the protest could readily misfire—and did. Other Protestants were in any case already preparing whole treatises, alike improbable, and alike splenetic. They include Simon Rosarius, who installed the hapless Joan at the very center of his scurrilous *Antithesis Christi et Antichristi* (1578); "H.S."—often assumed to be the German philologist Hermann Witekind—whose vitriolic tract, *Iesvitas, Pontificvm, Romanorvm emissarios, falso et frvstra negare Papam Ioannem VIII. fvisse mvlierem* (1588), was deemed worthy to be translated into both German (1596) and English (1599); and "I.M.," an Englishman, who in *The Anatomie of Pope Ioane . . . . : Necessarie for all those that . . . abhore the sottish illusions of Romish Antichrist* (1624) demonstrated that he was as capable as "H.S." to prove that the Catholic Church was "a sinke of wickedness." Such histrionic tracts were often accompanied by equally histrionic illustrations, even if in some cases—notably the title page of the Latin tract by "H.S." (Pl. 3)—the plate was not devised by Protestants but, as already noted, was first ventured by Catholics for Boccaccio's *De claris mulieribus* (Pl. 2).

Not every Protestant monomaniacally espoused abuse, however. A few aspired to some semblance of scholarly detachment, like the German polymaths Matthias Flacius surnamed Illyricus and Sethus Calvisius, the one reiterating the legend in the massive compilation known as "the Centuries of Magdeburg," the other endorsing it in his outline of chronology.[36] England could also pride herself on the relatively inoffensive discussions of the

[35] *Op.cit.* (above, note 30), p. 387.

[36] Illyricus, *Ecclesiastica historia* (Basle, 1559-1574), IX, 332-33, 337, and 500-502; Calvisius, *Chronologia* (Leipzig, 1605), p. 733.

fable by Gabriel Powel and especially by Alexander Cooke, who managed to overcome his evident anti-Catholic bias long enough to review the evidence as fairly as his ill-starred age could tolerate;[37] nor can it be held against Cooke that a posthumous adaptation of his work—*A Present for a Papist: or the Life and Death of Pope Joan* (1675)—carried opposite the title page yet another illustration of the inopportune birth of Joan's child (Pl. 4). The event is annotated in appropriately horrendous verses:

> *A Woman Pope* (as History doth tell)
> In *High Procession* Shee in Labour fell,
> And was *Deliuer'd* of a *Bastard* Son;
> Thence *Rome* some call *The Whore of Babylon.*

It is all the same disconcerting to find among Joan's defenders four individuals one had assumed were far less partisan: Bishop John Jewel, "a iuell rare indeed," as a contemporary epigram called him; John White, the liberal Anglican theologian; John Donne; and, lastly, Henry More, the Cambridge Platonist, whose acceptance of the fable was dictated by the common obsession to discern in Pope Joan "a palpable Hieroglyphick . . . that *Rome* was indeed the Seat of that great Apocalyptick Strumpet." For More, in fact, Joan's pontificate was not merely

---

[37] Powel, *Dispvtationvm theologicarvm & scholasticarvm de Antichristo & eius Ecclesia, libri II* (London, 1605), pp. 274-76; Cooke, *Pope Joane* (1610), translated into both Latin (Oppenheim, 1619) and French (Sedan, 1633), reissued in English as *A Dialogve betweene a Protestant and a Papist. Manifestly prouing, that a woman called Ioane was Pope of Rome* (1625), and adapted after Cooke's death as *A Present for a Papist* (1675; 1740; 1785). It may be noted that the Tudor antiquary John Leland also credited Joan's existence; but then he also defended the historicity of the Trojan Brutus and of King Arthur, and accepted the British origins of St. Helen, the discoverer of the Cross (T. D. Kendrick, *British Antiquity* [1950], p. 58).

a demonstration of God's intervention in history but a particular example of God's odd playfulness, one of those "notorious *Specimens* of *Festivity*, as I may so speak, that is sometimes observable in Divine Providence, answerable to that Lidibundness in Nature in her *Gamaieu's* and such like sportful and ludicrous Productions."[38] More's tortuous grammar and pretentious vocabulary are perfectly commensurate to his objectives.

Nevertheless, Parsons quite properly suggested that "the learneder sort of Protestants" were persuaded that the story of Pope Joan is "a meere fable." Earnestly questioned by Protestants in the sixteenth century, the fable was to be demolished in the seventeenth century again by Protestants—or, to be more exact, by one reputable Protestant in particular. The attempt was mounted by the Huguenot David Blondel (1590-1655), who had initially pleased his fellow-Protestants mightily by proving that the Isidorian decretals, until then regarded as genuine letters of the early popes, were in fact forgeries of the ninth century.[39] But those same Protestants were less than pleased when Blondel argued with equal impartiality against the legend of Pope Joan in *Familier Éclaircissement de la question si une femme a été assise au siège papal de Rome* (Amsterdam, 1647), later translated by himself into Latin as *De Ioanna Papissa: sive Famosæ Quæstionis, an fœmina ulla inter Leonem IV, & Benedictum III, Romanos Pontifices, media sederit. ἀνάκρισις* (Am-

---

[38] *Seriatim*: Jewel, "Dame Iohane Pope," *op.cit.* (as above, note 3), pp. 427-34, and *The Apologie of the Church of England*, trans. Anne Lady Bacon, (1600), p. 111 [the epigram is quoted from William Gamage, *Linsi-Woolsie* (Oxford, 1613), §42]; White, *The Way to the Trve Church*, 4th impr. (1616), pp. 416-18; Donne, *op.cit.* (as above, note 25), as well as VI, 249, and X, 146; and More, *A Modest Enquiry into the Mystery of Iniquity* (1664), p. 316.

[39] Owen Chadwick, *The Reformation* (1964), p. 218.

sterdam, 1657). Exhaustively detailed, the treatise displays its author's credentials in its impressive scholarly apparatus and especially in its tone, untouched as it is by the scorching fire of partisanship. Replies were not long in materializing, notably by Pierre Congnard and Samuel Desmarets;[40] but Blondel's treatise withstood such onslaughts to remain the definitive scholarly confirmation that the fable of Pope Joan is indeed but a fable.

IV

While Joan's existence engaged Catholics as well as Protestants and aroused the passions of both equally, two particular aspects of the legend appear to have exercized nearly everyone involved. Through these aspects one can appreciate the inflammable nature of the controverted legend and the alarming dimensions that it often assumed.

The first of these aspects involves the report by Adam of Usk in the early fifteenth century that an "image [of Pope Joan] with her son stands in stone in the direct road near St. Clement's"—i.e., the street between the Coliseum and the Lateran where Joan's son was born and where both of them died.[41] The report was soon confirmed by John Capgrave, who remarked in his description of Rome (c. 1450) that the Church "was decayued ones in a woman whech deyied on processioun grete with

---

[40] Congnard, *Traité contre l'eclarcissement donné par M. Blondel, en la question, Si vne femme a esté assise au Siège Papal de Rome, entre Leon IV. & Benoist III* (Saumur, 1655); Desmarets [Maresius], *Joanna Papissa Restituta* (Groningen, 1658).

[41] *Chronicon*, ed. and trans. Edward M. Thompson (1876), pp. 88 and 215.

child for a image is sette up in memorie of her as we go to laterane."[42] The question thereafter debated *ad nauseam* centered not on the actual existence of the statue, nor even on whether it was a representation of Joan and her son or—as a modern scholar has argued rather ingeniously—of Juno suckling Hercules.[43] What concerned the combatants from the fifteenth century on was an inscription which other accounts claimed to have been carved on the statue: *P.P.P.P.P.P.* Disregarding the obvious possibility that the six *P*'s are of classical origin in accordance with a standard monumental inscription—i.e., the formula "*P* (designating any given praenomen so beginning) *pater patrum* (title of the priests of Mithra) *propria pecunia posuit* ('has put up at his own expense')"—four other theories were proposed: *Petre pater patrum papisse prodito partum* ("O Peter, father of fathers, betray the giving birth of a popess"); *Parce pater patrum papisse edere partum* ("Spare, O father of fathers, that a popess should give birth"); *Papa, pater patrum, papisse pandito partum* ("O Pope, father of fathers, reveal the giving birth of a popess"); and *Papa pater patrum peperit papissa papellum* ("O Pope, father of fathers, a pope has given birth to a baby pope"). The first theory was often said to have been the inscription's intended meaning; the second was, evidently, a *cri de cœur*; the third was attributed to the devil; while the fourth was normally favored by the least forgiving Protestants.[44] In the light of such

[42] *Ye Solace of Pilgrimes*, ed. C. A. Milles (1911), p. 74.

[43] G. Tomassetti, "La statua della papessa Giovanna," *Bollettino della Commissione Archeologica Comunale di Roma*, XXXV (1907), pp. 82-95. Some sources refer not to a statue, however, but to a monument in stone.

[44] I have depended for this paragraph on both Daniel-Rops and Thurston (as above, note 7), but especially on the useful annotation provided by Mr. C.B.L. Barr of the York Minster Library.

convolutions, one can readily imagine the treatment reserved for a report on yet another statue of Pope Joan, said to have formed part of a sequence of statues of popes in the very cathedral of Siena![45]

The other aspect worthy of attention is the incredible ceremony said to have been introduced in order to preclude the election of another female pope. It appears that newly elected popes were wont to sit during their inauguration on a marble chair or throne as the choir chanted, "suscitans de terra inopem et de stercore elevat pauperem";[46] and the chair was in consequence termed the *sedes stercorata.* Somehow, however, the purpose of the ceremony and the nature of the chair were amended after the fashion reported by the Byzantine historian Laonikos Chalcocondylas (d. 1464?): καθίζουσι δὲ ἐπὶ σκίμποδος ὀπὴν ἔχοντος, ὥστε καὶ τῶν ὄρχεων αὐτοῦ ἐπικρεμαμένων ἅπτεσθαί τινα τῶν προσαχθέντων, ὥστε καταφανῆ εἶναι ἄνδρα εἶναι τοῦτον. δοκοῦσι γὰρ τὸ παλαιὸν γυναῖκα ἐπὶ τὴν Ῥώμης ἀρχιερατείαν ὠφικέσθαι.[47] Even the most frenetic of anti-Catholics understandably hesitated to translate Chalcocondylas' precise words. The English version of the vitriolic tract by "H. S.," for example, tactfully renders the passage thus:

---

[45] The statue, Cooke reported excitedly, "is to be seene there [Siena] at this day" (as above, note 37: *A Dialogve*, p. 3); and so, too, claimed the controversialist Thomas Bell in *The Survey of Popery* (1596), p. 191. Later in the seventeenth century, Jean Mabillon and Michael Germain confirmed the statue's existence (*Museum Italicum* [Paris, 1687], I, 159); but numerous others denied it.

[46] Psalm 112.7 (Vulgate): "[He] rais[es] up the needy from the earth, and lift[s] up the poor out of the dunghill" (Douay version). The last word also occurs in the King James Version (Psalm 113.7).

[47] *Historiarum libri decem*, Bk. VI; ed. I. Bekker, in *Corpus Scriptorum historiae byzantinae* (Bonn, 1843), XXXI, 303.

". . . they place him who is chosen [pope] vpon a sell [i.e., cell] hauing an open hole, by which his golden fleeces, hanging downe, of some one deputie to this office, they are handled, that it may be knowne whether he is a man: for they perceiue that in times past, a woman crept into the See of Rome."[48]

A number of Catholic reports to the same effect—notably those by Platina and Sabellicus—strenuously asserted that the ceremony had a different purpose, that "he who is plac'd in so great authority may be minded that he is not a God but a man, and obnoxious to necessities of Nature, as of easing his body."[49] But the more belligerent Protestants continued to sneer at what one of them called the "groping" of successive popes.[50] It hardly helped that prominent scholars like the French antiquary Jean Chifflet provided illustrations of the *sedes stercorata* (Pl. 5). These but assisted the visualization of a ceremony already insistently described by Catholics themselves—and in one case described with an explicitness that attests to some mental derangement:

". . . when any one comes to bee enstaulled Pope, they [the cardinals *et al.*] haue a Chaire purposely made open, like a Close-stoole, and by their passage vnderneath it, it is secretly and assuredly knowne, if *Habet testiculos*, hee bee a Man or Woman."[51]

[48] *Op.cit.* (above, note 4), sigs. C1-C1v.

[49] Platina, *The Lives of the Popes* (as above, note 26). See also Sabellicus (above, note 23); and among a number of similar reports, the one by Johannes Stella, *De vitis ac gestis summorum pontificum* (Amsterdam? 1650), pp. 112-13. For a scholarly explanation of the import of the ceremony, see the extensive footnote—a learned essay in itself—by Francesco Cancellieri, *Storia de' solenni possessi de' sommi Pontefici* (Rome, 1802), pp. 236 ff.

[50] "R.W.," *Pope Joan* (1689), p. 21.

[51] Pedro Mexía, in the version by Thomas Milles (as above, note 23).

The Catholic Church suffered some wounds during the controversy; but this one, in its essential premises largely self-inflicted, was by far the worst.

V

Blondel's definitive treatise on Pope Joan marks the end of an epoch. In the latter half of the seventeenth century attitudes began visibly to shift. On the Continent, the learned Friedrich Spanheim the Younger attempted belatedly to resuscitate the legend but failed; and his tone—like the illustration provided in one edition (Pl. 6)—was in any case dramatically different from the emotional outbursts of the increasingly more distant past.[52] In England an interesting representative of the new outlook was an erstwhile associate of the old, Thomas Fuller. He removed the legendary Joan from his list of English popes for rather novel reasons, not because he wished to eschew her at all costs. "Pope *John-Joan* is wholly omitted," he explained, "partly because we need not charge that See with suspicious and doubtful crimes, whose notorious faults are too apparent; partly because this *He-She*, though allowed of *English* extraction, is generally believed born at *Ments* in *Germany*."[53]

Yet Pope Joan survived, no longer indeed because any theological issues were involved, but because her fable could be made to carry a variety of other burdens. Thus the years of the Popish Plot in England (1678-1682) released anti-Catholic prejudices which displayed them-

[52] Spanheim, *De Papa foemina* (Leyden, 1691), with translations into French (Cologne, 1694; 3rd ed., 1736) and German (Frankfurt, 1737). Cf. Fridericus Montanus' scholarly *Disquisitio historica de Papa Foemina* (Leyden, 1690).

[53] *The History of the Worthies of England* (1662), p. 13.

selves most lucidly in Elkanah Settle's politically motivated play, *The Female Pope* (1680). Settle's heroine is a vastly ambitious, utterly egocentric woman who experiences her first defeat when she falls in love with the bombastic Duke of Saxony. "I die for the Duke," she proclaims; but he is so far from responding that he rouses the multitude against her. By the end of the "tragedy" order is fully restored; but Settle, bent on confirming the political argument of his play, went on to provide an explicitly anti-Catholic tract on *The Character of a Popish Successour* (1681).[54] As John Wilkes in conversation with Dr. Johnson was to say, *"Elkanah Settle* sounds so *queer*, who can expect much from that name?"[55]

Pope Joan's presence in the eighteenth century was minimal. Curiosity on the popular level was but spasmodically lively, in spite of the sensational accounts still furnished by persistent individuals like Maximilien Misson. The period's intellectuals, certainly, were laconic to the point of total indifference. The lexicographer Pierre Bayle, for example, rejected the legend outright, paying due tribute to Blondel's momentous labors; and Gibbon confined himself to a single scornful reference to "the fable of a female Pope."[56]

[54] *The Female Pope: being the History of the Life & Death of Pope Joan. A Tragedy* (1680). Settle's 1681 tract was reprinted in 1689 and again in *State Tracts* (London, 1693), pp. 148-64—the same collection that included a reprint of Marvell's *Account of the Growth of Popery.* To the same general period belong the reissue of Cooke's adapted account (above, p. 171) together with its sensational illustration (Pl. 4), and the account by "R.W." already quoted (note 50).

[55] Boswell, *Life of Johnson,* ed. G. B. Hill (Oxford, 1934), III, 76.

[56] Bayle, *op.cit.* (above, note 1); and Gibbon, *The History of the Decline and Fall of the Roman Empire,* ed. J. B. Bury (London, 1898), V, 298. Among the other responsible scholars who also rejected the fable was Pierre

But in the second half of the nineteenth century Pope Joan revived in the very different setting of a re-emergent Greece. The delightful novel of which she is the protagonist, Emmanuel Rhoïdes' *Pope Joan* (1866), was established in time as a classic of modern Greek literature. It gained an international audience too, in that it was translated thrice into French and twice into German and English; it appeared in Italian, Danish, and Russian; and, more recently, it was adapted by Lawrence Durrell (1954, revised 1960). Rhoïdes' Joan is a picaresque figure in the Byronic vein; and if one is also reminded of *Tom Jones*, it is in order to mark Rhoïdes' similarly "epic" range as well as the zest of his considerably more vulpine heroine. In a long "historical" introduction, Rhoïdes dutifully listed all the spokesmen in favor of the legend and somberly declared that his intention was "the delineation of the state of religion as well as of the customs and traditions in the ninth century." In fact, however, the novel is a caustic satire on ecclesiastical abuses everywhere: the ignorance, the illiteracy, the presumption, the commercialism of the Church whether East or West. The Holy Synod of the Greek Orthodox Church, not amused, promptly anathematized the novel as "anti-christian and maleficent." But Rhoïdes characteristically responded by suggesting that the Holy Synod was actually in collusion with himself since the anathema increased his sales thousandfold! He also added that his attack was directed against "the laughable ecclesiastics, not the Christian faith itself." "If my work has generated laughter," he wrote, "it was the result of

Nicolas Lenglet du Fresnoy, *A New Method of Studying History*, trans. Anon. (1728), I, 317. For Misson's sensational account, on the other hand, see his *A New Voyage to Italy*, 4th ed. (London, 1714), II, 82 ff. and 111 ff.

the absurdity of things as they are."[57] Therefore the details of his account of Joan—her cohabitation at Fulda with her first lover Frumentius, their years in Athens, her departure for Rome, her election to the papacy, her love affair with Florus the son (*sic*) of Leo IV, her childbearing, her death—are but the framework that sustains a remonstrance against the perverse traditions, practices, and attitudes openly endorsed by the Church. Often serious in the extreme, Rhoïdes protested with fiery indignation that hagiographers should recount the experiences of Christian martyrs but neglect those "charred by the flames of Christian injustice." Far more typical of his normal tone, however, is his conflation of the serious and the comic in the manner of Horace and Juvenal or the ethically oriented irony of Pascal's *Les Provinciales*.[58] The degree of the monks' dedication at Fulda, for example, is stated thus: "All submitted to the blessing on the Sabbath, but since it is not known for certain on which day God rested after the creation of the world, and they being fearful of falling into error, they remained idle the whole week long." The articulation of Charlemagne's proselytizing tactics is even more delectable: "No other missionary succeeded in so short a time in christianising so many unbelievers. The eloquence of the Gallic emperor was invincible. 'Believe or die,' he told the Saxon prisoner, in whose eyes the glitter of the executioner's sword shone with the light of persuasive

[57] Ἡ Ἱστορία τῆς Πάπισσας Ἰωάννας . . . Πρόλογος—Ἐπιμέλεια-Σχόλια, ed. Aghisilaos Tselalis (Athens, 1963), p. 255.

[58] These works are cited as precedents by Rhoïdes himself in his pseudonymous—and devastatingly ironic—"Letters of a Man from Agrini" (*ibid.*, pp. 262, 267).

argument. The mob jammed the fonts as geese do ditches after rain."[59]

Our own century has so far provided no comparable contribution. It began most inauspiciously, indeed, with a hysterical tract[60] reminiscent in its excessive zeal of the sensationalism of John Foxe or "H.S." Its title: "The End of the Papacy . . . never to rise again into political power over the nations of the earth. A brief review of the over-ruling providence of God in history. . . . With an appendix, including the history of the Woman Popess Joan." Far worse, however, was the legend's adaptation for the cinema. Produced in 1972, it featured two major stars but also a screenplay whose monotony—as a film critic remarked at the time—was "occasionally varied by a religious gathering or a rape."[61] The film's foreword proclaimed that the legend is one of "the most enduring." True enough; but it was interred at long last by the film's prodigious vulgarity.

Was it the ultimate manifestation of Providence, perhaps?

[59] *Pope Joan: A Romantic Biography*, trans. Lawrence Durrell (1960), p. 19; the other quotations from the novel are from pp. 65 and 106. Like others before him, Rhoïdes did not escape "responses"—as by Charles Buet, *Études historiques: La Papesse Jeanne. Réponse a M. Emmanuel Rhoïdis* (Paris and Brussels, 1878).

[60] By Edward Poulson (1901).

[61] *Pope Joan*, with Liv Ullmann in the title role, Trevor Howard as her predecessor Leo IV, and Franco Nero as the Emperor Louis II; directed by Michael Anderson, screenplay by John Briley; Columbia Pictures, 1972. The film critic quoted is Dilys Powell in *The Sunday Times* (London) for October 29, 1972.

⤠ 11 ⤟

"A horror beyond our expression":
The Dimensions of Hell

In Hell is Griefe, Paine, Anguish, and Annoy,
All threatening Death, yet nothing can destroy:
There's Ejulation, Clamor, Weeping, Wailing,
Cries, Yels, Howles, Gnashes, Curses (neuer failing)
Sighes and Suspires, Woes, and Vnpittied Mones,
Thirst, Hunger, Want, with lacerating Grones.
Of Fire or Light no comfortable beames,
Heate not to be endur'd, Cold in extreams.
Torments in ev'ry Artyre, Nerve, and Vaine,
In ev'ry Ioint insufferable paine.
In Head, Brest, Stomake, and in all the Sences,
Each torture suting to the foule offences,
But with more terror than the heart can thinke:
The sight with Darknesse, and the Smel with Stinke;
The Taste with Gall, in bitternesse extreme:
The Hearing, with their Curses that blaspheme:
The Touch, with Snakes & Todes crauling about them,
Afflicted both within and without them.

Thomas Heywood

I

The traditional conception of Hell is often said to have
been voiced by Jonathan Edwards. As he once told his
congregation: ". . . imagine yourself to be cast into a
fiery oven, all of a glowing heat, or into the midst of a
glowing brick-kiln, or of a great furnace, where your

182

pain would be as much greater than that occasioned by accidentally touching a coal of fire, as the heat is greater. Imagine also that your body were to lie there for a quarter of an hour, full of fire, as full within and without as a bright coal of fire, all the while full of quick sense; what horror would you feel at the entrance of such a furnace!" "But your torment," warned Edwards by way of conclusion, "your torment in hell will be immensely greater than this illustration represents."[1]

Yet Edwards and the other spokesmen for the Society of Saints in New England are not necessarily the most extreme dispensers of hell-fire in Christian history. Their predecessors in Western Europe had been no less enthusiastic. Painters like Breughel—not unjustly known as "Hell Breughel"—had already ventured in one medium what poets like Thomas Heywood had attempted with equal grimness in another.[2] The shared conception is that which Michael Wigmore articulated in 1619 thus:

". . . if all the agonies of the spirit of man, that euer were since life was first; if all the tyrannies of humane inuention: as hot glowing ouens; fiery furnaces; chaldrons of boyling oyle; roasting vpon spits; nipping of the flesh with pincers; parting of the nayles and finger ends with needles, and the like; if all these tortures were ioyned in one, to shew their force vpon one wretched soule, yet were they all as the biting of a flea, a very

[1] "The Future Punishment of the Wicked Unavoidable and Intolerable," in *Works* (1844), IV, 260-61. The ulterior motives underlying this stress on the fires of hell are discussed by Babette A. Boleman, "Success: The Puritan Highway to Hell," *Journal of Religion*, XXIII (1943), pp. 206-13. See further Edward K. Trefz, "Satan in Puritan Preaching," *Boston Public Library Quarterly*, VII (1956), pp. 71-84, 148-59.

[2] *The Hierarchie of the Blessed Angells* (1635), p. 347—quoted in the head-note, above.

nothing, in respect of hel, where God hath shewne the power of his vengeance, in preparing that infinite, endlesse, ineffable, insufferable place of torments."[3]

Protestants even transcended the bounds of their theological differences from Catholics by availing themselves of the host of intimidating details already accumulated on Hell by their nominal opponents. Accordingly, the descriptions of Hell by Wigmore in 1619 and Heywood in 1635 differ only in degree from the tradition set forth in the *Image du monde*, translated by Caxton in 1480, where the dolorous realm is envisaged as "ful of alle stenche and of sorowes, anguysshes, heuynes, hungre and thyrste," or in Cardinal Bellarmine's shattering vision of Hell in 1621, which is prefaced by the alarming observation that "the punishment of hell is not one particular punishment, but the heape of all punishments and torments togeather."[4] Central to

---

[3] *The Way of All Flesh* (1619), pp. 14-15. For other Protestant writers stressing the physical pains of hell, see Otto Werdmueller, *The Hope of the Faythful*, trans. Miles Coverdale (Antwerp? 1554), Ch. XXVII; Thomas Adams, *Workes* (1629), p. 242; and Humphrey Mill, *Poems* (1639), sigs. L7ᵛ ff. For a similar Catholic view, see Richard Crashaw, *Sospetto d'Herode*, stanzas 5 et seq., freely adapted from Marino's *La Strage de gli innocenti*.

[4] *Image du monde*, trans. William Caxton, *Mirrour of the World* (1480), ed. Oliver H. Prior, Early English Text Society: Extra Series, CX (1913), pp. 107-108, and Bellarmine, *The Art of Dying Well*, trans. Edward Coffin (St. Omer, 1622), Bk. II, Ch. III. See also the alarming remarks attributed to St. Anselm of Canterbury in *Man in Glory*, trans. Henry Vaughan (in the latter's *Works*, ed. L. C. Martin [Oxford, 1914], I, 200) and the lengthy exposition by Innocent III, *The Mirror of Mans Lyfe*, trans. H. Kerton (1576), Bk. III, Ch. IV-IX. The pertinent studies of this viewpoint include Howard R. Patch, *The Other World* (Cambridge, Mass., 1950), as well as Theodore Spencer, "Chaucer's Hell: A Study in Mediæval Convention," *Speculum*, II (1927), 177-200, and George B. Pace, "Adam's Hell," *PMLA*, LXXVIII (1963), pp. 25-35.

this tradition—Catholic at first, yet all too readily embraced by Protestants later—was the representation of Satan as a hideous monster, eventually involving the popular misconception that the fallen angels generally (as John Deacon and John Walker objected in 1601) "are vndoubtedly some *blacke, grim, griesly ghostes*, hauing goggled *eies*, fearefull *clawes*, with two clouen *feete*."[5] The tradition was thereafter extended in works like Pinamonti's *L' Inferno aperto al cristiano* (Bologna, 1688), itself destined to be the most probable "source" for the harrowing sermon heard by Stephen Dedalus in Joyce's *Portrait of an Artist as a Young Man* (1916).[6]

Yet Hell's "sorowes, anguysshes, heuynes" were not the only aspect of the infernal torments emphasized by either Catholics or Protestants. As John Donne correctly reminded his audience at Whitehall in 1620, the Christian tradition has consistently upheld "two sorts of torments in hell, *Poena damni* and *Poena sensus*, the Pain of Loss as well as the Pain of Sense."[7] Most brilliantly asserted by St. John Chrysostom in his homilies on Matthew (XXIII, 8), by St. Gregory the Great in his *Moralia* (VI, 47; IX, 97), and by St. Thomas Aquinas in the *Summa theologica* (I, lxiv, 4), the tradition was summarized early in the seventeenth century by the learned Robert Bolton as follows:

About HELL, Consider,

"1. The *Paine of losse*. Privation of GODs glorious presence, and eternall separation from those everlasting

---

[5] *Dialogicall Discourses of Spirits and Divels* (1601), p. 15.

[6] See James R. Thrane, "Joyce's Sermon on Hell: its Sources and its Background," MP, LVII (1960), pp. 172-98.

[7] *Sermons*, III, 51.

joyes, felicities and blisse above, is the more horrible part of hell, as Divines affirme. There are two parts (say they) of hellish torments; 1. *Paine of losse*; and 2. *Paine of sense*: but a sensible and serious contemplation of that inestimable and unrecoverable losse, doth incomparably more afflict an understanding soule indeed, than all those punishments, tortures, and extremest sufferings of sense.

"It is the constant and concurrent judgement of the antient Fathers, that the torments and miseries of many hels, come farre short, are nothing, to the kingdome of heaven, and unhappy banishment from the beatificall vision of the most soveraigne, only, & chiefest Good, the thrice-glorious *Iehovah* . . .

"2. *The Paine of sense.* The extremity, exquisitenesse and eternity whereof, no tongue can possibly expresse, or heart conceive . . . [The] severall paines of all the diseases and maladies incident to our nature [are] nothing to the torment which for ever possesse and plague the least part of a damned body! And as for the soule: let all the griefes, horrours and despaires that ever rent in peeces any heavy heart; and vexed conscience; as of *Iuda, Spira*,[8] &c. And let them all bee heaped together into one extremest horrour, and yet it would come infinitely short to that desperate rage and restlesse anguish, which shall eternally torture the least and lowest faculty of the soule!"[9]

Bolton's exposition of the traditional views parallels numerous similar accounts, variously addressed to

[8] A popular exemplar of the experience of despair, most fully expounded by Nathaniel Bacon, *A Relation of the Fearful Estate of Francis Spira* (1548; with more than ten editions in the seventeenth century).

[9] *Of the Foure Last Things*, 4th ed. (1639), pp. 95-96, 97, 99, 103.

Protestants[10] and to Catholics.[11] But elaborate treatises
and ponderous arguments were most often reduced to
fundamentals, as in Sir John Stradling's lines on the fallen
angels in 1625:

A two-fold punishment augments their anguish,
The sense of hellish paines, is but the least:
Losse of heau'ns ioyes
    constraines them fret and languish,
Hereby their torments chiefly are encreas't.[12]

Catholics and Protestants also agreed that Hell is no
less a condition than it is a place. Occasionally, it is

---

[10] See, for example, Thomas Adams, *A Divine Herball* (1616), pp. 153
ff.; William Bates, *The Four Last Things* (1691), pp. 495 ff.; Robert Be-
dingfeld, *A Sermon Preached at Pavls Crosse* (Oxford, 1625), pp. 24 f.; Thomas
Bilson, *The Svrvey of Christs Svfferings* (1604), pp. 37 ff.; John Boys, *An
Exposition of the Proper Psalmes* (1616-17), II, 107 f.; Jeremiah Burroughs,
Gospel-Revelation (1660), pp. 246 ff.; Richard Carpenter, *Experience, Historie, and Divinitie* (1642), I, 88; John Denison, *A Threefold Resolution*, 4th
ed. (1616), pp. 380 ff.; Johann Gerhard, *Meditations*, trans. Ralph Win-
terton (Cambridge, 1638), Med. XLIX; Henry Greenwood, *Tormenting Tophet*, 2nd ed. (1614), pp. 63 ff. [extracts from another edition of this work
are given by George W. Whiting in *N&Q*, CXXII (1947), pp. 225-30];
Sir John Hayward, *The Sanctvarie of a Troubled Soule* (1616), I, 122 ff.;
Richard Middleton, *The Heauenly Progresse* (1617), pp. 150 ff.; Robert Mossom, *Sion's Prospect* (1653), p. 103; William Sheppard, *Of the Four Last and
Greatest Things* (1649), pp. 39 ff.; Thomas Tymme, *A Silver Watch-Bell*,
18th impr. (1638), Ch. IV; *et al.*

[11] See particularly Cardinal Bellarmine, *De geminv colvmbæ, siue de bono
lacrymarum, libri tres* (Antwerp, 1617), p. 97-115 [trans. Thomas Everard,
Of the Enternall Felicity of the Saints (St. Omer, 1638), pp. 410-11]; Luis de
la Puente, *Meditations*, trans. John Heighan (St. Omer, 1619), I, 135-47;
Jean Pierre Camus, *A Dravght of Eternitie*, trans. Miles Carr (Douai, 1632),
Ch. XXIV-XXX; Nicolas Caussin, *The Holy Court*, trans. Sir Thomas
Hawkins *et al.* (1650), III, 430ff.; and Robert Southwell, *A Foure-fould
Meditation of the Foure Last Things* (1606), stanzas 52-86.

[12] *Divine Poemes* (1625), p. 290.

true, Catholics were wont to accuse their opponents with a reprehensible imbalance, witness Bishop Richard Smith's charge in 1631 that "Protestants expressly say, that hell is no place, no corporall place, no prison; that it is nothing but a wicked conscience."[13] But the charge was quite unfounded. "As for the situation of Hell," declared the royalist divine Thomas Tuke in an accurate summary statement of the Protestant view, "to say precisely where hell is, it is not easie: below its doubtlesse, as may appeare by sundry places of Scripture, and farre from heauen: but that there is a Hell, to wit, a place appointed for the tormenting of wicked Angels, and vngodly men, it is cleere ynough."[14] A few years later the antiquary and poet Abraham Fleming insisted that we must "take and esteeme this for a trueth, that there is a Hell, a denne of diuels and infernal fiends, where brimstone with flames of fire as blue as azure doth vnquenchably burne."[15] As with Hell, so with Heaven: in the words of that fervent champion of inflexible orthodoxy, Alexander Ross: "Though it be true, that where Gods presence is, there is Heaven; yet we must not therefore thinke, that there is not a peculiar *ubi* of blisse and happinesse beyond the tenth Sphere, wherein God doth more manifestly shew

[13] *A Conference of the Catholike and Protestante Doctrine* (Douai, 1631), pp. 509 f. By way of documentation Bishop Smith quoted Luther and Calvin, both out of context. The view of William Perkins he also cited ("We must not imagin, that hell is anie certaine definite and corporall place") is balanced by Perkins' *The Foundation of Christian Religion* (1591), sig. C4ᵛ.

[14] *A Discourse of Death* (1613), p. 102.

[15] *The Foot-path of Faith* (1619), p. 125. These "flames" were traditionally thought to shed no light: see the numerous references collected by John M. Steadman, "Milton and Patristic Tradition: The Quality of Hell-Fire," *Anglia*, LXXVI (1958), pp. 116-28. For a broader study of the controversial nature of hell-fire, consult Joseph Bautz, *Die Hölle* (Mainz, 1882), pp. 99-110.

his glory and presence, then any where else."[16] Admittedly a number of Protestant theologians, led by Calvin, regarded the "fire" of Hell as a metaphor, and affirmed further that all the torments of Hell are accommodated to our understanding, "figured to us by corporeal things."[17] However, neither Calvin nor any of the theologians in agreement with him was ever prepared to assert that Hell, and still less Heaven, are also mere metaphors and "no corporall" places. Their acceptance of the torments of Hell as symbols of the actual truth confined them, besides, to a minority; for the vast majority of Protestants would have concurred with Bishop Thomas Bilson's intimidating warning to all exponents of the "metaphoricall" fire of Hell: "they that go thither shall find it no metaphore."[18]

II

The Protestant extension of the traditional "two sorts of torments in hell" is reflected in the poetry of Marlowe and Milton. Faustus is initially led to believe that Hell

---

[16] *Medicus Medicatus* (1645), p. 57. Ross was protesting against Sir Thomas Browne's excessive stress on heaven and hell as states of mind (*Religio Medici*, I, §§49 and 51; in *BMP*, pp. 122-23 and 125). Browne, however, also regarded them as specific places (*ibid.*, I, §52; in *BMP*, pp. 125-26).

[17] *Institutes*, III, xxv, 12. Calvin's position is discussed by Heinrich Quistorp, *Calvin's Doctrine of the Last Things*, trans. Harold Knight (1955), pp. 187 ff. On the theory of accommodation operative here, consult the relevant authorities I cited in *Bright Essence: Studies in Milton's Theology*, by William B. Hunter, J. H. Adamson, and myself (Salt Lake City, 1971), pp. 159-63.

[18] *The Effect of Certain Sermons* (1599), p. 52. The observation is hardly original: I have encountered it a number of times, as in Richard Clerke's *Sermons* (1637), p. 549: "they shall find [the fire] no figure, that shall feele it."

is a state of mind—"ten thousand hells / In being de-priv'd of everlasting bliss"—only to discover that Hell is also a

vast perpetual torture-house.
There are the furies, tossing damned souls
On burning forks; their bodies boil in lead:
There are live quarters boiling on the coals,
That ne'er can die . . .[19]

Milton's Hell is likewise a condition as well as a place.[20] Located "in a place of utter darkness, fitliest call'd *Chaos*"—as the Argument to Book I of *Paradise Lost* expressly states—it comprehends both "a fiery Deluge" and "a frozen Continent" that serve as "fierce extreams, extreams by change more fierce" (I, 68; II, 587, 599). But the emphasis is clearly on that aspect of hell which has been phrased most memorably by Donne:

". . . when all is done, the hell of hels, the torment of torments, is the everlasting absence of God, and the everlasting impossibility of returning to his presence;

[19] *Doctor Faustus*, III, 81-82, and XIX, 117-21; ed. John D. Jump (1962). By way of contrast, in *The Historie of the Damnable Life and Deserved Death of Doctor Iohn Faustus*, trans. P. F. (1592), Ch. XV, XX, LXI, hell is said to have the usual "horrible torments, trembling, gnashing of teeth . . ." and the like (ed. H. Logeman, *The English Faust-Book* [Gand and Amsterdam, 1900], and P. M. Palmer and R. P. Moore, *The Sources of the Faust Tradition* [1936] Ch. IV).

[20] His *De doctrina christiana* provides a tradition-bound summary statement of the *poena damni* and the *poena sensus* (*Worke*, XVI, 371). Shakespeare's attitude, on the other hand, cannot be determined precisely. He was probably "sceptical" of the literal expositions of hell; and it is therefore with suitable caution that Claudio's well-known utterance in *Measure for Measure* (III, i, 119-27) has been discussed by Elizabeth M. Pope, "Shakespeare on Hell," *SQ*, I (1950), pp. 162-64.

Horrendum est, sayes the Apostle, *It is a fearefull thing to fall into the hands of the living God* [Hebrews 10.31] . . . but to fall out of the hands of the living God, is a horror beyond our expression, beyond our imagination. . . . What Tophet is not Paradise, what Brimstone is not Amber, what gnashing is not a comfort, what gnawing of the worme is not a tickling, what torment is not a marriage bed to this damnation, to be secluded eternally, eternally from the sight of God?"[21]

Milton's Hell might readily be defined as the state wherein the fallen angels lament their everlasting loss of Heaven. Satan is reportedly tormented by "the thought / Both of lost happiness and lasting pain" (I, 54 f.), yet the primacy of the former is soon established in his own case as well as in that of his companions. Just as Moloch bewails his expulsion "from bliss" (II, 86), and Beelzebub mourns the "loss / Irreparable" of "Heav'ns fair light" and its "happy state" (II, 151, 330 f., 398), so Satan's first words after his expulsion from Heaven concern the loss of "the happy Realms of Light" (I, 85) and the exchange of the "mournful gloom" of Hell for "that celestial light" (I, 244 f.). Light, indeed, deepens his heartfelt sense of loss, "wakes the bitter memorie / Of what he was" (IV, 24 f.)—and yet, divided as he is against himself, he is irresistibly drawn by light even while he expresses his utter hatred for the sun's overwhelming brilliance (IV, 37). The disjointed nature of Satan's personality is further confirmed by his contradictory experiences of Hell as a state of mind. On the one hand is his firm pronouncement that

[21] *Sermons*, V, 266 f. For parallel statements see also *ibid.*, I, 186; IV, 86; VII, 366.

> The mind is its own place, and in itself
> Can make a Heav'n of Hell, a Hell of Heav'n.
>
> (I, 254-55)

On the other hand, however, is the brutal reality:

> horror and doubt distract
> His troubl'd thoughts, and from the bottom stir
> The Hell within him, for within him Hell
> He brings, and round about him, nor from Hell
> One step no more then from himself can fly
> By change of place.
>
> (IV, 19-23)

In his own words,

> Me miserable! which way shall I flie
> Infinite wrath, and infinite despaire?
> Which way I flie is Hell; my self an Hell;
> And in the lowest deep a lower deep
> Still threatning to devour me op'ns wide,
> To which the Hell I suffer seems a Heav'n.
>
> (IV, 73-78)

Satan's alienation from God has clearly resulted in schizophrenia. The annotation provided by Origen is apposite: "When the soul is found apart from that order and connexion and harmony in which it was created by God for good action and useful experience and not at concord with itself in the connexion of its rational movements, it must be supposed to bear the penalty and torture of its own want of cohesion and to experience the punishment due to its unstable soul and disordered condition."[22] A modern commentator expands on the demonic soul's "want of cohesion" in even more explicit terms: "The soul which was made for God has sought in this life to love itself, and in Hell its free will is eternally fixed in an interior convulsion. As nature and being it still must seek God with all the energies of its being. But as a free being it continues to reject God as it did in life. The simultaneous natural searching for God and the rejection of God by his free will set up an interior division which almost tears his personality apart."[23] The terrible irony is that in Hell the efforts of the individual soul are finally crowned with success. Each soul has at last become the center of its own universe. But it is now an unbalanced center, buried in its isolation, "in solitary confinement walled up within itself, entombed alive within itself."[24]

III

The motif of the loss of Heaven and the consequent advent of an inner Hell is present not only in Marlowe and Donne and Milton. Widely sustained by their lesser contemporaries, it is encountered in the statement of James Forsyth in 1615 that "the greatest punishment that the damned shall receiue in hell torments will be the re-

[22] *De principiis*, II, x, 5; trans. G. W. Butterworth (1936).

[23] Robert W. Gleason, S.J., *The World to Come* (1958), p. 122. The essay, reprinted from "Hell: An Apology," *Thought*, XXXIII (1958), pp. 165-82, elaborates a thesis originally argued by Henri Rondet, S.J., "Les peines de l'enfer," *Nouvelle revue théologique*, LXVII (1940), pp. 397-427.

[24] *Ibid.*, p. 124.

membrance of their former pleasure."[25] Later, in 1647, Samuel Rutherford—the Principal of St. Mary's College, St. Andrews, and well-known to Milton—observed that "the want of *God* and of Heaven is the greater Hell."[26] "Hell is intolerable," Sir John Hayward also wrote, "but innumerable hels are more tolerable then to be depriued of the glory of heauen"; indeed, added Jeremy Taylor, such a loss is "a Hell in Hell, worse than a thousand Hells."[27] In the parallel statement of Richard Sibbes, ". . . when God the Fountaine of all good shall hide his face altogether from the creature, that is Hell: The place where God shines not outwardly with comforts nor inwardly, nor there shall be no hope of neither, but a place of horrour and despaire, that is hell, as the hell of this life is when God shines not on our soules."[28] Behind these and the numerous similar statements stood not only the affirmations of the guiding spirit of the Reformation, St. Augustine,[29] but also the Scriptural "proof" perennially in demand by Protestants—in this case the specific claim in the First Letter to the Thessalonians that at the Last Judgment the reprobates "shall be punished with everlasting destruction from the presence of the Lord."[30]

[25] *The Bitter Waters of Babylon* (1615), p. 17.

[26] *Christ Dying and Drawing Sinners to Himselfe* (1647), p. 20. Rutherford is mentioned in Milton's poem "On the New Forcers of Conscience" (1646?), l. 8.

[27] Hayward, *The Sanctvarie of a Troubled Soule* (1616), I, 129, and Taylor, *Contemplations of the State of Man* (1684), p. 221.

[28] *Beames of Divine Light* (1639), I, 323.

[29] e.g. *Enchiridion*, CXII: "to be lost out of the Kingdom of God . . . would be a punishment so great that, if eternal, no torments that we know could be compared to it, no matter how many ages they continued" (trans. A. C. Outler in *LCC*, VII, 407).

[30] 1 Thes. 1.9. Conversely, to "see" God is regarded as the supreme joy (e.g. Matthew 5.8 and 18.10, 1 Corinthians 13.12, 1 John 3.2, etc).

The more particular conception of an inner Hell reached the Renaissance with impressive credentials, endorsed as it had been by St. Thomas Aquinas and St. Bonaventura among others. Generously extended thereafter, its adherents ranged from the humanists Cristoforo Landino and Coluccio Salutati to the mystics Jakob Boehme and Angelus Silesius, the Florentine Neoplatonist Ficino and the Cambridge Platonists Benjamin Whichcote and John Smith, Bishop Joseph Hall as much as Thomas Traherne, and Robert Burton no less than Sir Thomas Browne.[31] When all is said, however, the most emphatic celebrants of the idea in England were the Cambridge Platonists. Ralph Cudworth's affirmation in his magnificent sermon in 1647 represents the views of the entire group:

---

[31] These and many other writers are cited by Margaret L. Bailey, *Milton and Jakob Boehme* (1914), p. 158; Rufus M. Jones, *Spiritual Reformers in the 16th and 17th Centuries* (1914), pp. 147, 186-88, 301 f., 312 f., 334 f.; Frederic Palmer, "Angelus Silesius: A Seventeenth-Century Mystic," *HTR*, XI (1918), pp. 171-202 *passim*; William D. Briggs, "Marlowe's *Faustus*, 305, 548-70," *MLN*, XXXVIII (1923), pp. 385-93; Robert H. West, *The Invisible World* (Athens, Ga., 1939), pp. 82, 238; Grant McColley, *"Paradise Lost": An Account of its Growth and Major Origins* (Chicago, 1940), pp. 140-41; Paul O. Kristeller, *The Philosophy of Marsilio Ficino*, trans. Virginia Conant (1943), pp. 360-62; John K. Ryan, "John Smith: Platonist and Mystic," *New Scholasticism*, XX (1946), pp. 1-25 *passim*; Ernst Cassirer, *The Platonic Renaissance in England*, trans. J. P. Pettegrove (1953), pp. 32 f.: Roland M. Frye, "The Teachings of Classical Puritanism on Conjugal Love," *SR*, II (1955), pp. 156-58; D. C. Allen, *"Paradise Lost*, I, 254-5," *MLN*, LXXI (1956), pp. 324-26; Merritt Y. Hughes, " 'Myself Am Hell,' " *MP*, LIV (1956), p. 80-94; J. B. Broadbent, *Some Graver Subject* (1960), pp. 80-82; *et al.* Several distinctly "popular" if minor exponents of the idea could also be cited, e.g., George Meriton, *A Sermon preached . . . at Glascoe* (1611), sig. A2ᵛ; Samuel Rowlands, *A Most Excellent Treatise*, 3rd ed. (1639), p.84; Timothy Rogers, *A Faithfull Friend* (1653), p. 33; Thomas Bilson, *The Svrvey of Christs Svfferings* (1604), pp. 633 f.; Richard Holdsworth, *A Sermon preached in St Maries in Cambridge* (Cambridge, 1642), p. 34; *et al.*

"We have dreadfull apprehensions, of the Flames of Hell without us; we tremble and are afraid, when we hear of *Fire and Brimstone*, whil'st in the meantime, we securely nourish within our own hearts *a true and living Hell*,

—*Et cæco carpimur igni:*

the dark fire of our Lusts, consumeth our bowels within, and miserably scorcheth our souls, and we are not troubled at it. We do not perceive, how Hell steales upon us, whilest we live here. And as for Heaven, we onely gaze abroad, expecting that it should come in to us from without, but never look for the beginning of it to arise within, in our own hearts."[32]

It is evident that for Cudworth the burden of interest has shifted from the predicament of the fallen angels to that of man. Henry More was to agree, seeking as he habitually did "to understand what that Kingdome of God is that is amongst *Men*, being less curious touching that part of his Dominion that he exercises over *Angels*, whether lapsed or unlapsed."[33] In *Paradise Lost*, too, the emphasis changes from the inner Hell portrayed in relation to Satan and his disciples, to the same experience delineated in connection with fallen man. Adam after the Fall, torn by "fierce passion," curses his very existence:

[32] *A Sermon preached before the Honourable House of Commons, at Westminster, March 31, 1647* (Cambridge, 1647), pp. 72 f.; reprinted in *CP*, p. 123. On Whichcote and Smith, see above (note 31), especially the studies by Jones, Ryan, and Hughes. Consult also the exposition by Henry More (as in the next note), Dialogue IV, §§5-15.

[33] *Divine Dialogues: The Two Last Dialogues, treating of the Kingdome of God Within Us and Without Us* (1668), p. 26.

>   miserable
> Beyond all past example and future
> To *Satan* onely like both crime and doom.
> O Conscience, into what Abyss of fears
> And horrors hast thou driv'n me; out of which
> I find no way, from deep to deeper plung'd!
>
> (X, 839-44)

Adam's ascription of the emerging inner Hell to his conscience parallels Milton's earlier affirmation that Satan's predicament has also been the result of conscience (IV, 23). The two instances, we realize, are meant to remind us of the promise of the Father in Book III, made immediately after the Son's offer to die for fallen man:

>   I will cleer their senses dark
> What may suffice, and soft'n stonie hearts
> To pray, repent, and bring obedience due . . .
> And I will place within them as a guide
> My Umpire *Conscience*, whom if they will hear,
> Light after light well us'd they shall attain,
> And to the end persisting, safe arrive.
>
> (III, 188-97)

Satan's inner Hell, we see in retrospect, is not only a result of the loss of "Heav'ns fair light." In addition, it must be attributed to God's "Umpire *Conscience*," placed within the fallen angels in order to intensify their remorse, and within fallen humanity in order to direct them back to their Creator.

Milton's interpretation once again reflects the views of his contemporaries; and indeed one of them, Samuel Purchas, anticipated Milton's metaphor by describing conscience as "a iust Vmpire betwixt God and Man, giuen as a Guardian to the Soule and Vertues keeper."[34] Still others maintained that conscience was placed within man "in Gods stead," becoming, as it were, "a little God" or "a second God" in man,[35] and leading to the creation of an inner Hell for sinners and an inner Heaven for the elect. "Know for a truth," wrote Jean Puget de la Serre, "that the repose of the Conscience bringeth forth peace to the Soul; and as both these together make up a Heaven upon Earth, so there is no other Hell but that which consists in the privation of them."[36]

"No other Hell": we are far removed at this point from the attention paid on other occasions to Hell's "Cries, Yels, Howles, Gnashes, Curses"—and the like. In retrospect, indeed, one may even grant that Bishop Smith's charge in 1631 ("Protestants expressely say, that hell is no place, no corporall place") was becoming a reality in the decades after its utterance. This is not to say, of course, that Hell was dismantled during the seventeenth century.[37] It proved on the contrary durable enough to inform the mode of thought characteristic of the Victorians, even if some of them credited—perhaps too anx-

[34] *Purchas his Pilgrim* (1619), p. 222.

[35] *Seriatim*: Richard Bernard, *The Isle of Man*, 12th ed. (1648), p. 94; Joseph Fletcher, *The Historie of . . . Man* (1629), p. 12; James Robinson, *Essayes*, 2nd ed. (1638), p. 423.

[36] *Ethice Christiana, or the School of Wisdom*, trans. J. A. (1664), pp. 11 f. See also John Rawlinson, *Qvadriga Salvtis* (Oxford, 1625), II, 1-2; John Bodenham and Nicholas Ling, *Politeuphuia* (1641), pp. 17, 390; John Dod, *Seven . . . Sermons* (1614), p. 85; Joseph Hall, *Select Thoughts* (1648), pp. 218 f.; etc.

[37] See D. P. Walker's authoritative study *The Decline of Hell: Seventeenth-Century Discussions of Eternal Torment* (1964). The attitudes of the radicals are best explicated by Christopher Hill, *The World Turned Upside Down* (1972; Penguin Books, 1975), pp. 170-82.

iously—that Hell was by their time relegated "to the far-off corners of the Christian mind . . . there to sleep in deep shadow as a thing needless in our enlightened and progressive age."[38] Was such optimism warranted, whether by the Victorians or their heirs in the twentieth century?

[38] W. E. Gladstone (1898), quoted by Geoffrey Rowell, *Hell and the Victorians: A Study of the Nineteenth-Century Theological Controversies concerning Eternal Punishment and the Future of Life* (Oxford, 1974), p. 212.

❦ 12 ☙
"A Principle of infinite Love":
The Salvation of Satan

post multa saecula atque unam omnium restitutionem id ipsum fore Gabrihel, quod diabolum, Paulum, quod Caiphan, uirgines, quod prostibulas.—Origen

I

Dr. Slop in *Tristram Shandy* (1760-1767) is not a very nice man. He does not quite understand Uncle Toby, but then Uncle Toby does not quite understand Dr. Slop. At one point they discuss Satan:

"He is the father of curses, replied Dr. *Slop.*—So am not I, replied my uncle.—But he is cursed, and damn'd already, to all eternity, replied Dr. *Slop.*

"I am sorry for it, quoth my uncle Toby."

Coleridge a few decades later was not so much sorry as indignant. While reading *Religio Medici* he had come across Sir Thomas Browne's renunciation of the "error" ". . . that God would not persist in his vengeance for ever, but after a definite time of his wrath hee would release the damned soules from torture; Which error I fell into upon a serious contemplation of the great attribute of God his mercy." "To call this opinion *an error!*" exclaimed Coleridge. "Merciful God! how thy creatures blaspheme thee!"[1]

[1] *Seriatim*: Sterne, *Tristram Shandy*, Bk. II, Ch. XI, in the Everyman ed.

The responses of Sterne's Uncle Toby and of Coleridge form part of the long and complicated history of belief in Satan's eventual restoration to Grace ("apocatastasis"). This history begins properly with St. Clement of Alexandria (*c.* 150 to *c.* 215). From the outset one element clearly emerges: the conviction that God's love is all-inclusive and irresistible. The crucial issue, which orthodox theologians failed to grasp, was never whether Satan should be, or could be, redeemed, but whether Divine Love may be limited in any way, even to the extent of Satan's exclusion from Grace. St. Clement, having pondered the matter, could determine only that the love of God is ecumenical in its compass. "I think it is demonstrated," he wrote, "that the God being good, and the Lord powerful, they save with a righteousness and equality which extend to all that turn to him, whether here or elsewhere. For it is not here alone that the active power of God is beforehand, but it is everywhere and is always at work."[2]

Yet Origen's was the name destined most closely to be associated with apocatastasis. Origen (*c.* 185 to *c.* 254), Clement's younger contemporary, became a legend in his own lifetime both as a philosopher and as the possessor of a kind and loving nature.[3] Περὶ ἀρχῶν (*De principiis*), the work in which he deals with apocatastasis, survives largely in the inadequate translation of Rufinus of Aquileia, who elected to alter a number of

---

(1912), repr. 1961), p. 129; Browne, *Religio Medici*, Part I, Sect. 7, in *BMP*, p. 67; and *Coleridge on the Seventeenth Century*, ed. Roberta F. Brinkley (Durham, N.C., 1955), p. 440.

[2] *Stromata*, VI, vi, 47 (in *ANF*, XII, 331).

[3] Thus Eusebius, *Historia ecclesiastica*, VI, 3; but see also the oration on Origen by St. Gregory Thaumaturgus, especially IX and XV (in *ANF*, VI, 31 and 36).

Origen's controversial views in an attempt to make him more palatable to Western theologians.[4] Inevitably, the precision of Origen's statement concerning the possibility of Satan's restoration to Grace has suffered, though fortunately not to such an extent that we cannot establish his opinion with some degree of accuracy. Rufinus' version of the crucial passage in *De principiis*[5] reads as follows:

"It is on this account, moreover, that the last enemy who is called death,[6] is said to be destroyed; in order, namely, that there may be no longer any sadness when there is no death nor adversity when there is no enemy. For the destruction of the last enemy must be understood in this way, not that its substance which was made by God shall perish, but that the hostile purpose and will which proceeded not from God but from itself will come to an end. It will be destroyed, therefore, not in the sense of ceasing to exist, but of being no longer an enemy and no longer death."

The idea of apocatastasis, we should remember, has respectable Biblical antecedents. The word itself occurs in Acts 3.21, where reference is made to "the times of restitution of all things [χρόνων ἀποκαταστάσεως πάντων] which God hath spoken by the mouth of all his holy prophets." Moreover, St. Paul's view that God will ultimately be "all in all" (I Corinthians 15.28), and the Johannine affirmation that "God is love" (I John 4.8

[4] See Francis X. Murphy, *Rufinus of Aquileia* (Washington, D.C., 1945), Ch. I *passim*; but cf. Samuel Laeuchli, "Origen's Interpretation of Judas Iscariot," *CH*, XXII (1953), pp. 253-68. Rufinus' express denial that Origen believed in apocatastasis is in *PG*, XVII, 624-25.

[5] III, vi, 5; trans. G. W. Butterworth (1936), pp. 250-51.

[6] According to 1 Corinthians 15.62; but Origen's actual reference—suppressed by Rufinus for obvious reasons—was to the devil.

and 16), appeared to justify the belief of Origen and all subsequent exponents of apocatastasis that, in the final state of existence, evil will necessarily be abrogated. In Origen's spectacular conception of the universe, the punishments of God, including the pains of Hell, were regarded as curative, not penal, as remedies intended to restore all sinners to their original state of righteousness and purity. In other words, the course of world history constitutes a long process of education aimed at the purgation of sinners and the gradual elimination of evil in preparation for the final state of "all in all" beyond history. Origen, as a commentator has observed, evidently believed that "in the end God's patient love will succeed in making all his creatures weary of their unfaithfulness. The most stubborn will eventually give in and consent to love him, and at last even his enemy death will be overcome."[7]

But the champions of orthodoxy were less than impressed by such considerations. Shocked by the mere thought of Satan's salvation, they agreed with the Emperor Justinian I in protesting against the idea that "for all wicked men, and for demons too, punishment has an end, and both wicked men and demons shall be restored to their former rank."[8] The inevitable condemnation of

---

[7] Jean Daniélou, *Origen*, trans. Walter Mitchell (1955), p. 287. See further; Charles Bigg, *The Christian Platonists of Alexandria* (Oxford, 1886), pp. 228 f.; Eugène de Faye, *Origène* (Paris, 1928), Vol. III, Ch. XV; W. R. Inge, "Origen," *Proceedings of the British Academy*, XXXII (1946), 134 ff.; Jaroslav Pelikan, *The Shape of Death* (1962), Ch. IV; *et al.*

[8] *Liber Imp. Justiniani adversus Origenem*; trans. G. W. Butterworth (1936), p. 146. See also *PG*, LXXXVI, 989; Jean Hardouin, ed., *Acta conciliorum* (Paris, 1714), III, 283-88; and Karl Joseph von Hefele, *Conciliengeschichte* (Freiburg, 1875), II, 786-89. Justinian's canons against Origen were reputedly confirmed by Pope Vigilius (Heinrich Denzinger, *Ehchiridion sym-*

apocatastasis occurred during the Second Council of Constantinople—the Fifth General Council of the Church—which Justinian convened in the year 553.

It is not an accident that the successors of Origen who propounded the theory of apocatastasis were, like him, men of exceptional kindness and all-embracing love. This was true especially of Didymus of Alexandria (*c.* 313-398), the blind teacher of Gregory of Nazianzus, Jerome, and Rufinus. Although Didymus' personal qualities were never questioned, his opinion that Infinite Love would ultimately end the torments of hell and restore the damned to Grace[9] brought condemnation at the Second Council of Constantinople upon himself as upon Origen. Didymus' views were shared in many respects by his more eminent contemporaries, St. Gregory of Nyssa and St. John Chrysostom. Origen's influence on both is demonstrable. Yet John Chrysostom only implied the idea of apocatastasis. While trying to interpret the Pauline statement that "God shall be all in all," he observed that "where there is no sin, it is evident that God shall be all in all."[10] Even this hint was enough to secure his condemnation for "Origenism," though we know now that the exaggerated charges brought against him were largely fabricated by his rival, the Patriarch Theophilus of Alexandria.

---

bolorum, trans. Roy J. Deferrari, *The Sources of Catholic Dogma* [St. Louis, 1957], p. 211). For an early and standard censure of apocatastasis see the observations by St. Maximus the Confessor (7th cent.), *The Earlier Ambigua* ("Studia Anselmiana," XXXVI, Rome, 1955), Ch. VI.

[9] According to a report, Didymus agreed with Origen in teaching "the termination of hell and the restoration (ἀποκαταστάσεις) of the devils" (*PG*, XXXIX, 248). See further Gustave Bardy, *Didyme l'Aveugle* (Paris, 1910), Ch. VIII, "Didyme et les controverses origénistes."

[10] *Homiliae in epistolam primam ad Corinthios*, XXXIX, 6 (in *A Library of the Fathers: Homilies . . . on the First Epistle* etc. [Oxford, 1854], p. 562).

What John Chrysostom elected only to imply, Gregory of Nyssa affirmed more openly. Gregory, in his discussion of the same Pauline statement, argued that God's ultimate presence "in all" necessarily means the elimination of all evil from the universe: ". . . if God will be 'in all' existing things, evil, plainly, will not then be amongst them."[11] Gregory even went so far as to declare that eventually all things will be restored to their primal state of innocence, including Satan and the fallen angels: ". . . when, after long periods of time, the evil of our nature, which now is mixed up with it and has grown with its growth, has been expelled, and when there has been a restoration of those who are now lying in sin to their primal state, a harmony of thanksgiving will arise from all creation, as well as from those who in the process of purgation have suffered chastisement, as from those who needed not any purgation at all."[12]

Theologians in the West, less permissive in matters of theology and more inclined toward dogmatism, were unable to generate much enthusiasm over the speculative views emanating from the East. St. Jerome, although fully aware of Origen's greatness as a thinker,[13] was never very patient when confronted by the prospect of Satan's redemption. His frequent references to apocatastasis reveal him as highly irritated at best, or totally unsympathetic at worst[14]—and given always to exaggerations concerning Origen's views, which, when disseminated

---

[11] *De anima et resurrectione* (in *NPF*, 2nd ser. V, 452).

[12] *Oratio catechetica*, XXVI (in *NPF*, 2nd ser., V, 496).

[13] See his tributes to Origen in *Epistulae*, XXXIII and LXII.

[14] See particularly *Epistulae*, LXXXIV, 7 [which provides Origen's statement partially quoted in the headnote, above] and *Liber contra Joannem Hierosolymitanum*, VII. Jerome's translation of Theophilus' attacks on Origen are in *Epistulae*, XCII and XCVI (*Corpus scriptorum ecclesiasticorum latinorum*, [Vienna, 1812], LV, 129, 148-50, 165-66).

throughout Latin Christendom, did little to endear the Greek Father to Western theologians. Origen is least offensively censured in *De civitate Dei*, in which St. Augustine patronizingly undertook "a gentle disputation with certain tender hearts" for dreaming that God will finally deliver the damned from their torments, and thereafter turned his ire on "pitiful" Origen because he maintained that "the devils themselves after a set time expired should be loosed from their torments, and become bright angels in heaven, as they were before" (XXI, 17). Throughout the millennium after Augustine, the notion of apocatastasis is rarely mentioned in the West and then only by theologians like John Scotus Erigena who were exposed to Greek thought.[15] Augustine's extreme popularity during the Reformation strengthened the traditional standpoint even more.

II

The attitude of the Protestant Reformers toward apocatastasis was conditioned by their legalistic theory of the Atonement; for now the punitive purpose of the divine judgments was stressed much more as Christ's work was expounded in terms of a "contract" between the Father and the Son, a "contract" whose capital provision called for punishment to be diverted from guilty mankind to the Filial Godhead, so that the exacting demands of Divine Justice would be "satisfied," the wrath of God "pa-

[15] On Erigena's acceptance of apocatastasis see Henry Bett, *Johannes Scotus Erigena* (Cambridge, 1925), p. 78; Etienne Gilson, *History of Christian Philosophy in the Middle Ages* (1955), pp. 127 and 613; and Frederick Copleston, *A History of Philosophy* (repr. 1962), Vol. II, Pt. 1, pp. 144 ff.

cified."[16] In such a scheme the idea of God as the very embodiment of infinite love and mercy tended in practice to retreat before the conception of God as the stern guardian of Divine Justice—a loving God indeed, but loving only *after* full penalty for man's transgression had been rigorously exacted. Since the "contract" excluded Satan, his salvation was automatically removed from the realm of possibility. The leading theologians of the Renaissance, trailed by a host of minor ones, closed ranks to oppose any display of mercy toward Satan. As Théodore de Bèze categorically put it, the devils are "fallen withoute anye hope of rysyng againe."[17] We can tell how widely the sentiment was accepted in England from Sir John Hayward's flat statement that "the Angels that did sinne, shall neuer be blessed,"[18] to Richard Montagu's more elaborate declaration of a view that had become commonplace:

"Before the creating of man upon earth, millions of Angels, created in glory, and subsisting with God in place of blisse, abandoned that first and originall state, which they did then enjoy, and might with their Maker have enjoyed for ever. This act of Apostasie, and aversion from God, instantly ensued their first creation, it was *irrecoverable*, and their sin *impardonable; God sware unto them in his wrath, they should never more return unto his rest.* For that one act of rebellion and disobedience, God threw

---

[16] See my study "Milton and the Protestant Theory of the Atonement," *PMLA*, LXXIV (1959), 7-13, and my further comments in *Milton and the Christian Tradition* (Oxford, 1966; repr. Hamden, Conn., 1979), Ch. V.

[17] *A briefe and pithie summe of the Christian Faith*, trans. Robert Fyll (1565?), sig. Clv. For another Continental censure of all who "promyse saluation at length euen untoo the diuells," see Augustin Marlorat, *A Catholike Exposition vpon the Reuelation*, trans. Arthur Golding (1574), fol. 211v.

[18] *Davids Teares* (1623), p. 94.,

them everlastingly out of heaven: They are and shall be ever Ταρταρωθέντες, as the Apostle phraseth it,[19] cast into, and irremediably detained in chaines of outward darknesse, unto the judgement of that great day."[20]

In *Paradise Lost*, where the dramatic context demanded that Satan's redemption should at least be entertained as a possibility, the fallen archangel soliloquizes thus:

> But say I could repent and could obtaine
> By Act of Grace my former state; how soon
> Would highth recall high thoughts, how soon
>   unsay
> What feignd submission swore: ease would recant
> Vows made in pain, as violent and void . . .
> This knows my punisher; therefore as farr
> From granting hee, as I from begging peace.
>
> (IV, 93-104)

Satan's decision coincides with the decree pronounced by God the Father before the rebellion in Heaven that disobedient angels would be confined to Hell "without redemption, without end" (V, 615). In *Paradise Regained*, finally, Satan appears fully convinced that "all hope is now lost / Of my reception into grace" (III, 204 f.).

The refusal of Renaissance theologians even to consider the possibility of Satan's salvation was voiced authoritatively by John Donne. To the rebellious angels, Donne repeatedly maintained, "can appertaine no reconciliation"; once fallen from Heaven, they fell also into "an absolute incapacity of reconciliation," and so will

---

[19] Adapted from 2 Peter 2.4.
[20] *The Acts and Monuments of the Church* (1642), p. 7.

"never be forgiven," "never return to mercy."[21] On another occasion he asserted that "When the Angels were made, and when they fell, we dispute; but when they shall return, falls not into question."[22]

As Protestant theologians consistently denied that Satan's restitution was possible, Origen's contrary suggestion had many Renaissance thinkers questioning his very sanity. His misunderstood theory was all too often termed a "dreame," a "wilde fancy," or a vile "error" that "we condemne, and detest."[23] Bishop John Woolton's cen-

[21] *Sermons*, IV, 299; II, 139; V, 78; V, 86.

[22] *Ibid.*, V, 86. Calvin's similar view is expounded by Heinrich Quistorp, *Calvin's Doctrine of the Last Things*, trans. Harold Knight (1960), pp. 190-91.

[23] Seriatim: John Wall, Alæ serapicæ (1627), p. 67; Humphrey Sydenham, *Sermons vpon Solemne Occasions* (1637), p. 177; and Hieronymus Zanchius, *Confession of Christian Religion* (Cambridge, 1599), p. 269. For parallel attacks on Origen and the idea of apocatastasis generally, see: Gulielmus Bucanus, *Institutions*, trans. Robert Hill (1606), pp. 87, 400; John Bramhall, *The Catching of the Leviathan*, appended to *Castigations of Mr. Hobbes* (1658), pp. 489-90; Heinrich Bullinger, *Fiftie . . . Sermons*, trans. H. I. (1587), pp. 746 f.; Jean Pierre Camus, *A Draught of Eternity*, trans. Miles Car (Douai, 1632), Ch. X; Richard Clerke, *Sermons* (1637), pp. 22, 550; Samuel Gott, *An Essay of the True Happiness of Man* (1650), p. 280; Peter Hausted, *Sermons* (1632), pp. 137 f.; Stephen Jerome, *Origens Repentance* (1619), sig. A2; Henry King, *An Exposition vpon the Lords Prayer* (1634)l, pp. 332 f.; Christopher Lever, *The Holy Pilgrime* (1618), p. 81; Augustin Marlorat, *A Catholike Exposition vpon the Reuelation*, trans. Arthur Golding (1574), fol. 211v; John Salkeld, *A Treatise of Angels* (1613), pp. 349 f.; Richard Sibbes, *Light from Heaven* (1638), II, 17; Thomas Sutton, *Lectures* (1632), p. 443; Thomas Tymme, *A Silver Watch-Bell*, 18th impr. (1638), p. 90; Pierre Viret, *A Christian Instruction*, trans. John Shute (1573), p. 497, and *The Christian Disputations*, trans. John Brooke (1579), fols. 272 f.; John Wall, *Christian Reconcilement* (1658), p. 9; Otto Werdmueller, *The Hope of the Faythful*, trans. Miles Coverdale (Antwerp? 1554?), Ch. XXVIII; Thomas Wilson, *Theologicall Rules* (1615), p. 66; et al. See also *Confessio Augustana* (1530), Art. XVII (in *Bibliotheca symbolica ecclesiae universalis*, ed. Philip Schaff, 3rd ed. [1877], III, 18).

sure of Origen in 1576 is one of the few that we may select as at all reasonable:

"I thinke it rather expediĕt to admonish my reader in this part, of the heresie of the *Chiliastes*, who supposed, that both al mĕ & diuels shuld be saued at the last day.[24] Of the which opinion was Origen: who also helde that the benefite of Christ should extende it selfe as largely as the offence of Adam. But there is playne & euident mention made in the holy scripture of the paynes of damned men. *Their worme shall neuer dye* [Isaiah 66.24, Matthew 9.44-8]. Nether is it expressed in the scripture that Christes binefite shuld be extĕded as ample as the fall of Adã. And albeit some . . . do affirme that by his meanes al men are partakers of the resurrectiõ: vnto this it may be inferred, that as the resurrectiõ is a benefit to the godly, so is it a punishment to the vngodly. For the resurrectiõ of the wicked is vnto thĕ partly an execution of gods seueritie and wrath."[25]

Woolton's statement is typical of the way attacks on apocatastasis frequently became censures of "universalism." The latter was regarded as a considerable threat to orthodox Protestantism, if one is to judge by the numerous denunciations of "that erroneous, detestable, and damnable doctrine of the Arminians, dreaming of an vniuersall grace as they call it."[26] Yet the Arminians were not alone in their espousal of universalism. Support had come, and continued to come, from the many Anabaptists on the Continent, notably Jakob Kautz and

---

[24] The "heresie" was by no means limited to chiliasts. Origen himself, after all, did not endorse the millenarian expectations then current.

[25] *A Newe Anatomie of Whole Man* (1576), fols. 48v-49.

[26] William Narne, *Christs Starre* (1625), p. 281.

Johann Denck.[27] England had its share of universalists,[28] and therefore the widely respected William Perkins tried to clarify the issue by affirming that "Vniuersal redemption of all men, we grant: the Scripture saith so: and there is an vniuersalitie among the Elect and beleeuers: but vniuersall Redemption of all and euery man as well the damned as the elect & that effectually, we renounce as hauing neither footing in the scripture, nor in the writings of any auncient and orthodox diuine."[29] We can be certain that Perkins, in appealing to "auncient and orthodox" authorities, was not thinking particularly of Origen.

III

Yet the balance had already begun to shift, however imperceptibly at first, in Origen's favor. The single most decisive factor in the improvement of his reputation was

[27] Kautz is especially well known to us for proposing a number of topics for public debate, among them the probability that "in Christ shall *all* men be quickened and blessed forever" (*apud* Samuel M. Jackson, *Selected Works of Huldreich Zwingli* [Philadelphia, 1901], p. 148n). On Denck, see G. H. Williams, ed., *Spiritual and Anabaptist Writers*, in *LCC*, XXV, 88-111.

[28] The English universalists included Richard Coppin, William Erburg, and particularly Gerard Winstanley (*fl.* 1648-52); see the latter's *Works*, ed. George A. Sabine (Ithaca, N.Y., 1941). Universalism was later defended in modified form by Richard Baxter, *Universal Redemption of Mankind* (1694), and even more openly by Isaac Barrow, *Theological Works*, ed. Alexander Napier (Cambridge, 1859), IV, 273-370 [Sermons LVIII-LIX, "The Doctrine of Universal Redemption asserted and explained"]. On the other side were treatises such as Obadiah Howe's *The Vniuersalist Examined and Convicted* (1648).

[29] *Works* (Cambridge, 1605), p. 357. For a full exposition of this standpoint, see Walter Sweeper, *Israels Redemption by Christ. Wherein is Confuted the Arminian Universall Redemption* (1622).

the judgment of Erasmus that, among Christian philosophers, Origen was infinitely superior to St. Augustine.[30] By the early seventeenth century in England, therefore, we find authorities of the order of Donne cautiously warning that Origen's precise views on apocatastasis are "hard to state": *"Origen* was not, herein, well understood in his owne time; nor do we understand him now, (for the most part) but by his accusers, and those that have written against him."[31] In time such cautious observations were replaced by the wholly partisan protests of individuals like Alexander Gill, Milton's one-time schoolmaster: "Ah, blessed Origen! hath thy too much charity been blamed so long?"[32] There followed detailed public defenses of Origen's position, notably in *A Letter of Resolution concerning Origen and the chief of his Opinions* (1661).

The *Letter* was published anonymously. Its author was

[30] *Opvs epistolarvm Des. Erasmi Roterodami*, ed. P. S. Allen (Oxford, 1913), III, 337; cf. below, note 45. On this crucial judgment consult Frederic Seebohm, *The Oxford Reformers* (1914), p. 274; Ernst Cassirer, *The Platonic Renaissance in England*, trans. J. P. Pettegrove (Austin, 1953), pp. 106 f.; and Henry Chadwick, *Early Christian Thought and the Classical Tradition* (Oxford, 1966), p. 123. Orthodox theologians in the West were of course utterly opposed to Erasmus' view, witness its criticism by Luther as well as by Dr. John Enck, Luther's Catholic opponent (see P. O. Kristeller, "Augustine and the Early Renaissance," *Review of Religion*, VIII [1944], 352). The distinctly favorable attitude toward Origen on the part of the Italian humanists is indicated by Nesca A. Robb, *Neoplatonism of the Italian Renaissance* (1935), pp. 139 f., 168 f., and Ernst Cassirer, "Giovanni Pico della Mirandola," *JHI*, III (1942), 330. See further Edgar Wind's indispensable study of "The Revival of Origen," in *Studies in Art and Literature for Belle da Costa Greene*, ed. Dorothy Greene (Princeton, 1954), p. 412-24.

[31] *Sermons*, III, 115-16.

[32] *Apud* J. H. Adamson, in *Bright Essence*, by W. H. Hunter *et al.* (Salt Lake City, 1971), pp. 57-58.

almost certainly George Rust, who had been Fellow of Christ's College, Cambridge, until 1659, but had settled in Ireland from 1661 and was appointed Bishop of Dromore in succession to Jeremy Taylor.[33] The Vice Chancellor at Cambridge, Theophilus Dillingham of Clare, spoke on behalf of the Western Christian tradition when he declared Rust's work to be "a dangerous book."[34] In general, however, the reaction was rather temperate: the *Letter*, as John Worthington observed, contains only "such arguments as are paradoxal according to common esteem and apprehension."[35] On a more positive note, Henry More, the Cambridge Platonist, expressed himself in favor of Rust's thesis because of its "witt and learning"[36] but equally because he had himself upheld a number of Origen's ideas, notably that of the pre-existence of the soul.[37]

Rust's declared motive in expounding and defending

[33] The *Letter* has been reproduced for the Facsimile Text Society with a bibliographical note by Marjorie H. Nicolson (1933). The best introduction to Rust is by W. C. de Pauley, *The Cambridge Platonists* (1937), Ch. VIII; and the best study of the immediate context of his thesis: D. P. Walker, *The Decline of Hell: Seventeenth-Century Discussions of Eternal Torment* (1964), Ch. VIII. Walker also reminds us (pp. 124 ff.) that not every scholar accepts Rust's authorship of the *Letter*.

[34] *Conway Letters: The Correspondence of Anne, Viscountess of Conway, Henry More, and their Friends 1642-1684*, ed. Marjorie H. Nicolson (New Haven, 1930), p. 194.

[35] *The Diary and Correspondence of Dr. John Worthington*, ed. James Crossley (Chetham Society, XIII [1847], 312).

[36] As above, note 34.

[37] More's view of Origen was extremely favorable: he called him "the greatest Light and Bulwark that ancient Christianity had" (as above, note 32), else "that Miracle of the Christian World" (in "The Preface General" to his *Collection of Several Philosophical Writings*, 2nd rev. ed. [1662], pp. xxi-xxiii). But More was not himself partial to apocatastasis (cf. his *Philosophical Poems*, ed. Geoffrey Bullough [Manchester, 1931], p. xlix).

Origen's views was his "infinite desire to doe the *Father* right" (*A Letter of Resolution*, p. 2). In this goal he was eminently successful. His approach to Origen constitutes a step in the right direction, for he studied Origen's works in the original Greek, discarding all translations he found to be "so sacrilegiously mangled and performed with so little judgement and faithfulness" that Origen's own statements were confounded with the interpolations of "some very mean Author" (p. 95). Having separated the genuine from the spurious, Rust saw clearly that the "errors" of Origen were derived from his "over-great solicitude of rendring the wayes of *Providence* clear, righteous and benigne" (p. 71). Rust sympathized with this prejudice of Origen's, for he was, like Origen, a man of infinite benevolence[38] and totally unable to comprehend the harshness of the traditionalists who condemned the "calamitous Souls" of sinners to a region of eternal night because, we may presume, "they darkly fancy God himself does" (p. 133). Rust rightly concluded that their attitude had been fortified by the legalistic theory of the Atonement, particularly its demand that Christ undergo infinite punishment for the infinite sin committed by Adam. But could it not be, asked Rust, that theologians have rendered "an excess of complement to the Justice of God"? (p. 74.) After all, he reminded his readers, God is not merely just; he is above all the embodiment of love. The world was created "out of a Principle of infinite Love" (p. 72), yet we have been led to believe that God, who had so enthusiastically approved his own creations as "very good," nevertheless "omitted to cast

---

[38] See Jeremy Taylor's testament concerning Rust, quoted by John Tulloch, *Rational Theology and Christian Philosophy in England*, 2nd ed. (1874), II, 208 and 433.

his all-comprehensive Eyes to all possible conditions they might afterward fall into. For certainly if he had done so, & seen this never-to-be-ended doom of intolerable pain and anguish of body and minde, the infinite compassionateness of his blessed Nature would scarcely have given so chearful an approbation to the works of his hands" (p. 76). But the divine approbation *was* extended, and cheerfully, because God knew that in the long run—after an αἰών or a "remarkable period of duration"[39]—he would be reconciled to all his wayward creatures, even those confined to the πῦρ αἰώνιον of the realm of darkness (pp. 71 ff., 130 ff.). Under such circumstances the very prospect that had alarmed St. Jerome so much was likely to be fulfilled: the devils would become angels again. But of such a prospect, Rust disarmingly observed: "I shall not say much, but onely ask, what difference is there in the distance betwixt a *devil* made an *angel*, and an *angel* made a *devil*? I am sure the advantage is on the ascending part rather than on the descending; for the mercy and compassion of God to all the works of his hands may reasonably be supposed to help them up though undeserving" (p. 131). As for the thesis argued by the exponents of the legalistic theory of the Atonement, Rust limited himself to the devastating observation that "to imagine that God suffers any real injury and detriment from the transgressions of a peccable Creature, which must (say they) be infinite, because he is so, and therefore to deserve a punishment

---

[39] *A Letter*, p. 132. Rust's interpretation of αἰώνιος does not violate its Biblical orientation. See Hermann Sasse, *"αἰών," Theological Dictionary of the New Testament*, ed. Gerhard Kittel, trans. G. W. Bromiley (Grand Rapids, Mich., 1964), I, 197-209; and cf. Ian T. Ramsey, *On Being Sure in Religion* (1963), Ch. I, "Eternal Punishment."

in all respects infinite, is to talk of God very meanly and too much after the manner of men" (p. 75).

The main argument in Rust's *Letter* is amply confirmed in one of his sermons.[40] Centered on the Johannine affirmation that "God is love," the sermon is a celebration of that "Ocean of Love and Goodness, that delights to overflow his Banks, and break in upon his Creatures, and make them happy." The nature of God, proclaimed Rust, is "an all-spreading and diffusive Love"; and therefore, he added, "it is more impossible for God not to be good, and consequently not to doe good, than it is for the Sun to turn into a Cloud, and to be no longer the Treasure of Light." He concluded: ". . . from such Premisses as these, it will follow, that his infinite Goodness must infinitely communicate it self unto all degrees of Being, in all the possible differences of Place or Duration, or else he must contradict his own Nature, and cease to be what he is."[41] The possibility of Satan's restoration to Grace is not mentioned even once. But the implications of the argument point to no other direction.

The eminence in which Origen today rejoices as "the most creative mind of the early church"[42] is not solely the achievement of our time. His resuscitation was begun early in the sixteenth century by Erasmus and carried on by George Rust in seventeenth-century England. Rust may not have been—and indeed was not—the first to perceive Origen's "stupendious worth,"[43] but he was

[40] *Remains* (1686), pp. 1-20. The sermon is sustained throughout by the patterns of thought characteristic of the Cambridge Platonists. It is indeed followed by another sermon on their favorite verse, Proverbs 20.27 ("The Spirit of Man is the Candle of the Lord").

[41] *Ibid.*, pp. 5, 7, 12, 15.

[42] Jaroslav Pelikan, *The Shape of Death* (1962), p. 50.

[43] *A Letter*, p. 5.

certainly one of the very first reasonably to expound Origen's views and thereby to foster an intellectual atmosphere in which those views might be received far more favorably than was possible before.

Leibniz some fifty years after the publication of Rust's *Letter* reported that "much stir" was caused by yet another revival of "the opinion of Origen" that the fallen angels "will become at last holy and blessed."[44] But the thesis did not arouse its opponents to fury; for tempers were now likely to flare up—if at all—only in a manner akin to Coleridge's, on the positive side of God's mercy as we saw at the outset (p. 200). Origen's heirs in the Eastern Orthodox Church, meanwhile, continued serenely to endorse apocatastasis. They include in our day the Russian theologian Nicolas Berdyaev,[45] who shares with Nikos Kazantzakis, the Greek novelist and poet, the vision of a far-off divine event: "One day Lucifer will be the most glorious archangel standing next to God; not Michael, Gabriel, or Raphael—but Lucifer, after he has finally transubstantiated his terrible darkness into light."[46]

[44] *Theodicy* (1710), ed. Austin Farrer, trans. E. M. Huggard (1951), p. 132. The occasion was the appearance of Johann Wilhelm Petersen's Μυστήριον 'Αποκαταστάσεως Πάντων *Das ist: Das Geheimnisz der Wiederbringung aller Dinge* (1770-10). The work and related developments are discussed by Walker (as above, note 33), Ch. XIV. Subsequent events are outlined by Paul C. Davies, "The Debate on Eternal Punishment in Late Seventeenth- and Eighteenth-Century Literature," *Eighteenth-Century Studies*, IV (1971), 257-76.

[45] *The Destiny of Man*, trans. Natalie Duddington (1937), Pt. III, Ch. II. Berdyaev's central conviction that "there is more moral truth in Origen than in St. Augustine" (p. 347) indicates the Eastern origin of Erasmus' view cited earlier (above, note 30).

[46] *Saint Francis*, trans. P. A. Bien (1962), p. 21.

Index nominum

Index rerum

Library of Congress Cataloging in Publication Data

Patrides, C. A.
   Premises and motifs in English Renaissance thought and literature.

   Includes indexes.
   1.   England—Intellectual life—16th century—Addresses,
essays, lectures.   2.   England—Intellectual life—17th
century—Addresses, essays, lectures.   3.   English literature—Early modern, 1500-1700—History and criticism—
Addresses, essays, lectures.   I.   Title.
DA320.P34   942.05   81-47940
ISBN 0-691-06505-5   AACR2